Microservices: Up and Running
A Step-by-Step Guide to Building
a Microservices Architecture

Ronnie Mitra and Irakli Nadareishvili

Beijing · Boston · Farnham · Sebastopol · Tokyo

Microservices: Up and Running

by Ronnie Mitra and Irakli Nadareishvili

Published by O'Reilly Media, Inc., 1005 Gravenstein Highway North, Sebastopol, CA 95472.

O'Reilly books may be purchased for educational, business, or sales promotional use. Online editions are also available for most titles (*http://oreilly.com*). For more information, contact our corporate/institutional sales department: 800-998-9938 or *corporate@oreilly.com*.

Acquisitions Editor: Melissa Duffield	**Indexer:** nSight, Inc.
Development Editor: Melissa Potter	**Interior Designer:** David Futato
Production Editor: Deborah Baker	**Cover Designer:** Karen Montgomery
Copyeditor: Charles Roumeliotis	**Illustrator:** Kate Dullea
Proofreader: Piper Editorial, LLC	

December 2020: First Edition

Revision History for the First Edition

2020-11-25: First Release

See *http://oreilly.com/catalog/errata.csp?isbn=9781492075455* for release details.

978-1-492-07545-5

[LSI]

To every person who took the time to chronicle and share their experiences. And to Kairav, who didn't help me write this dedication.

—Ronnie Mitra

To Lucas, who was born shortly after we started working on this book and whose smiles gave me the strength to complete this book in the middle of a global pandemic; to my wife Ana, for her support; and to my amazing students at Temple University, in Philadelphia, who kindly "test drove" early versions of a lot of the content in this book.

—Irakli

Table of Contents

Preface

Ten years ago a group of software architects gathered together and coined the term *microservices* to define a style of software architecture that had evolved. Since that time, there's been an explosion of classes, videos, and written works for the microservices style. In fact, in 2016 we coauthored *Microservice Architecture*, a book that offered an introductory guide to the principles of a microservices system.

Since the publication of that book, we and many others have had a chance to live with the microservices systems we've built. Our own experiences, as well as conversations with other practitioners, have led to a better understanding of the practical problems that implementers face. A lot of that understanding comes from success, but some of the most useful insights have come from mistakes.

We've endeavored to package up the experiences of practitioners into a highly opinionated guide. We live in an age with an abundance of practitioner advice available. But, it can be difficult to navigate this sea of information and put it together in a way that works. This book offers a practical, prescriptive model that spans team design, domain design, infrastructure, engineering, and release. Our goal is to give you a unified view of a microservices implementation and a strong first step in your journey to adoption.

Who Should Read This Book

We've written this book for microservices implementers. While we touch on some of the principles and patterns of a microservices system, the focus of the book is on practical design and engineering. If you are an architect or engineer tasked with building microservices or a microservices architecture, this is the book for you.

But this book is also a useful guide for readers who simply want to get "up close and personal" with a microservices implementation. No matter what your role is, if you're interested in understanding the work that goes into building a microservices system, you'll find this book enlightening.

What You'll Need

Since the scope of microservices is quite large, we use a number of different tools and methods. If you want to follow along with all of the examples, you'll need to install or subscribe to use the folllowing tools and platforms:

- Docker
- Redis
- MySQL
- GitHub
- GitHub Actions
- Terraform
- Amazon Web Services
- kubectl
- Helm
- Argo CD

We provide instructions on where and how to access these tools in their relevant sections.

Conventions Used in This Book

The following typographical conventions are used in this book:

Italic
> Indicates new terms, URLs, email addresses, filenames, and file extensions.

`Constant width`
> Used for program listings, as well as within paragraphs to refer to program elements such as variable or function names, databases, data types, environment variables, statements, and keywords.

`Constant width bold`
> Shows commands or other text that should be typed literally by the user.

`Constant width italic`
> Shows text that should be replaced with user-supplied values or by values determined by context.

This element signifies a tip or suggestion.

 This element signifies a general note.

 This element indicates a warning or caution.

Using Code Examples

Supplemental material (code examples, exercises, etc.) is available for download at *https://oreil.ly/MicroservicesUpandRunning*.

If you have a technical question or a problem using the code examples, please email *bookquestions@oreilly.com*.

This book is here to help you get your job done. In general, if example code is offered with this book, you may use it in your programs and documentation. You do not need to contact us for permission unless you're reproducing a significant portion of the code. For example, writing a program that uses several chunks of code from this book does not require permission. Selling or distributing examples from O'Reilly books does require permission. Answering a question by citing this book and quoting example code does not require permission. Incorporating a significant amount of example code from this book into your product's documentation does require permission.

We appreciate, but generally do not require, attribution. An attribution usually includes the title, author, publisher, and ISBN. For example: "*Microservices: Up and Running* by Ronnie Mitra and Irakli Nadareishvili (O'Reilly). Copyright 2021 Mitra Pandey Consulting, Ltd. and Irakli Nadareishvili, 978-1-492-07545-5."

If you feel your use of code examples falls outside fair use or the permission given above, feel free to contact us at *permissions@oreilly.com*.

O'Reilly Online Learning

 For more than 40 years, *O'Reilly Media* has provided technology and business training, knowledge, and insight to help companies succeed.

Our unique network of experts and innovators share their knowledge and expertise through books, articles, and our online learning platform. O'Reilly's online learning platform gives you on-demand access to live training courses, in-depth learning paths, interactive coding environments, and a vast collection of text and video from O'Reilly and 200+ other publishers. For more information, visit *http://oreilly.com*.

How to Contact Us

Please address comments and questions concerning this book to the publisher:

O'Reilly Media, Inc.
1005 Gravenstein Highway North
Sebastopol, CA 95472
800-998-9938 (in the United States or Canada)
707-829-0515 (international or local)
707-829-0104 (fax)

You can access the web page for this book, where we list errata, examples, and any additional information at *https://oreil.ly/Microservices_Up_and_Running*.

Email *bookquestions@oreilly.com* to comment or ask technical questions about this book.

For news and information about our books and courses, visit *http://oreilly.com*.

Find us on Facebook: *http://facebook.com/oreilly*

Follow us on Twitter: *http://twitter.com/oreillymedia*

Watch us on YouTube: *http://www.youtube.com/oreillymedia*

Acknowledgments

We'd like to thank our editors Melissa Potter and Deborah Baker, and the team at O'Reilly, without whom we'd never have finished this book. We'd also like to thank Pete Hodgson, Chris O'Dell, Lorinda Brandon, JP Morgenthal, Mike Amundsen, and David Butland for the incredible insight, feedback, and observations they provided. Finally, we'd like to thank Capital One and Publicis Sapient for the support they provided in allowing us to bring this book to life.

## CHAPTER 1

Toward a Microservices Architecture

The goal of this book is to help you build a working microservices architecture. In pages you'll find opinionated and prescriptive advice for building software. That advice comes from real practitioner experiences that we've gathered, both from successful implementations and the ones that could have gone better. We've refined these lessons into a model that we hope will get you up and running faster with your own system.

Recently, the microservices style of building software has exploded in popularity. In the early 2010s, the term *microservices* emerged as a way to describe a new style of software architecture. Applications built in this newly named style are built with small, independent components that work together. Since then, adoption rates for the microservices style have skyrocketed. Startups, enterprise companies, and everyone in between have been learning and implementing microservices-style architectures. The growing ecosystem of tools, services, and solutions in this space is testament to its widespread popularity. At the time of this writing, Allied Market Research (*https://oreil.ly/cugsz*) has predicted that the global market for microservices architectures will grow to $8.07 billion USD in 2026, from the current $2.07 billion USD. These kinds of numbers indicate a lot of interest, a lot of adoption, and lots and lots of microservices work.

For many, building software in the microservices way has turned out to be a challenge. The truth is that implementing a microservices system isn't easy. Making lots of independent parts work together is harder to do than it might sound. Management, maintenance, support, and testing costs add up in the system. At scale, those costs can become prohibitive. If you aren't careful, the pain of managing the system can make microservices seem like a bad idea.

But the benefits of building microservices make the risks worthwhile. Microservices done well enable you to make software changes faster and safer at scale. Faster and safer change means more agility for your business. That agility translates to better outcomes for your business and your organization.

The trick to unlocking all that value is to have the right architecture in place to support the services. It needs to reduce system costs, without diminishing the value of independent services. To build that architecture, you'll need to make important decisions early. Those decisions will span methods, processes, teams, technologies, and tools. They'll also need to work together to form an emergent, optimized whole.

A good way to build a system like this is through evolution. You could start with a few small decisions and learn and grow as you go. In fact, most early adopters ended up with microservices through iterative experimentation. They didn't set out with a goal of building a microservices-based application. Instead, they ended up with them through a continuous process of optimization and improvement.

Starting from scratch and iterating takes time. But the good news is that you can use the experiences of these practitioners to help you build your system faster. Begin your build with a foundation of patterns, methods, and tools that have been used together successfully. Then optimize the system to meet the unique goals and constraints of your organization.

In this book, we've documented the decisions that form a strong microservices foundation. Before we can dive into the details of the model, let's address an important question. What exactly do we mean by "microservices"?

What Are Microservices?

There isn't one official, canonical definition for *microservices*. A good starting place is James Lewis and Martin Fowler's seminal article (*https://oreil.ly/guhCP*) on microservices from 2014. In that piece, they describe microservices as:

> an approach to developing a single application as a suite of small services, each running in its own process and communicating with lightweight mechanisms. [...] built around business capabilities and independently deployable by fully automated deployment machinery.

The real heart of Lewis and Fowler's article is the set of nine characteristics that microservices possess. Their list starts with the core microservice characteristic of *componentization via services*, which means breaking an application into smaller services. From there they go on to cover a wide breadth of capabilities. They document the need for organizational and management design with the characteristics of *organization around business capabilities* and *decentralized governance*. They hint at DevOps and Agile delivery practices when they introduce *infrastructure automation* and *products not projects*. They also identify a few key architecture principles, such as *smart endpoints and dumb pipes*, *design for failure*, and *evolutionary design*.

Each of these characteristics is worth understanding, and we encourage you to read their article if you haven't already. Together, these characteristics form a holistic solution with a very large set of concerns. It includes technology, infrastructure, engineering, operationalization, governance, team structure, and culture.

For contrast, here is another definition for microservices from the book *Microservice Architecture* by Irakli Nadareishvili, Ronnie Mitra, Matt McLarty, and Mike Amundsen (O'Reilly):

> A *microservice* is an independently deployable component of bounded scope that supports interoperability through message-based communication. *Microservice architecture* is a style of engineering highly automated, evolvable software systems made up of capability-aligned microservices.

This definition is similar to Lewis and Fowler's, but it pays special attention to bounded scopes, interoperability, and message-based communication. It also makes a distinction between microservices and the architecture that enables them.

These are just two examples from a sea of microservices definitions. As with these examples, most definitions are broadly similar, but each of them differs slightly in their focus. But they're usually different enough that it becomes hard to gauge if you've built a textbook microservices system.

In the world of technology, names are important because they give us a simple way of communicating complex concepts. In this case, the "microservices" label allows us to describe a *style* of software architecture that has three general design traits:

1. The application architecture is primarily composed of machine-invocable "services" that are made available on a network.
2. The sizes (or boundaries) of services are an important design factor. These boundaries include runtime, design-time, and people factors.
3. The software system, organization, and way of working are holistically optimized to achieve a goal.

This is a pretty general set of design traits. For example, it doesn't document organizational styles, specific tools, or architectural principles that should be used. There also aren't any formal patterns or practices defined. Instead, this gives us just enough characteristics to be able to identify a microservices system when we see one.

The truth is, you can get away with calling almost any API-based system a microservices architecture if you try hard enough. But the real focus should be on the goal of your system. We think that question of why you'd build microservices is much more enlightening than the question of what they are. While there are lots of potential benefits to microservices, we believe the best reason to build software this way is to reduce your coordination costs.

Reducing Coordination Costs

Companies around the world have had success implementing microservices architectures. Almost universally, the practitioners we've talked to have reported an increase in speed of software delivery. We believe that improvement comes from the fundamental benefit of the microservices style: a reduction in coordination costs.

It should be pointed out that there are many ways to increase speed in software engineering. Building software the microservices way is just one option. For example, you could build a system quickly by cutting corners and incurring "technical debt" (*https://oreil.ly/PBMHU*) that you'll deal with later. Or, you could focus less on stability and safety and just get your product out the door. In some situations and for some businesses these are reasonable approaches.

But systems developed for the financial, healthcare, and government sectors, among others, are not allowed to compromise on safety for the sake of speed. And yet, competitive and market forces demand higher speed from these industries just like any other. This is where a microservices system can shine. It provides an architectural approach that allows you to increase speed without compromising safety. And it lets you do that at scale.

The Coordination Cost Problem

Building complex software is hard work. In films and on TV, a brilliant programmer can heroically engineer a world-changing product over the course of a sleepless weekend. In real life it takes lots of people and a whole lot of time to produce a quality result. Multiple teams working on a complex project are typically implementing different parts of said system, following independent roadmaps, at independent paces. Periodically, these parts need to be integrated to resolve dependencies, at which point the mostly autonomous teams need to coordinate their work (see Figure 1-1).

Imagine that Jane is the team lead in charge of the Accounting workstream. Her team just finished a sprint and has a dependency on a component being developed by the team in charge of the Shipment module, led by Tyrone. Since roadmaps are independent, it could be that Tyrone's team is not actually done with their implementation of the needed component, in the Shipment workstream. At this point Jane has one of two choices: she can either wait for the component to be delivered (prioritizing safety but sacrificing speed by putting her team on halt) and do a proper integration test, or she can rely on an agreed interface contract between her team and Tyrone's, assuming that his team will deliver the component exactly as planned. In the latter case, Jane would proceed without interruption, increasing her team's speed, but potentially compromising the overall safety of the system since integration testing didn't occur at the earliest possible stage and a "happy path" assumption was made.

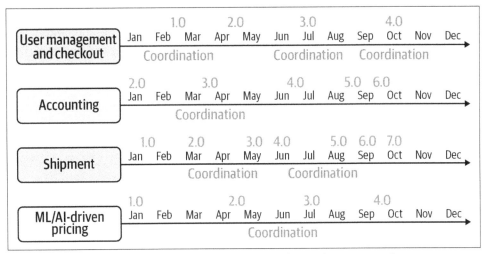

Figure 1-1. Sample timeline of a complex project with coordination touchpoints

Any team lead in a complex, multiteam environment regularly faces this choice between ignoring coordination costs and keeping momentum versus acknowledging the need for coordination and slowing down. Typically we choose one or the other using our intuition on risk versus benefits, but overall, in a sufficiently complex system, when these choices occur frequently enough there is a very pronounced tension between speed and safety.

The tension is real; however, it is not related to our primal instincts and there is a way to fix it. Since coordination costs cause the tension, what if we had a system specifically designed in a way to *minimize* those coordination costs? What if instead of choosing one way or the other, teams did not even face the choice most of the time? You can have such a design, emphasizing the minimization of coordination, if you have autonomous teams working on small batches of isolated work. And that is exactly what microservices architecture is all about, in its essence.

Understanding that the fundamental force of building successful microservices architectures is aiming for the minimization of coordination is extremely useful. It gives us a universal litmus test. Building complex distributed systems such as a microservices architecture isn't easy, and when in doubt we should always ask ourselves, "Is this decision I am facing going to reduce coordination costs for my teams or not?" The right answer will be much more obvious when we view decisions from the perspective of coordination costs.

Ultimately, microservices have become popular because they help businesses succeed. Modern organizations are under incredible pressure to adapt, change, and improve more often and more quickly. Investing in a technology architecture that is purposefully designed to change speed and change safety at the scale of a large organization makes a lot of sense. The microservices style enables companies operating in complex domains to have the agility of a simpler, smaller company while continuing to harness the power and reach of their actual size. It's incredibly appealing and the growth in adoption proves that—however, the benefits don't come for free. It takes a lot of up-front work, focus, and decision making to build a microservices architecture that can unlock that value.

The Hard Parts

One of the biggest hurdles that first-time microservices adopters face is dealing with the enormous scope and breadth of a microservices system. You might start by focusing on creating smaller, bounded services. But very soon you'll find yourself having to come up with the right infrastructure, data models, frameworks, team models, and processes to support them. It's a lot of ground to cover and dealing with all of that scope can lead to some unique challenges. Here are the three big design problems that microservices architects and engineers usually face:

Long feedback loops

One big challenge is that impactful decisions in a microservices system aren't easy to measure. From the decisions you make today problems may emerge, but they may not show up until much later. For example, when you start out you might decide to use a shared communication library to make it easier for your services to talk to each other. Over time it may become clear that keeping that library up to date across all of your microservices and teams turns out to be a huge problem. The crux of the problem here is that it's difficult to understand the impact of the decision you're making until problems arise, which makes it difficult to evaluate options and choose among them.

Too many moving parts

At its heart, a microservices system is a complex adaptive system. This means that each part of the system impacts the other parts in some way. When all those parts come together an emergent system behavior is produced. If you've ever introduced a new tool or a new process into an organization, you've probably seen this firsthand. Some teams take to new stimuli and change immediately, others need help and support to adapt, but no matter what, you almost always end up with consequences as to the way people work and the decisions that are made. For example, technology teams who introduce Docker containerization tooling inevitably end up adapting their development and release life cycle as a consequence of their adopting the container deployment model. Sometimes these consequences are planned, but often we need to deal with the unintended consequences of the changes that are introduced. This complexity is what makes microservices system design difficult. It's difficult to predict the specific impacts of the changes that are introduced, leading to a risk that we'll do more harm than good with a new architecture model.

Analysis paralysis

When we compound the problem of long feedback loops for our decision with the complex system we need to design, it's easy to see why microservices architecture is a challenge. The decisions you need to make are both highly impactful and difficult to measure. This can lead to endless speculation, discussion, and evaluation of architectural decisions because of the fear of making the wrong kind of system. Instead of building a system that can achieve business outcomes, we end up in a state of indecision, trying to model the endless permutations of our choices. This condition is commonly known as *analysis paralysis*. It doesn't help that the web is full of horror stories, "bumper sticker" advice, and contradictory best practices for building a microservices architecture.

Ultimately, the real challenge of building a microservices architecture is that of dealing with a big, complicated system that spans a huge scope. The good news is that this is not a unique problem to solve. In this book, we'll be bringing together and using a set of practices and patterns that have evolved for this type of domain. We'll also be introducing and implementing tools that embody these ways of working and make the work that happens in a microservices system easier, safer, cheaper, and faster.

Learning by Doing

So far, we've established that the microservices style can help you deliver software faster without compromising on safety. But we've also identified that the path to a good microservices architecture is difficult and fraught with challenging and complex decisions. Many of the successful microservices implementers we've talked to have built their systems through continual iteration and improvement. Frequently, they've had to build architectures that failed before they unlocked an understanding of how to build a system that works.

If you had unlimited time, you could build a great microservices architecture solely through experimentation. You could adopt endless organizational models, try every methodology, and build microservices of various sizes. As long as you could measure your results, you'd continue to improve the system. With enough trials, you'd end up with a system that works for you as well as a lot of experience building microservice systems.

Chances are, though, that you don't have the luxury of unlimited time. So, how do you build the expertise you need to build better microservices?

To help address this challenge, we've developed a prescriptive microservices model. We've made decisions about team design, process, architecture, infrastructure, and even tools and technologies. We'll cover a large scope of topic areas while building a solution that brings those areas together. Our decisions are built on opinions based in experiences building microservices systems for large organizations. If you follow our instructions, by the end of the book you'll have built a simple, operational microservices system in a cloud-based architecture.

To help bring our microservices examples to life, we'll be using the backdrop of a fictional airline reservations system. It will be a vastly simplified version of what a real reservations system would look like. Our very basic airline reservations system will include two functions: a read-only flight information service and a seat reservation service.

Our goal is to guide you in building your first microservices implementation as quickly as possible. In our experience, the act of building a real system is the best way to gain a true understanding of the work involved and the key decisions. We don't expect you to agree with all of our decisions. In fact, questioning the decisions we've made for you is a big part of the learning journey! We hope that the model we build together is only the first of many microservices systems that you'll build.

The Dreyfus Model of Skill Acquisition

Starting a learning journey by following instructions is a tried-and-true path to gaining expertise. In Stuart and Hubert Dreyfus's Five-Stage Model of Adult Skill Acquisition (*https://oreil.ly/vs3ao*), the first stage involves following prescriptive guidance before proficiency and expertise are established.

The "Up and Running" Microservices Model

The scope of a microservices architecture is quite large. Unfortunately, we can't cover the entire scope in this single book. However, we've made an effort to cover the topic areas that are the most relevant to a microservices system and have the biggest impact on success. Let's take a quick look at what we'll be covering in our "up and running" microservices model.

Team design

We'll kick off our build in Chapter 2 by tackling the people side of a microservices system. We'll uncover the challenges of effective team design and the fundamental factors that influence microservice coordination. We'll also introduce the teams we'll be using within our example system along with a tool called Team Topologies to help design them.

Microservice design

After designing the teams, we'll introduce the SEED(S) process in Chapter 3. This is a design process that will help us create microservices that fulfill the needs of users and consumers with actionable interfaces and behaviors. Then, in Chapter 4, we'll take on the problem of designing the right boundaries for our example microservices. We'll also introduce some important Domain-Driven Design concepts and use a process called Event Storming to "rightsize" our services.

Data design

Data is one of the most difficult aspects of a microservices design. In Chapter 5, we'll take a look at the data factors you'll need to consider in a microservices system. We'll introduce the concept of data independence and lay the groundwork for the data architecture in our example project.

Cloud platform

Our microservices implementation will be built on top of a cloud-based infrastructure. In Chapter 6, we'll introduce and implement the principles of immutable infrastructure and infrastructure as code (IaC) as the foundation for our microservices infrastructure. We'll also introduce AWS as our cloud platform and build a GitHub Actions–based CI/CD pipeline. Then, in Chapter 7, we'll use that pipeline to design and develop an AWS-based microservices infrastructure that will include networking, a Kubernetes cluster, and a GitOps deployment tool.

Microservices development

With our infrastructure platform in place, we'll dive into the work of engineering the microservices. We'll start by covering the principles and tools you'll need to succeed in Chapter 8. Then in Chapter 9, we'll implement two independent, heterogeneous microservices for our example application.

Release and change

We'll bring the whole solution together in Chapter 10, where we'll deploy one of the example microservices we've engineered onto the cloud-based platform we've developed. To do this, we'll use a set of technologies including DockerHub, Kubernetes, Helm, and Argo CD. Finally, after release, we'll take a retrospective look at the system in Chapter 11.

 The model we've developed is built on a set of five guiding principles, including the twelve-factor app (*https://12factor.net*) pattern. If you're interested, you can read about our model's guiding principles at this book's GitHub repository (*https://oreil.ly/MicroservicesU pandRunning*).

Hopefully this short overview gives you an idea of the scope of our model and example application. By the end of the book we'll have implemented a full-fledged system. To get there, we'll need to make a lot of decisions. So, the first tool we'll need is a way of keeping track of the really important ones.

Decisions, Decisions…

When it comes to building software, decisions are a big deal. Professional software engineers and architects get paid a lot for the decisions that they make and the problems they solve. The quality of the software and the business outcomes they drive depend on the quality of those decisions.

But decisions aren't always easy to make. They also aren't always correct. We make the best decisions we can given the information, experience, and talent that we have. When any of those variables change, our decisions should change too. Some decisions are correct at the time, but become outdated when technology, people, or situations change. Some decisions were never good ones in the first place. In either case, we need a way of capturing the decisions that matter so we can re-evaluate and improve on them over time.

To address that need, we're going to use a tool called an *architecture decision record* (or ADR). We're not sure who invented the term *ADR* or when it was first used, but the idea of documenting design decisions has been around for a long time. The real problem is that most people don't take the time to do it. In our experience, ADRs are an extremely useful tool and a good way of getting clarity on the decisions that need to be made.

A good decision record needs to capture four important elements:

Context
> What is the challenge? What is the problem that we are trying to solve? What are the constraints? A decision record should give us a summary of these contextual elements. That way we can understand the rationale for a decision and why it may need to be updated.

Alternatives
> A decision isn't a decision unless there is a choice to be made. A good decision record should help us to understand what the choices are. This helps us to better understand the context and the "selection space" at the time the decision was made.

Choice
> At the heart of a decision is the choice. Every decision record needs to document the choice that was made.

Impact

Decisions have consequences and a decision record should document the important ones. What are the trade-offs? How will our decision choice impact the way we work or other decisions that need to be made?

You can create decision records however you like. You can write them up as text files, use a project management tool, or even track them in a spreadsheet. The format and tooling is less important than the content. As long as you capture the areas we've described you'll have a good decision record.

For our example project, we'll use an existing format called a *lightweight architectural decision record* (LADR). The LADR format was created by Michael Nygard (*https:// oreil.ly/_mVoC*), and is a nice concise way of documenting a decision record. Let's get to know LADR by building one together.

 If you want to use something other than LADR, Joel Parker Henderson maintains a great list of ADR formats and templates (*https://oreil.ly/T3Tc-*).

Writing a Lightweight Architectural Decision Record

The first key decision we'll record is the decision to keep a record of decisions. Put more simply, we'll create an ADR that says we intend to keep track of our decisions. As we've mentioned, we'll be using the LADR format. The nice thing about LADR is that it's designed to be lightweight. It lets us keep track of decisions in simple text files that we can write quickly. Since we're dealing with text files, we can even manage our decision records in the same way we manage source code.

LADRs are written using a text format called Markdown (*https://oreil.ly/oRyx0*), which provides an elegant and simple way of writing documentation. What's great about Markdown is that it's easy for humans to read in its raw form and most popular tools know how to render it. For example, Confluence, GitLab, GitHub, and Share-Point can all process Markdown and present it as a formatted, human-readable document.

To create our first Markdown-based LADR, open your favorite text editor and start working on a new document. The first thing we'll do is lay out the structure.

Add the following text to your LADR file:

```
# OPM1: Use ADRS for decision tracking

## Status
Accepted

## Context

## Decision

## Consequences
```

These are the key elements of our decision record. The # characters preceding the lines are Markdown tokens that will let the parser know that these lines are meant to be headings. Notice that we've given this decision a title that corresponds to the decision we're making. We've also given the decision the slightly cryptic title: "OPM1." This is just a short form code that will help us label and understand which part of the system the decision relates to. In this case, "OPM1" indicates that this is the first decision we're recording related to the operating model.

The `Status` header of our record lets us know what life-cycle stage this decision is in. For example, if you're drafting a new decision that you need to get agreement on, you might start with a status of `Proposed`. Or, if you're considering changing an existing decision, you might change its status to `Under Review`. In our case, we've already made the decision for you, so we've set the status to `Accepted`.

The `Context` section describes the problem, constraints, and background for the decision being made. In our case, we want to capture the need to log important decisions and why that's important. Add the following text (or your own variation of it) to the `Context` section of your record:

```
## Context
A microservices architecture is complex and we'll need to make many
decisions. We'll need a way to keep track of the important decision
we make, so that we can revisit and re-evalute them in the future.
We'd prefer to use a lightweight, text-based solution so that we
don't have to install any new software tools.
```

With the context in place, we can move on to recording the actual decision we've made. We can list some of the alternatives considered as well as our choice to use LADR. Add the following to the `Decision` section to document this fact:

```
## Decision
We've decided to use Michael Nygard's lightweight architectural
decision record (LADR) format. LADR is text based and is
lightweight enough to meet our needs. We'll keep each LADR record
in its own text file and manage the files like code.

We also considered the following alternative solutions:
```

```
* Project management tooling (not selected, because we didn't want
  to install tools)
* Informal or "word of mouth" record keeping (not reliable)
```

All that's left is to document the consequences. In our case, one of the key consequences is that we'll need to spend time actually documenting our decisions and managing the records. Let's capture that as follows:

```
## Consequences
* We'll need to write decision records for key decisions
* We'll need a source code management solution to manage decision record files
```

That's all it takes to write an LADR. This is an incredibly useful way of capturing your thinking and has the added benefit of forcing you to make rational, thoughtful decisions in the first place. As we build our example flights application, we'll be keeping a log of the key decisions we make. To save time, we won't write out the entire decision record. Instead we'll highlight that a key decision has been made as in the following note.

Key Decision: Use ADRs for Decision Tracking

Use ADRs to log the key decisions we've made in our system design and build.

You'll be able to find a detailed version of each decision record at this book's GitHub repository (*https://github.com/implementing-microservices/ADRs*).

Summary

In this chapter we introduced some foundational concepts for this book. We provided a loose definition of a microservices system, including a set of three key traits. We identified the reduction of coordination costs as the key microservices benefit. We also explored how complexity and analysis paralysis present challenges to microservices adopters.

To help address these challenges, we introduced the "up and running" microservices model—an opinionated, prescriptive implementation that will accelerate the learning process for implementers. We covered the aspects of the model and the topics we'll discuss. Finally, we introduced the concept of the architectural decision record (ADR) that we plan to use throughout the rest of the book.

With the overview out of the way, all that's left is to build the system. We'll kick things off in Chapter 2 by tackling how microservices work is done with a special focus on team coordination.

Designing a Microservices Operating Model

In this book, we'll be building a microservices-based application. To do that, we'll design and build microservices as well as the infrastructure and tools you need to support them. However, the truth is that success with microservices takes more than writing code and deploying it. To really succeed, you need to have the right people, the right ways of working, and the right principles in place to make the whole system work. That's why we want to start our journey by designing a general operating model for our application.

An *operating model* is the set of people, processes, and tools that underlies your system. It shapes all the decision making and work that you do when you build software. For example, an operating model can define the responsibilities of teams. It can also define governance over decision making and work.

You can think of the operating model as the "operating system" for your solution. All the work needed to build microservices happens on top of the team structures, processes, and boundaries you define. In practice, operating models can have a big scope and can be very detailed. But for our build, we'll reduce the scope and focus on the most important parts of a microservices system—how the teams are designed and how they work together.

That's what we'll be covering in this chapter: the relationship between teams and microservices implementations. We'll introduce a tool called Team Topologies and by the end of the chapter we'll have a team-based design that we can use as the foundation for the rest of our build.

You don't need to actually assemble the people and teams we've defined in order to follow along with our "up and running" microservices build.

Let's get started by taking a look at why teams and team design are so important in the first place.

Why Teams and People Matter

The model we're using in this book is mostly concerned with technology and tool decisions. But technology alone won't give you the value you need from a microservices system. Technology is important. Good technology choices make it easier for you to do things that may have been prohibitively difficult. At its best, technology opens doors and unlocks new opportunities. However, it's useless on its own.

You can have the world's best tools and platforms, but you'll fail if you don't have the right culture and organization in which to use them. The goal we're trying to reach in our model is to put good technology in the hands of independent, high-functioning teams. So we'll need to start by considering the types of teams and structure that will work best for the model we're going to develop.

In a microservices system, culture and team design matters. In our research for this book and in our own implementation experiences we've learned an important truth: people and process are critical success factors. A microservices implementation is valuable when it gives you the freedom to make changes easily and quickly. In practice, however, change is a byproduct of your organization's decision-making capability. If you can't make quality decisions quickly, you'll have a difficult time getting value from your microservices. It'd be like building a racing car with a very poor engine. No matter how well the car is built, it's never going to run the way it should.

The idea that team design and culture is important isn't a new one. Mel Conway captured the impact of team structure on system design eloquently in his now-famous article, "How Do Committees Invent?" (*https://oreil.ly/oRyx0*) Mel Conway's insightful observations spawned an even more famous paraphrasing of his thesis, called "Conway's Law":

> Any organization that designs a system (defined broadly) will produce a design whose structure is a copy of the organization's communication structure.
>
> —Attributed to Fred Brooks

Conway tells us that the output of an organization reflects the way its people and teams communicate. For example, consider a microservices team that must consult a centralized team of database experts whenever they need to change a data model. Chances are that the data model and data implementation will also be centralized in the system that gets produced. The system ends up matching the organization and coordination model.

The takeaway from all this is that the people in a microservices system matter. The way that they make decisions, do their work, and communicate with each other has a big impact on the system that gets produced. Generally speaking, there are three people factors that have the biggest impact on a microservices system: team size, team skills, and interteam coordination. Let's take a closer look at each of them, starting with size.

Team Size

The "micro" in microservices implies that size matters and smaller is best. To be honest, that's a bit of an oversimplification. But the truth remains: buliding smaller deployable services is an important part of succeeding with microservices. It also turns out that the size of the teams building those services matters a lot too.

If you have too many people on a team, they'll need to spend more time communicating with each other. That internal coordination will end up slowing the team down, resulting in slower delivery of changes. If you have too few people, you won't have enough minds and hands to get the work done. "Rightsizing" teams is an important part of your system design. While there isn't a specific size that works for everyone in all situations, a body of experience and studies on team sizes has evolved into accepted practice.

Bill Gore, cofounder of the Gore-Tex company, W. L. Gore, limited the size of company teams to keep them effective. To make that happen, he instituted a built-in size limit: everyone on a team must have a personal relationship (*https://oreil.ly/wduQE*) with one another. When a team gets so big that its members don't know each other, the unit has grown too large.

Anthropologist Robert Dunbar, in his studies of the social behavior of chimpanzees, observed that the group sizes of chimpanzees correlated to their brain size. By extrapolating these findings to his understanding of the human brain, he established a set of group sizes for people. The Dunbar number (*https://oreil.ly/-DbyT*) states that we can only comfortably maintain 150 stable relationships, based on the size of our brains. Dunbar also determined that humans could keep about 5 intimate, familial relationships and only about 15 trusted friends.

Perhaps most famously, Amazon CEO Jeff Bezos gave us the "two pizza rule" (*https://oreil.ly/ccT85*). It states that an Amazon team should be small enough that it can be fed with two pizzas. Although the specific details about the size of the pizzas and the appetite of the team members are unclear, a two-pizza team is probably going to land somewhere in the 5 to 15 person range that Dunbar describes and stands a good chance of maintaining the personal relationship heuristic that Gore describes.

All of these stories point to a size limit based on the ability for people to communicate effectively. Our experiences and our research align with this intuitive concept. To keep the rate of change high, we'll need to limit the size of the teams in our system. In our microservices model, we're going to keep the size of teams to somewhere between five to eight people.

Key Decision: Team Size Should Be Limited

The teams that perform work in our system should have no more than eight people each.

Keeping the team size down will help us limit the internal interaction needed. But it will have a knock-on effect. Smaller team sizes usually mean more teams. So, we'll need to be careful in how we design the rest of the system. It's no good to have small teams if they have to spend all their time coordinating with each other. To avoid that, we'll need to enable independent and autonomous work as much as safely possible.

Another side effect of making our teams smaller is that it limits the number of specialists we can have. With less people on the team, we'll need to make sure we have enough talent collectively to deliver a quality output. That's why we'll need to consider how we populate our teams from a skills perspective.

Team Skills

A team can only be as good as its members. If we want high-performing teams, we'll need to pay special attention to the way we decide who gets to be on a team. For example, which roles and specializations will our teams need? How talented and experienced should individual team members be? What is the right mix of skills and experience?

The truth is that these are difficult questions for us to answer universally. That's because people and culture are often the most unique thing about the place where you work. For example, a handful of companies spend a lot of money to have the top 1% of technology talent from around the world working for them. Another company might mostly hire local talent with a focus on career growth and learning on the job from a small number of experts. Good team design in these two companies will probably look quite different.

We want this book to be focused on building a microservices implementation. So, we won't go very deep into organizational and culture design. The good news is that there is a general principle we can adopt that seems to help microservices implementers universally. That's the principle of the cross-functional team.

In a cross-functional team, people with different types of expertise (or functions) work together toward the same goal. That expertise can span both technology and business domains. For example, a cross-functional team could contain UX designers, application developers, product owners, and business analysts.

Cross-functional teams have been around for a long time, dating back to at least the 1950s at the Northwestern Mutual Life Insurance Company.

A big advantage of building a team this way is that you can make better decisions faster. We've already established an upper limit on team size, by limiting membership to eight people. A "rightsized" team with the right people on board can move at high velocity with authority.

But who are the *right people*? When it came to team size, we had anecdotes, experience, and academic studies to draw on. But for team profiles, it's much more difficult to find consistent stories. For example, when we've seen a large cloud vendor work on microservices, they've used four to five experts with cross-domain knowledge, coupled with a single testing expert. Conversely, we've seen consulting companies use a large mix of specialized engineers, product owners, project managers, and testing experts on each team. The talent, experience, and culture of your organization will inform the precise mix of people.

So, rather than dictate exactly which roles you'll need on your teams, we'll make two general decisions for our model. First, teams should be cross-functional. Our experience shows that microservices work better when teams can make good decisions on their own. Cross-functional teams enable that. Second, teams should be comprised of members who directly influence the output. In this way, we'll pick people who we know can add value to the team. We don't need observers on the team or people who are only tangentially related to the work and decisions that are being made.

Key Decision: Principles for Team Membership Should Be Defined

Teams should be cross-functional and consist only of members who can add value to the team's deliverable, service, or product.

With the right size and the right people, we should be able to build effective teams that can get things done. As the number of teams grow, we'll also need to consider how teams coordinate with each other. That's the last team property we need to address.

Interteam Coordination

Building a team with the right size and filling it with the right people will help us create high-performing teams. But it's the communication among teams, rather than inside them, that can really bog down a microservices system. We highlighted the problem of coordination costs in "The Coordination Cost Problem" on page 4. If we can reduce the amount of coordination that takes place between teams, our microservices teams will be able to deliver changes faster.

It would be nice if our microservices teams could act completely autonomously and independently. If teams were free to make their own design, development, testing, and deployment decisions, there would be no "organizational friction" to slow things down. In our experience this isn't a practical method of operation.

That's because coordination and collaboration are important for the success of an organization. We might want our microservices teams to act independently, but we also want them to create services that are valuable to customers, users, and the organization. This means communication is required to establish shared goals, communicate change requests, deliver feedback, and resolve problems.

On top of this, when teams operate completely independently, there's less opportunity to share. Microservices teams working independently can pick the right tools for the right job and build highly efficient systems. But that efficiency is localized to the team. Sometimes, that means we lose out on *system-level* efficiency. For example, if all our teams design and build their own cloud-based network architectures, we've lost an opportunity to do that work once and share it.

 It's possible to build an organization that enables efficient team independence and autonomy through self-organization. For example, microservices pioneer Fred George has described a method he calls Programmer Anarchy (*https://oreil.ly/C1N0f*), in which technology teams have full autonomy (and responsibility) to form teams, choose work, and design their own solutions. But in our experience most enterprise organizations would have difficulty pulling this off consistently.

If we go too far towards team independence and autonomy, we'll introduce system-level inefficiencies and misalignment with organizational goals. If we introduce too much coordination, we risk bogging the whole system down and losing the benefits of highly changeable microservices. The challenge is to strike the right balance between independent work and coordinated efforts. That takes some experimentation and continuous tuning of your team design.

Most importantly, optimizing team coordination requires an active design effort. One of the mistakes we've seen practitioners make is to focus solely on the technical architecture. When that happens, the team design forms around the technology that's been created. It's only then that the problems with the coordination model become obvious. By that point, it's often too costly or too difficult to make changes.

To avoid this problem, we'll address team coordination and team design as the first step of our system design process. Some people call this an "inverse Conway maneuver," because the communication structure we design will end up informing the system that gets created. Whatever you want to call it, we've found that starting with a focus on team design and coordination can really help you succeed with your microservices design. In fact, this point is so important that we'll log it as a decision.

> ## Key Decision: When to Design Teams and Coordination Models
>
> Team and coordination design should start before the design of the system architecture or microservices. The team and coordination models must continually be updated and improved for the life of the system.

We'll cover this in the rest of this chapter. First, we'll introduce a useful tool for designing microservices team models called Team Topologies.

Introducing Team Topologies

Since we're going to start our design work with a focus on teams, we'll need a way of cataloging and communicating our decisions. There are plenty of ways of documenting team designs. For our model, we'll use a design tool called Team Topologies.

Team Topologies (*https://teamtopologies.com*) is a design approach invented by Matthew Skelton and Manuel Pais. We like using it because it provides a formal language for talking about team design, with a special focus on the way teams work with each other.

We won't be using every aspect of the Team Topologies approach in our design work. Instead, we'll be drawing on three elements: team types, team interaction modes, and diagramming. With these parts, we'll be able to build a simple, working design for our microservices teams.

Next, we'll look at different parts of the Team Topology approach, starting with the types of teams we can define.

Team Types

One of the core concepts of Team Topologies is *team types*. These are archetypes or categories that describe the basic nature of a team, from the perspective of its communication with the rest of an organization. There are four team types defined in Team Topologies: stream-aligned, enabling, complicated-subsystem, and platform. Let's take a quick look at each of them:

Stream-Aligned

A stream-aligned team owns and runs a deliverable piece of work. The key characteristic of this team is a continual delivery of something relevant to the business organization. The stream-aligned team embodies Amazon CTO Werner Vogel's comment (*https://oreil.ly/bIwkK*) on the responsibilities of Amazon teams: "You build it, you run it." Stream-aligned teams don't disband after a release. Instead, they continue to own and implement a "stream" of changes, improvements, and fixes to their business deliverable. For example, microservices teams are usually stream-aligned as they continually release features to the services they own.

Enabling

An enabling team supports the work of other teams with a consulting engagement model. These teams are usually composed of specialists and subject matter experts who can bridge gaps in expertise or capability. But they can also help individual teams understand the bigger picture of the organization or industry they are operating in. For example, an enabling architecture team can help microservices teams understand emerging technical standards and conventions in the organization.

Complicated-Subsystem

This type of team works on a domain or on subject matter that is difficult to understand. Or at least, it's difficult enough that there is a lack of available resources in the organization. Some problem areas don't scale well and can't be embedded in every team. For example, tuning software for cryptographic security requires a special kind of expertise and experience. Rather than trying to scale that skill across all teams, most organizations create a complicated-subsystem security team who can engage with individual teams as needed.

Platform

Like enabling teams, the platform team provides support to the rest of the organization, with one important difference—platform teams deliver a self-service enablement experience to their users. While the enabling and complicated-subsystem teams are limited by the bandwidth of their people, a platform team invests in building supporting tools and processes that can scale easily. This requires more up-front investment and continual maintenance and support. The platform becomes a product, whose users are the rest of the teams in the organization. For example, operations teams can become platform teams when they offer build and release tools to development teams for them to use.

With an understanding of these four team types, we can start communicating how we want our teams to operate. To really communicate our team design, we will need one more part of the model: the ways in which teams interact with each other, which we'll cover next.

Interaction Modes

Our goal in designing teams for the microservices build is to reduce the amount of coordination that needs to happen for work to get done. The Team Topology team types help us identify the basic characteristics of a team. To really understand how and where we can reduce coordination costs, we'll need to articulate the way our teams are coordinating with each other. That's where the Team Topology interaction modes come in. In their book, Skelton and Pais discuss three interaction modes, which describe different levels of coordination:

Collaboration

This interaction mode requires both teams to work closely together. Collaboration provides opportunities for teams to learn, discover, and innovate. But it requires high levels of coordination from each team and is difficult to scale. For example, a security team might collaborate with a microservices team to develop a more secure version of their software. The collaborative work might entail designing, writing, and testing code together.

Facilitating

A facilitating interaction is similar to a collaborative one, but it is unidirectional. Instead of teams working together to solve a shared problem, one team plays a support role to help the other team deliver their desired outcome. An example of a facilitating interaction would be when an infrastructure team helps a microservices team understand how to troubleshoot issues with the network architecture they've been provided.

X-as-a-service

Sometimes team collaboration takes on a consumer-provider flavor. In this type of interaction, one team provides a service to other teams in the organization with minimal levels of coordination. This usually occurs when a team releases a shared process, document, library, API, or platform. *X*-as-a-service interactions tend to scale well because they require less coordination. They are also a natural fit for platform teams, but other team types may incorporate this mode as well. For example, an enabling architecture team might document a list of recommended software patterns and offer those to all microservices teams in a "patterns as a service" model.

There's a lot more to Team Topologies then we've outlined here. Taken together, this categorization of team types and interactions gives us a great palette of terms we can use to paint a picture of what our microservices teams should look like, with particular emphasis on when and how much our teams will need to coordinate. In the next section, we'll use the terms we've borrowed from Team Topology to design a microservices team model.

Designing a Microservices Team Topology

The Team Topology approach gives us a language for talking about team coordination. What makes it really special, is that it's a language built for visual representations. In this section, we're going to create a design for our microservices teams that communicates the teams we need and how they will work together. When we're done, we'll have a diagram that highlights the main points of team coordination and interaction.

To create a team design and Team Topology, we'll follow this step-by-step approach:

1. Establish a system design team.

2. Create a microservices team template for future teams.

3. Define platform teams.

4. Add enabling and complicated-subsystem teams.

5. Add key consumer teams.

As we go through each of the steps, we'll be documenting our team design and building our Team Topology. For each step we'll identify one or more teams, create and populate a team design document, and draw the key interactions for that team. Let's get started by focusing on the system design team.

 There isn't a single Team Topology that is a good fit for everyone. It would be impossible to account for your organization's size, people, skills, and needs. The topology we've created here is a consolidated version of large enterprise-scale implementations that we've seen work well.

Establish a System Design Team

A microservices system is a complex system with lots of parts and lots of people doing work. The software that gets built emerges from the collective decision making and work of all those people together. In our experience, getting everything to work together the way you want isn't easy. That's why you'll need to designate a group of people who can shape the vision and behavior of the system. In our model, we'll call this group the system design team.

In our model, the system design team has three core reponsibilities:

Design team structures

The system design team is the first team we're putting together. It's also the team that we expect to design the teams that will do the work of building the system. That's the work we'll be doing in our subsequent team design steps. In effect, we're playing the role of the system design team together.

Establish standards, incentives, and "guardrails"

In addition to forming teams, the system design team should shape the decisions that individual teams can make. This ensures that teams produce results that align with our system goals. One way to do this is by enacting standards that dictate what teams can and can't do. That's the prescriptive approach we've taken for many of the decisions in this book. In practice, too much standardization is difficult to maintain and too restrictive for a healthy system. Good designers will introduce incentives to get more of the behavior they want and "guardrails" that act as lighter recommendations and references rather than outright rules.

Continually improve the system

Finally, the system design team needs to continually improve all the team designs, standards, incentives, and guardrails that have been introduced. To do that, they'll need to establish a way of monitoring or measuring the system as a whole so that they can make changes and introduce improvements.

It's useful to document these team responsibilities so that we can clearly communicate what each team does. In fact, we should document all of the key properties of our teams to make it easier to understand and improve them as the system evolves. At a minimum, we should cover the Team Topology type, the size of the team, and the responsibilities we've defined earlier.

Let's start by deciding on a Team Topology type. After the initial setup of team designs and standards, we expect the system design team to focus on helping other teams build microservices and supporting components. We expect most of their work to be consulting based, facilitating delivery teams and helping them navigate the system. Although the system design team delivers a system, the work we want them to do is characteristic of an enabling team type.

We also want the system design team to be small. It should consist of just a few senior leaders, architects, and system designers who can quickly make decisions together for the system as a whole. To that end, we'll limit the size of the team to between three to five people—even less than our general team size that we decided on earlier.

Let's capture these decisions and team properties by creating a lightweight design document for the system design team. Using your favorite text or document editor, create a file named *system-design-team.md* and populate it with the following content:

```
# System Design Team

## Team Type
Enabling

## Team Size
3-5 People

## Responsibilities
* Design team structures
* Establish standards and "guardrails"
* Continually improve the system
```

The nice thing about using a text file for our team documentation is that we can treat it like code. Because of this, we can store the documentation in a code repository and version it whenever we need to make changes. Alternatively, you can use a wiki, document repository, or whatever works best in your company. We'll leave it to you to decide how you want to manage your team design files. You can find all of the examples for our team designs in our GitHub repository (*https://oreil.ly/ Microservices_UpandRunning_team-designs*).

At this point, we'd typically diagram the team visually and map out its interactions with other teams in the system. This is the heart of our team design work and allows us to visualize how teams will work together. For example, we can expect the system design team to use a facilitating interaction model with microservices teams. But since this is the first team we've defined, we don't have anything to interact with. So we'll leave the diagramming work for later.

With the system design team document created, we can move on to documenting and diagramming our microservices teams.

Building a Microservices Team Template

In the "up and running" model, every microservice is owned by a team. This single team owns the decisions and work of designing, building, delivering, and maintaining a microservice. In practice, a single team may own multiple microservices. This is fine, and avoids unnecessary growth of teams. The most important constraint is that the responsibility for a microservice is not shared across multiple teams. Microservice ownership will be limited to an accountable and responsible team.

As your system matures, you'll end up with lots of microservices. You'll also likely end up with lots of microservices teams. Since we expect to have multiple microservices teams operating in our system, we won't design each of them individually. Instead, we'll define a microservices team template that can be applied to any new teams we create. Think of this as creating a cookie cutter that we can use to "punch out" some microservices teams later on when we need them. Or, if you have a programming background, you can think of this as defining a "class," for which we'll be creating "instances" later.

To get started, we'll do the same thing we did for our system design team—define some essential team properties. Just like before, we'll document the team type, team size, and responsibilities. As we mentioned before, our microservices teams are expected to own one or more microservices independently. That ownership includes running the service and releasing a continuous stream of improvements, fixes, and changes as needed.

With that characteristic, it makes sense to classify the microservices team as stream-aligned. We'll also stick to the team-sizing decision we made earlier in this chapter and keep the team size between five to eight people. Let's document all of these properties like we did before. Create a file named *microservice-team-template.md* and populate it with the following content:

```
# Microservices Team Template

## Team Type
Stream-Aligned

## Team Size
5-8 People

## Responsibilities
* Designing and developing microservice(s)
* Testing, building, and delivering the microservice(s)
* Troubleshooting issues
```

With the template definition documented, we can start diagramming our team interaction model. To do that, open a drawing or diagramming tool and draw a horizontal rectangle as shown in Figure 2-1. We have used yellow for this; each type of team should have its own color.

Figure 2-1. A stream-aligned microservices team

 If you don't have a favorite diagramming tool, diagrams.net (*https://www.diagrams.net*) and Lucidchart (*https://www.lucid chart.com*) are good browser-based options that are free to get started with. Of course, you're also free to diagram the old-fashioned way, with a pen and a napkin!

In the previous section we defined our system design team. Now that we have our microservices team diagrammed, we can add the systems team into the picture. Draw the system design team using a vertical rectangle, as shown in Figure 2-2.

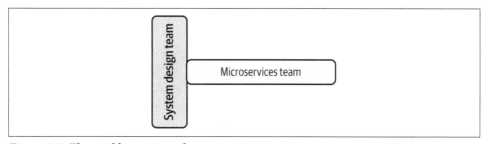

Figure 2-2. The enabling system design team

Use a unique color (we have used violet) for the system design team to denote that it's an enabling team. We've placed it vertically and to the left of the microservices team to show an interaction between the two teams. In this case, we expect the system design team to facilitate the microservices teams. To keep things simple, we aren't going to model the specific details of the interaction mode. Highlighting that the teams will need to interact is enough now.

 Our color choices for the team types in this chapter are based on the illustrations shown on the Team Topologies website (*https:// oreil.ly/dgEUz*).

In practice, as your system evolves, you'll need to replace this generic "Microservices team" box with the actual names of your teams and the services they are working on. Over time, you may also need to capture the interactions that must take place between your microservices teams. For example, if one microservice needs to invoke another service, chances are there will be some coordination work that is worth capturing.

We use a particular color to denote that our microservices team is stream-aligned. We'll be updating this diagram as we go through the team design steps, so keep your drawing tool handy for later on. You may also want to save the diagram so you don't lose any work.

Now that we have our first two teams modeled, let's take a look at the cloud platform team.

Platform Teams

Platform teams are an important part of a microservices system. Most of the microservices work is done by independent, stream-aligned teams. Without support, however, they'll need to figure out how to solve a lot of development, testing, and implementation problems on their own. Our facilitating system design team can enable some of their decision making, but the microservices teams will still need to deal with the complexities of an entire technology stack and architecture.

That's where platform team types can help. There are a lot of common components in a microservices system. A platform team can make those common components available for microservices to use "as a service." The service model improves the scalability of platform components, reducing the coordination problems that usually occur when shared components are centralized.

In our model, we've decided to instantiate a cloud platform team that offers a network, application, and deployment infrastructure to the rest of the organization as a service. We'll get into the details of what this offering looks like in Chapter 7, when we dive into infrastructure design. The key point for now is that the teams in our system will be able to create new environments on demand using the infrastructure services that our platform team provides.

With those details understood, we can document our cloud platform team in a file called *cloud-platform-team.md* with the following team properties:

```
# Cloud Platform Team

## Team Type
Platform

## Team Size
5-8 People
```

```
## Responsibilities
* Design and develop a network infrastructure
* Design and develop an application infrastructure
* Provide tools for building a new environment
* Update network and application infrastructure when required
```

Notice that one of the responsibilities of our cloud platform team is to update the infrastructure that is being offered. This is a key part of a platform team's responsibility. They need to treat the users of the platform as if they are customers. In this relationship, the platform offering needs to be continually improved to meet their customer's requirements and expectations.

As we've done before, we'll add the cloud platform team to the Team Topology diagram that we've been working on. But this time we need to model a platform team. To do that, draw a horizontal rectangle (again, using a unique color; we've used light blue) below the microservices teams and connected to the system design team, as shown in Figure 2-3.

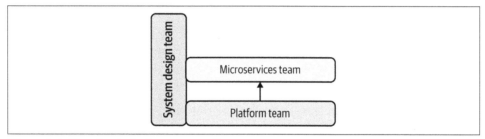

Figure 2-3. The cloud platform team offering a service

Note that we've also drawn a small black arrow between the platform and microservices teams. This is to show that the platform team is implementing the x-as-a-service model for its interaction with the microservices team. Our diagram also shows that the system design team will be enabling the work of the platform team. This will ensure that the platform fits the goals and vision for the overall system.

For our "up and running" model, we've only defined a single instance of a platform team. But, in practice, you'll probably need to roll out multiple platform teams to keep the teams to a manageable size. When that happens, you'll also need to be consider how multiple platform teams will coordinate together to offer services to the rest of the organization.

Enabling and Complicated-Subsystem Teams

With the three teams we've designed, we have enough people in place to be able to deliver a microservices system. Beyond these core capabilities, there may be additional capabilities that we want a team to own. That may be because there is an important set of skills that we want to provide enablement for. Or, because there is a complicated system feature that requires a dedicated team.

In our microservices model, we've decided to create a specialized release team. This additional team owns the responsibility of releasing (or deploying) microservices into a production-like environment. While a microservices team could deploy its own services directly into a production environment, in our experience this isn't always what happens.

That's because in most organizations there is usually an additional testing and acceptance check that needs to happen before a service can go live. Instead of deploying directly into production, microservices teams deliver a built and tested container. That container is then automatically deployed by a release team who coordinates the work of tests, approvals, and deployment of the change.

The release team embodies the complicated-subsystem team type. It contains specialist knowledge of the release, approval, and deployment process and collaborates with stream-aligned teams to make that work happen. To document the design of our release team, create a file called *release-team.md* with the following properties:

```
# Release Team

## Team Type
Complicated-Subsystem

## Team Size
5-8 People

## Responsibilities
* Releasing microservices to production
* Coordinating approvals for releases
```

Next, we'll add the release team to the developing picture of our Team Topology. Complicated-subsystem teams are modeled with yet another specific color.

So, open your Team Topology diagram and add a square (we've colored it red) near the end of the microservices team's box, as shown in Figure 2-4.

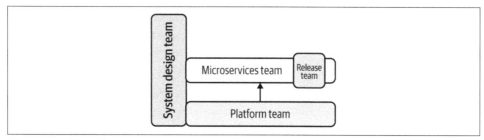

Figure 2-4. The release team

As we can see from our emerging topology, one of the trade-offs to the release team approach is the coordination costs it brings. At scale, this can become a big problem. For example, if you want to perform daily releases across multiple microservices, the release team will struggle to coordinate all of that activity. If you find yourself in that situation, you'll need to change the team design and shift the responsibilities for deployment to the individual microservices teams.

The release team is the final team at the core of our microservices model. But to finish our design, we need to consider the teams that will have to use our microservices. We'll cover that next.

Consumer Teams

Microservices are only useful if they are used. So, it's worthwhile identifying the consumers of our microservices and how they'll interact with our system teams. In some architectures, that could include mobile application development teams, web development teams, or even third-party organizations. In our model, the main consumer of our microservices system is the API team.

The API team is responsible for exposing our microservices to other development teams as an application programming interface (API). For example, a mobile application development team would interact with the API released by this team and never call our microservices directly.

We'll get into the details of the API and the architecture later in the book. For now, it's worth detailing the properties of our API team and its responsibilities. We can do that by creating a file named *api-team.md* and populating it as follows:

```
# API Team

## Team Type
Stream-Aligned

## Team Size
5-8 People

## Responsibilities
* Design, develop, and maintain APIs at the boundary of the system
* Connect API to internal microservices
```

Just like the microservices team, the API team is a stream-aligned team. That's because it needs to continually deliver changes to the API that reflect business needs and consumer demands. A special nuance of the API team is that, because the API needs to call microservices to function, it is dependent on the microservices team.

We can model these interaction properties in our Team Topology model by adding another rectangle at the top of our diagram to represent the API team. It should be of the same color as the microservices team (we've used yellow), as it is also a stream-aligned team. To reflect the dependency between our microservices and API teams, we'll again use a black arrow to show an *x*-as-a-service engagement model. This indicates that the microservices team will need to make sure their services are invocable and usable in a self-service fashion.

When you're finished, the diagram should look something like Figure 2-5.

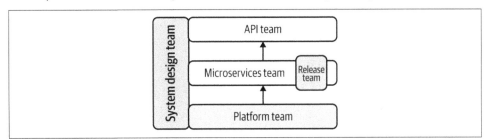

Figure 2-5. The finished Team Topology with the API team

With this final team defined an in the picture, our topology looks a lot like the finished product we showed you at the start of this section. With the topology defined, we can see where the main coordination points are where the work is being done. Overall, our model enables a fairly independent, autonomous way of working. However, we'll need to invest some time and effort into building a cloud platform as a service to make our model work.

With our basic Team Topology defined, we can see how this work ties back to the goal of our chapter—building an operating model.

Summary

Taken together, the decisions, team definitions, and topologies we've just created form our microservices operating model. With it, we've defined the teams that need to be created, their characteristics and responsibilities, and the way we expect our teams to work together. It's an important design step and will influence the rest of our microservices work. In fact, every decision we make from this point on will be heavily influenced by the operating model we've just established.

In truth, we didn't go very deep with our operating model design. In practice, it's worthwhile drawing out more than one Team Topology diagram to reflect different types of interaction modes. For example, the toubleshooting problems with our system would likely require a different engagement model from the one we've shown. Similarly, we haven't diagrammed the interactions required to change the deliverables that the cloud platform, system design, and release teams provide.

In addition to the initial design, the operating model design should be continually improved. One of the nice things about capturing our team definitions and topologies as documents is that we can treat them like code. So we can version and manage changes as the system evolves. You may even want to add additional design assets to your collection. For example, you could define service-level agreements for platform teams and skill inventories for your stream-aligned teams.

Ultimately, our goal in this chapter was to create a foundation for the rest of our design and development work. Our lightweight approach to the Team Topology and team designs does just that. With our operating model in hand, we can move on to designing the actual microservices. That's what we'll cover in Chapter 3.

Designing Microservices: The SEED(S) Process

If you recall, in Chapter 1, we stated that the main benefit of adopting microservices architecture is the ability to increase development speed without compromising safety of a system, at scale. This is an extremely important benefit for organizations tackling significantly complex problems. Note though that this certainly happens as a result of a conscious design, not by accident. In all but the simplest cases, it is impossible to iterate toward a successful microservices architecture without an effective and explicit, end-to-end system design.

In this chapter, we introduce an evolutionary process for designing microservices. This methodology was first formulated by one of the authors at a healthcare startup he cofounded, and later successfully implemented on numerous projects at other companies. The flexible approach has proven equally as effective for smaller organizations tackling complex problems; for eaxmple, a pioneering startup revolutionizing the vast healthcare industry and a large organization with thousands of software engineers across hundreds of teams.

Key Decision: Use a Standard Process for Service Design

Use a standard, repeatable process to achieve consistently high-quality, customer-centric design for the services in your system.

The microservices design system described in this chapter is a top-down, multistep methodology, and a collection of reusable processes, where each later step evolves from a previous one. Due to its evolutionary nature, we call the system *Seven Essential Evolutions of Design for Services* or *SEED(S)*. We find the tongue-in-cheek name fitting, given that the analyses performed with this methodology often prove to be the essential seeds from which a beautiful, complex microservices system emerges. Just as a beautiful, flourishing garden starts with planting of some key seeds, the SEED(S) analysis and design process is an essential first step of your microservices implementation that facilitates the later, coding part.

Introducing the Seven Essential Evolutions of Design for Services: The SEED(S) Method

As James Lewis and Martin Fowler point out in their seminal article about microservices, one of the main traits of the microservices architecture is componentization of a system via services (*https://oreil.ly/DVxRp*). By "services," they mean software components that are independently deployable and accessible over standard network protocols, such as a web service request or a remote procedure call. By exposing system components as services, among other things, we commit to defining explicit public interfaces for them. Increasing the flexibility and usability of these interfaces through good design can have a profound impact on the robustness of the system's architecture and on developer productivity.

The SEED(S) process provides a repeatable, reliable, and battle-tested methodology for designing service interfaces that are user-friendly and robust.

It should also be noted that, as a generic approach, the SEED(S) methodology is useful beyond just microservices and can be effective in the design of any number of service types, including RESTful and GraphQL APIs created for frontend UIs. This wide range of applicability should not be surprising. After all, from a technical perspective, a microservice is also a kind of API, just developed with a specific type of boundaries in mind—those that minimize coordination needs.

Without further ado, the seven steps of the SEED(S) process are:

1. Identifying actors
2. Identifying jobs that actors have to do
3. Discovering interaction patterns with sequence diagrams
4. Deriving high-level actions and queries based on jobs to be done (JTBDs) and the interaction patterns
5. Describing each query and action as a specification, with an open standard (such as the OpenAPI Specification [OAS] or GraphQL schemas)
6. Getting feedback on the API specification
7. Implementing microservices

Let's explore each of these steps in greater detail and see how we can master using them for service design.

Identifying Actors

In addition to being an evolutionary methodology, SEED(S) takes a distinctly customer-centric approach, viewing as products the services it is used to design. By now the "APIs are products" mantra is not particularly novel; we have been shouting it (*https://oreil.ly/y8CHg*) from all possible mountaintops for years. The good thing is that a product-oriented perspective on APIs and services allows us to reuse a wealth of techniques from the business world, where it is nothing new; in fact, the science and art of product management significantly predates that of APIs and even the internet itself. Many people track product management as a field (*https://oreil.ly/lunbc*) back to the 1930s with Procter & Gamble and Neil H. McElroy's (*https://oreil.ly/yYLlg*) attempts to improve the sales of P&G's Camay brand of soap. In the ensuing decades product management has evolved significantly, and there are a lot of lessons learned that we can reuse in the much more nascent API/services management space. If APIs are products, we should be able to use similar techniques to design APIs as what we use in product management.

When designing a product, and consequently an API or a service, we have to understand the "customer"; who is the service designed for? Typically, in the API and service management space, we don't call these personas "customers" but rather the less commerce-oriented denomination of "actor," removing any accidental, unintended connotation of a financial transaction or interest being present between the service consumer and a publisher.

Usage of "actors" in the first modeling step of SEED(S) methodology is inspired by the interaction design's heritage of using "user personas" for a similar need. The notion of personas, as an interaction design tool, was introduced by Alan Cooper in his 1998 book, *The Inmates Are Running the Asylum* (Sams Publishing), and has gained significant adoption since. To be completely transparent, at this point personas have also received their share of criticism (*https://oreil.ly/g1SYg*) (which methodology has not?), and some product teams passionately advocate using real user data instead. Discussing the pros and cons of personas in product management is far, far beyond the scope of this book. Actors are inspired by, but are not identical to, user personas. The purpose of actors is to aid in the modeling exercise at the stage in the design process when actual user data is typically limited.

The main motivation for starting modeling with the definition of actors is to aid in scoping and prioritization. Typical plagues of API and service design in our industry are overabstraction and lack of clarity regarding user needs. Too many APIs are simply exposures of some database tables over HTTP or an attempt to provide direct networked access into application internals, via remote procedure calls (RPCs). Such approaches often struggle in delivering for customer needs and achieving business goals. It should not be surprising. If we don't even ask, "Who will be using this API?" and "What are their needs?" how can we possibly design solutions that solve for their needs? And yet too many APIs and services are designed exactly this way: using a service publisher's goals, rather than that of the consumer. SEED(S) addresses this upside-down problem from the very first step, by identifying the actors first.

Key Decision: Scope Service Design Using Key Actors

Start service design by identifying key actors in your domain, to achieve customer-centric scoping of the capabilities represented by the services.

There are several fundamental rules for identifying the right set of actors for your goals:

1. Much like with Cooper's user personas, each actor must be *specific*, more so than *precise*. By this we mean that identifying the boundaries of what key traits differentiate various actors of our design is more important than identifying an excruciating level of detail for who the actors are. We ought to always remember that we are in the process of modeling and so any modeling exercise is by definition imprecise: it's not that we cannot capture the details, rather that we don't care about every single detail and are trying to capture the prioritized view of the reality relevant to us.

2. Overlapping or too-broad actor definitions are usually red flags. Actors also must be defined in context. Having a company-wide "portfolio" of actors that are reused for each application design is more than an indication of trouble—it's an "all alarms on, call 911" sure sign that the process has derailed and has been compromised.

3. As models, actor definitions first and foremost represent the needs, pain points, and behaviors inherent to each actor archetype. These needs and behaviors that distinguish one actor type from another are relevant, and there should be very limited overlap.

4. Less is more—you should use as few distinct actors as possible to describe your problem area, but no fewer than necessary. In most cases, if you have more than five actors for a service, it may be either an indication of prioritization gone awry, or service boundaries that are too broad.

Example Actors in Our Sample Project

Following are some of the possible actors relevant to the sample project we introduced in Chapter 1; an airline's online reservation system, or, more specifically, its flight reservation subsystem:

Frequent flyer
Emma travels for work, has elite loyalty status with the airline, manages her travel through her work's reservation system, and uses a number of connected apps to stay on top of her busy schedule. Due to her loyalty status, she is eligible for many perks. Often planning trips on short notice, when traveling with family, she typically uses loyalty miles.

Family vacationer
Riley and their spouse are mostly traveling for vacations with their kid(s). They usually plan trips well in advance, and travel infrequently.

Airline customer service agent
Sean is an experienced customer service agent assisting travelers with booking, rebooking, and resolving issues during travel and after through phone and online chat.

Once we have identified actors for our design effort, we can analyze the jobs that they have to do using our system. Let's explore what we mean by this in the next section.

Identifying Jobs That Actors Have to Do

Once we identify a target class of customers (actors, in our case), we need to spend a significant amount of our time understanding the jobs they have to get done, and only then create a solution that best addresses their needs. This is a critical point often misunderstood or ignored in the design of services and APIs, so let us try to explain the rationale behind its importance.

Any effective API or service design methodology, including SEED(S), is based on a fundamental premise we mentioned earlier: that APIs and microservices are types of products, and in their design we can successfully employ the rich product management toolset that has been developed over many decades. We already applied one such tool to our modeling process: the identification of actors, in the manner of user personas from interaction design. In this second step we will dive even deeper into product design, so it may be worth reiterating: why do we believe APIs are products? After all, a technical capability that is exposed over a network, using standard protocols, i.e., what we call an "API," doesn't necessarily have an obvious resemblance to hand soaps, winter jackets, smartphones, and other physical products that we are more accustomed to.

Well, what is a general definition of a *product*, anyway? There is no one, true definition that we are aware of, so we might as well use the one Wikipedia references (*https://oreil.ly/blWDL*):

> We define a product as anything that can be offered to a market for attention, acquisition, use or consumption that might satisfy a want or need. Products include more than just tangible objects, such as cars, computers or mobile phones. Broadly defined, "products" also include services, events, persons, places, organizations and ideas, or mixes of these.
>
> —Kotler et al., *Principles of Marketing*, 7th edition (Pearson)

Services, whether web APIs or microservices, do satisfy this definition: producers offer services to their respective consumer(s), they satisfy the needs of their consumers, and this supply/demand can create a "market."

Consumers of APIs are typically frontend (web, mobile) or third-party (partner) applications, while consumers of microservices are various parts of the system itself, but that's a distinction largely irrelevant to their design process. We will dive into defining differences between APIs and microservices later in this chapter.

So if APIs and microservices *are* products, how do we create better ones? The identification of actors is the first step, but what comes next? They must solve a customer's problem. Alas, the unfortunate reality is that too many products are designed from the perspective of a solution provider obsessing about what *they* have to offer rather than concentrating on the problems customers need to solve. Probably the most succinct explanation of this problem comes from the famous words of Harvard Business School marketing professor Theodore Levitt: "People don't want to buy a quarter-inch drill. They want a quarter-inch hole!"[1] Indeed, if you are a product company producing drills, you need to realize that the real job customers are trying to get done may be hanging a picture on their walls, not shopping for the most perfect general-purpose drill. If you fail to realize this, continuing your pursuit of perfecting a drill, you will eventually be outmaneuvered by an inventor who comes up with a simpler, alternative solution to getting quarter-inch holes in customer walls. It may be a chemical reaction of sorts or something else—we wouldn't know—but it will happen.

If you look at the history of technological advancement, it's the problems that are timeless; solutions change and evolve all the time. Case in point—nobody uses magnetic tapes or floppy disks to save data anymore, but the job of needing to save and transport data has not gone anywhere, even if it is all cloud-based now. Innovators must concentrate more on solving problems, and less on perfecting the tools that are typically transient.

---

1 Quoted in Clayton M. Christensen et al., "What Customers Want from Your Products," Harvard Business School, 2016, *https://oreil.ly/NKolz*.

Harvard Business School professor Clayton Christensen names this observation the "theory of jobs to be done," explaining that:

> [Customers] often buy things because they find themselves with a problem they would like to solve.
>
> —Clayton Christensen, *The Innovator's Solution* (Harvard Business Review Press)

In the Harvard Business School article quoted previously, "What Customers Want from Your Products," Christensen and his coauthors further explain that product designs are successful and customers find them desirable when "the job, not the customer, is the fundamental unit of analysis."

Key Decision: Use Jobs as the Unit of Analysis

Use jobs that key actors have to get done, in your domain, as the unit of analysis for collecting requirements.

Using Job Story Format to Capture JTBDs

For each of the actors we identify, we need to discover top JTBDs for that actor. For the sake of uniformity, as well as to make sure key data points are well-documented, we capture JTBDs in a standard format. The SEED(S) process uses the *Job Stories* format as defined by Paul Adams (*https://oreil.ly/VJQui*): "when <a circumstance>, I want to <motivation>, so I can <goal>" (see Figure 3-1).

Figure 3-1. Structure of a Job Story format

A Job Story centers around circumstances, the actor's motivations for a job to be done, and the goal that they are trying to achieve.

Please note that in Adams's original format, Job Stories are written in first person. In SEED(S), as you will see further in this chapter, we prefer to write Job Stories in third person, highlighting who the actual actor for the Job Story is.

If you are familiar with *User Stories* (*https://oreil.ly/PT6-v*) from Scrum or other Agile methodologies, you may have noticed that the Job Story looks almost identical. However, as Alan Klement explains in his blog post, "Replacing the User Story with the Job Story" (*https://oreil.ly/UGXy_*), there are crucial differences between the two. User

Stories revolve around a user persona; they start with "as a <persona>," while Job Stories disregard the persona and instead emphasize the circumstance.

This is important and aligned with Christensen's "the job, not the customer, is the fundamental unit of analysis." It is also spot-on, because in the context of describing a specific job, persona does not matter anymore. If I need to hang a painting on a wall, it doesn't really matter whether I am a licensed contractor or a novice homeowner, I will need a quarter-inch hole in the wall (or several). It is the context, the circumstance in which we have a motivation to achieve a goal that matters, not who we are. Long story short, we identify actors to scope the list of jobs, but at the point of describing each job for that actor, we need to identify circumstances and not just repeat 10 times "as a frequent flyer…"

> ## Key Decision: Use the Standard Job Story Format
>
> Use a standard format for capturing JTBDs (known as Job Story) to uniformly capture circumstances, motivations, and goals for all your jobs.

Example JTBDs in Our Sample Project

Let's pick some JTBDs for a family vacationer actor:

1. *When* Riley is planning a flight for their family vacation, *they want to* be able to filter available flights by multiple criteria, including: four adjacent seats available on the flight, the number of connections, connections that go through airports that have facilities friendly to young children, etc., *so that their family can* fly with maximum comfort.

2. *When* Riley is planning a quick, unplanned family getaway for a long weekend, *they want to* get suggestions for interesting available trips that are affordable and a short flight *so they can* have a list of choices they can consider.

And now, let's look at some jobs for a frequent flyer actor:

1. *When* Emma's plans change and she is unable to travel on a previously booked flight, *she wants to* easily reschedule her flight, *so she can* get a flight that works for her new plans.

2. *When* Emma prefers an available seat other than the one she has been currently assigned, *she wants to* select the alternative seat, *so she can* enjoy her flight more.

Finally, this is what JTBDs may look like for a customer service agent:

1. *When* a customer calls Sean, *he wants to* have a servicing ticket open pre-filled with customer information, *so he can* start tracking the progress towards the resolution of the customer need.

2. *When* a customer is asking Sean to find them a convenient flight for their trip, *he wants to* be able to find a fitting flight using a flexible set of filtering criteria, *so he can* meet the customer need and book a flight.

When possible, it is always a good idea to derive the Job Stories from user research. The simple, nontechnical, and consistent format is very helpful for capturing the research in a consistent way.

Job Stories provide a great format for conversations with subject matter experts and actual customers, but they are not convenient for deriving actual technical requirements. Rather, we need to translate them into a more developer-friendly format, which is what the next few sections of the SEED(S) process are all about.

Discovering Interaction Patterns with Sequence Diagrams

Job Stories are typically written by product managers from the business-value perspective and rarely correspond to our target services in any direct way. To proceed with a good design, we need to understand the service interaction patterns of our subdomain, i.e., the one that these services belong to. For complex interactions, a linear list of Job Stories will not be able to sufficiently support the design effort. Instead, you will want to draw an interaction diagram, explaining the sequence of events within your model.

In the spirit of reusing existing, familiar standards, SEED(S) recommends employing Unified Modeling Language (UML) sequence diagrams for this task. You can use any other diagramming approach to express your model, since the whole purpose here is to communicate the intent and the model. However, if you do wish to use UML sequence diagrams, then we highly recommend using one of the Markdown-based diagramming formats, such as PlantUML (*http://plantuml.com*).

We recommend this kind of approach because modeling in a microservices team is a team activity. Using a text-based format instead of a graphical file will allow team members to:

- Keep modeling separate from everyone's personal choice of editor. PlantUML and other similar formats can be edited in many different editors. As an example, PlantUML is supported in Atlassian's Confluence, a knowledge-management software used by many software teams. There are also free online editors you can use, such as LiveUML (*https://liveuml.com*) and PlantText (*https://oreil.ly/VpjNq*).

- Easily and effectively version-control sources of the diagrams. Text files are easy to diff, merge, and review in pull requests, none of which would be true for a binary graphic file.

- Conveniently integrate modeling into the release process. The diagrams become code and anything you can do with the code, you can now do with your diagrams as well; if you also version-control them in a system like Git, for example.

Key Decision: Use PlantUML Sequence Diagrams to Discover Interaction Patterns

To discover interaction patterns in SEED(S) methodology, we choose to use UML sequence diagrams expressed in a textual (Markdown) format such as PlantUML.

At this point in our design, we are in the phase of coming up with a technical model for the requirements gathered in the physical world. The Job Stories and actors represent the requirements of the physical world. They do not generally map to technical interactions one-to-one. As such, in your interaction model the events do not necessarily have to occur between the actors described in the first step of the SEED(S) process. Neither do they have to correspond to the jobs directly. Rather, your interaction diagrams may go a level deeper and show how the user-centric requirements translate into interactions between services at a technical level.

For instance, a very simple diagram describing interactions related to the JTBDs we already identified earlier in this chapter, may read something like the following:

```
@startuml

actor Agent
participant "Agent Servicing" as AS
participant "Reservations API" as rAPI
participant "reservationCRUD" as rCRUD

AS -> rAPI: checkRes(reservationId)
rAPI -> rCRUD: reserve(data)
```

```
rAPI -> rCRUD: cancel(reservationId)

@enduml
```

In LiveUML, this would render as in Figure 3-2.

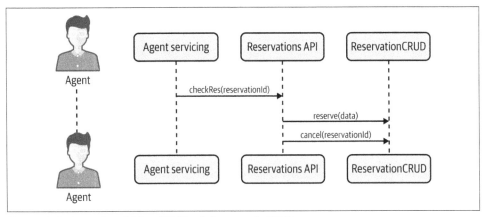

Figure 3-2. A rendered PlantUML of the sample UML sequence

Here, Agent Servicing is a user interface (web or mobile app) that agents can use directly, Reservations API is a REST or GraphQL API that the app invokes, and reservationCRUD is one of the microservices that fuels said API.

Once we have the sequence diagrams of the interactions, we can capture the technical requirements for a microservice, or an API, in the form of a set of actions and queries described using a standard syntax. Let's explore in the next section what those are and how they look.

Deriving Actions and Queries from JTBDs

Job Stories provide a great format for having fluid conversations with subject matter experts and acquiring insights into customers' needs. They may, however, be troublesome starting points for actually designing API specifications. Once we understand service interaction patterns and have had a chance to visualize those, we can transform jobs into more technically oriented interface contracts and greatly simplify our design process. Following Bertrand Meyer's command query separation (CQS) principle,[2] in SEED(S) we model a system's interface contracts as collections of two distinct types of interactions: the actions ("commands" in CQS) and the queries.

---

2 Bertrand Meyer, *Object-Oriented Software Construction*, 2nd ed. (New York: Prentice Hall, 2000).

In SEED(S), queries are lookups with defined inputs and outputs. They should be clearly formulated contracts between a client and a server: what input a client sends and what response they expect. They are distinctly different from actions, in that queries do not modify the system state (they "have no side effects").

Actions, in contrast, are requests that cause some sort of state modification—they not only do have side effects, but their whole purpose is to cause side effects. Much like queries, actions also have well-defined contracts—for inputs, expected outcomes, and expected responses.

Similar to Job Stories, we recommend using a standard format for capturing queries and actions. The template for queries looks something like this:

- An expressive description of a query
  - Input: list of input variables
  - Response: list of output data elements

Likewise, the standardized format for actions would look like the following:

- An expressive description of an action
  - Input: list of input variables
  - Expected outcome: description of the induced side effect
  - Response (optional): list of data elements in the response (if any)

Please note that Job Stories do not always produce exactly one query or action. A Job Story can be translated into multiple queries and actions, and a resulting query or action may combine multiple Job Stories as its source. SEED(S) is a process of modeling, design, and discovery, not a robotic process that is ripe for removal of the human judgment factor.

Example Queries and Actions for Our Sample Project

Let's see some examples of our existing Job Stories translated into a bunch of queries and actions.

Queries

One of our Job Stories described a family vacationer actor (Riley) who wants to find a flight that matches the travel comfort requirements of their family, by indicating detailed preferences such as: number of adjacent seats, maximum number of connections, etc. To satisfy the needs of such a job, we need a query contract that allows indication of all such preferences as inputs to the search query. Therefore, our query definition may look like the following:

Query 1: Flight Search
- Input: `departure_date`, `return_date`, `origin_airport`, `destination_airport`, `number_of_passengers`, `baby_friendly_connections`, `adjacent_seats`, `max_connections`, `minimum_connection_time`, `max_connection_time`, `order_criteria [object]`, `customer_id` (optional; to check loyalty privileges)
- Response: list of flights satisfying the criteria

Another one of our Job Stories described a circumstance in which a frequent traveler's plans suddenly change, and they are unable to travel on a previously scheduled date/flight. This actor needs to reschedule their existing booking. To achieve this task, we can imagine that at minimum we will need to know:

- The unique reservation identifier of the previous booking so that we can grab origin and destination airports, as well as any other preferences, so that we can automatically set those for the new search without asking the traveler to re-enter them
- A new departure date and return date that works for the traveler

Once we run the search, we will need to receive a list of flights that matches the input criteria for the new dates, so that we can present it to the customer and let them choose which flight they would like to rebook their travel ton.

Based on this analysis, we can conclude that the "rebooking" query specification could look like the following:

Query 2: Lookup of Alternative Flights for a Date Change
- Input: `reservation_id`, `new_departure_date`, `new_return_date`
- Response: list of alternative flights

Actions

Using an analysis similar to the one we used for deriving queries from Job Stories, you can produce actions that are required for rebooking and seat change jobs:

Travel Rebooking
- Input: `original_reservation_id`, `new_flight_id`, `seat_ids[]`
- Expected outcome: new flight booked or error returned; if new flight is successfully booked, old one is canceled
- Response: success code or a detailed error object

Seat Change
- Input: `reservation_id`, `customer_id`, `requested_seat_ids[]`
- Expected outcome: new seat reserved if the seat is available and the traveler is qualified; old seat canceled if the new seat ends up being successfully reserved
- Response: success code, or a detailed error object

In some sophisticated cases, you may find that the actions and queries approach of defining interface contracts may not be sufficient. In these cases, to capture the more complex requirements, we highly recommend using Matt McLarty's (*https://oreil.ly/lLRpj*) Microservice Design Canvas (*https://oreil.ly/tIxEi*). The design canvas and "actions and queries analysis" are substitutable techniques in the same phase of the SEED(S) process. The canvas is a more powerful tool that we do not cover in this book, but it is well worth getting acquainted with.

Once we have a set of actions and queries, or a Microservice Design Canvas, we can translate those into a formal interface specification.

Describing Each Query and Action as a Specification with an Open Standard

As a general rule, it is important to formally describe the interface contract of an API or a microservice before we start implementing it in code. Such codified contracts serve as a mutually agreed-upon understanding between a service producer and consumers, or API client developers. The contracts are also easily convertible into user-friendly documentation and interactive playgrounds. Contracts implemented using open standards such as the Open API Spec (*https://www.openapis.org*) and GraphQL (*https://graphql.org*) are widely supported by a rich set of tooling that allows easy rendering of documentation, streamlined creation of developer portals, etc.

In this section we will take the definition of an action that we described in the previous SEED(S) phase and design a RESTful endpoint for it, using the Open API Specification (*https://oreil.ly/JoiGg*) (OAS).

The OAS describes RESTful APIs in a standard, tech stack–agnostic manner. It is governed by OpenAPI Initiative, a Linux Foundation Collaborative Project. At the time of writing, the latest version of OAS is version 3.0.2 (*https://oreil.ly/c9U2V*).

Microservices interconnections do not have to be RESTful APIs. Other popular choices include GraphQL (*https://oreil.ly/C1c2h*), gRPC (*https://grpc.io*), and asynchronous event communications. At the time of writing, using JSON-, ProtoBuf-, or Avro-encoded messages on Kafka Streams seems to be a popular choice. It does not matter which communication style you choose; any one of them will assume exchange of messages and the format of those messages should be well-documented and part of the exchange "contract." For each of those styles you can apply the SEED(S) methodology in a way appropriate for the particular style. Since RESTful APIs are probably easiest and still the most ubiquitous, we demonstrate the approach using a RESTful design, but the methodology works with others, as well.

You can use any tooling to edit and author your OASs. If you are looking for suggestions, however, an open source setup that is available on most platforms, and seems to work well is the VS Code (*https://code.visualstudio.com*) editor with the Open API Designer (*https://oreil.ly/LySwF*) plug-in. Once you have the plug-in installed and a descriptor YAML file open inside the active tab, press CTRL+ALT+P on Windows or CMD+ALT+P on macOS and choose the appropriate preview command to see the rendering of the specification, as shown in Figure 3-3.

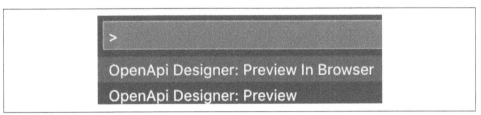

Figure 3-3. Selecting OAS Preview in VS Code

Example OAS for an Action in Our Sample Project

A simple version of the OAS for the rebooking action we described earlier in this chapter may look something like the following:

```
openapi: 3.0.0
info:
  title: Airline Reservations Management API
  description: |
    API for Airline Management System
  version: 1.0.1
servers:
  - url: http://api.example.com/v1
    description: Production Server
paths:
```

```
/reservations/{reservation_id}:
  put:
    # @see https://swagger.io/docs/specification/describing-parameters
    summary: Book or re-book a reservation
    description: |
      Example request:
      ```

        PUT http://api.example.com/v1/reservations/d2783fc5-0fee
      ```

    parameters:
      - name: reservation_id
        in: path
        required: true
        description: Unique identifier of the reservation being created or
                     changed
        schema:
          type : string
        example: d2783fc5-0fee

    requestBody:
      required: true
      content:
        application/json:
          schema:
            type: object
            properties:
              outbound:
                type: object
                properties:
                  flight_num:
                    type: string
                    example: "AA 253"
                  flight_date:
                    type: string
                    example: "2019-12-31T08:01:00"
                  seats:
                    type: array
                    items:
                      type: string
              returning:
                type: object
                properties:
                  flight_num:
                    type: string
                    example: "AA 254"
                  flight_date:
                    type: string
                    example: "2020-01-07T14:16:00"
                  seats:
                    type: array
                    items:
                      type: string
```

```
        example: [
          {
            outbound: {
              flight_num: "AA 253",
              flight_date: "2019-12-31T08:01:00",
              seats: [
                "9C"
              ]
            },
            returning: {
              flight_num: "AA 254",
              flight_date: "2020-01-07T14:16:00",
              seats: [
                "10A"
              ]
            }
          }
        ]


    responses:
      '200':    # success response
        description: Successful Reservation
        content:
          application/json:
            schema:
              type: object
              properties:
                reservation_id:
                  type: string
                  description: some additional description
      '403':
        description: seat(s) unavailable. Booking failed.
        content:
          application/json:
            schema:
              type: string
              description: detailed information
```

The rendered output with the VS Code plug-in should look something like
Figure 3-4.

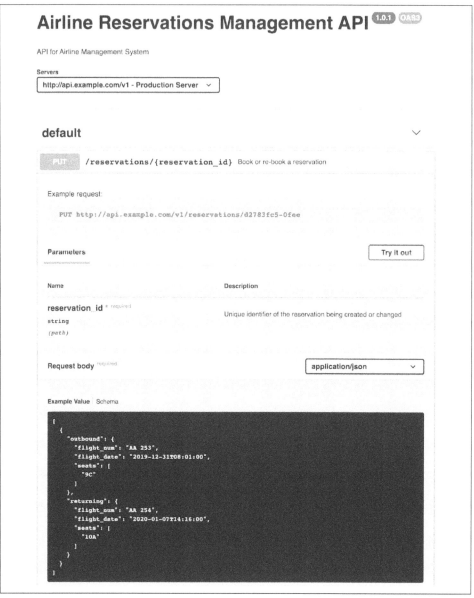

Figure 3-4. Rendering of a sample OAS document

Producing a formal API contract is a huge milestone for the design of APIs and microservices. Some may even consider it a job well done at this point. However, good API designs cannot end at this stage. We wish things were that simple, but there is actually an additional, critical activity that still needs to be completed. The next step in the SEED(S) process captures this activity.

Getting Feedback on the API Specification

The initial version of the API and service design as captured by an OAS-based description, or some other standard, is an important milestone, but there is more modeling work that is necessary for a well-designed API.

We need to show the draft design of the endpoints to the client developers who will be asked to use these APIs and services, and collect their feedback. If the previous steps involved active brainstorming and work, this is the stage of careful listening and reflection. It is an incredibly important step for designing APIs, if you care to design the kind of APIs and microservices that will stand the test of time and which your clients will love to use.

Key Decision: Collect Feedback on Your Service Designs

Service design is not done until it is presented to the target audience for the service and feedback is collected and applied to the initial designs.

Generally, you need to keep in mind two groups of customers when designing services and APIs:

- *End users of the system.* Your APIs enable the user experiences for them.
- *Client developers who will code against your services (APIs or microservices).* They build end users' experiences, such as web or mobile applications.

At the beginning of the SEED(S) process, we interview the end users to collect and understand the Job Stories relevant to them. However, later in the process we start receiving feedback from the client developers. This can happen as early as the interactions design phase, and then again once the OAS is produced, before coding. This second group, API client developers, must be interviewed to test the usability of the designs, to avoid coding something that may end up being rejected by them due to poor usability.

Both of the research activities are critical. The first study makes sure we build the right thing. The latter one makes sure we build it the right way!

Implementing Microservices

The last step in the SEED(S) methodology is actually implementing microservices. It is intentionally done at the very end of the process. Coding is one of the most expensive activities any software engineering team can undertake. Recoding a functionality that was initially designed based on wrong assumptions is a horrible, time-consuming, and expensive task. This is why we engage in a carefully thought-out process such as SEED(S) before we jump into coding microservices. Overall, it saves time and delivers better outcomes.

Before we wrap up this chapter, we need to clarify an important detail. Throughout this chapter, we have been saying "APIs and microservices" and we started by mentioning that the SEED(S) methodology can be equally successfully applied to both the design process of APIs as well as that of microservices. This is in part true because APIs and microservices have a lot of similarities. But how are they different? Are microservices just small APIs? In the next section, we will try to shed some light onto this important question.

Microservices Versus APIs

APIs and microservices do indeed have a lot in common. Microservices are capabilities exposed via standard network protocols, most commonly HTTP. But capabilities exposed as HTTP endpoints had been known as web APIs, way before the coining of the term *microservices*. So are the two essentially the same thing? Are microservices just a new flavor of APIs—smaller APIs? More importantly, do we even need conventional APIs once we start writing microservices, or do the smaller APIs (microservices) replace the bigger (conventional) APIs? We have often seen these questions cause a lot of confusion on teams trying to adopt microservices architecture.

With some frequency we have encountered developers referring to any small, focused APIs as "microservices." In such an approach microservices have the same role as APIs had before them, so they do indeed replace the APIs of old. In our experience, this is not an ideal approach for successful microservices thinking, and we offer an alternative, albeit opinionated, definition of what separates microservices from legacy APIs. Our approach builds on the experience of some notable experts in the space, and is rooted in our own experiences with successful microservices projects and teams.

Microservices Are Not Just Smaller APIs

Microservices are not just smaller replacements for the APIs of the old days. Microservices provide the implementation of your system, while APIs should still be the outward-facing interface of a system.

We think that if microservices replace anything, the things they replace are the modular components you used to build your systems with. If before you would build a large system by linking (statically or dynamically) various submodules together, in a microservices architecture the building blocks are networked services we call "microservices." This approach is depicted in Figure 3-5.

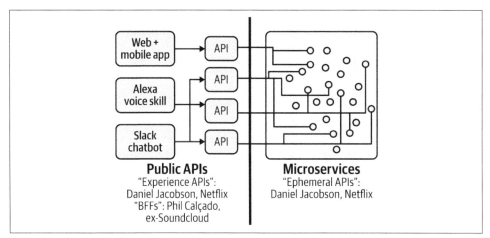

Figure 3-5. Relationship between microservices and APIs

Note that a similar approach—of separating APIs into "internal ones, the ones you build with"; and "external ones, the ones that are optimized for consumption by frontends"—has been described by Phil Calçado as the Backend for Frontend pattern (*https://oreil.ly/ef8jV*) when he was at SoundCloud, and by Daniel Jacobson (*https://oreil.ly/CxTka*) during his time at Netflix. Daniel Jacobson explained how at Netflix they separated APIs into Experience (frontend) and Ephemeral (backend) APIs.

Key Decision: Web APIs Are Layered on Top of Microservices

Differentiate between web APIs that represent the public interface of your subsystem and microservices that represent the implementation of the same system. Avoid thinking of microservices as "just small APIs."

There is no one, true way of organizing microservices and connecting them up with "frontend" APIs. This is the part where we live up to the promise of providing unabashedly opinionated guidance in this book. Our opinions are rooted in what we have witnessed to have worked well, but we also acknowledge that other strategies may have worked for other practitioners.

In our experience, the ideal separation of duties happens when all of the business logic (capabilities) is implemented by microservices, while APIs act as a thin layer of orchestration in front of those microservices. Additionally, we recommend that teams try to avoid microservices directly "invoking" each other. Instead, for the sake of loose coupling, it's best if any orchestrating workflow is implemented in the API layer, in front of microservices, without microservices knowing anything about each other.

Note that there is no 1:1 relationship between an API and the microservices that implement the corresponding capability. These two assets are parts of fundamentally different layers of your architecture.

We believe that such a "microservices should be unaware of each other and be orchestrated externally" approach is where the Unix philosophy (*https://oreil.ly/GVjJV*) of building a system as a collection of composable tools resonates well with microservices architecture principles. One of the most powerful aspects of the Unix philosophy is that you can combine Unix tools (e.g., GNU tools) in a variety of ways using input and output piping on the command line or in shell scripts. However, in order to achieve this, it's critical that various Unix tools act the same way for any input—they should not care who "calls" them or where their output goes. Components cannot explicitly know about each other for them to become composable. Loose coupling is what makes the whole thing work, not just that the tools are small-ish and focused. The same holds true for microservices.

Keep Microservices Unaware of Each Other

Avoid microservices directly "knowing" about each other and directly calling each other via synchronous interfaces. Instead, try to orchestrate processes involving multiple microservices in the API layer. If this is not possible, consider using asynchronous interfaces between microservices where an upstream microservice publishes data to an event log (e.g., Kafka) and a downstream microservice can subscribe to that event log without the upstream microservice having tight coupling with the subscriber(s).

Summary

In this chapter, we set up a critical foundation for understanding the process of designing robust microservices. By establishing an effective and repeatable methodology, the SEED(S) method, we acquired a powerful understanding of many aspects of what traits make projects successful in their microservices journey and learned how to adapt these traits for our own circumstances.

In the following chapters we will leverage the insights gained from an understanding of SEED(S). In Chapters 4 and 5 we will dive deeper into the design process for microservices, and in Chapter 9 we go through the code implementing several microservices of our sample project, reusing, demonstrating, and expanding efforts started in this chapter.

## CHAPTER 4

Rightsizing Your Microservices: Finding Service Boundaries

One of the most challenging aspects of building a successful microservices system is the identification of proper microservice boundaries. It makes intuitive sense that breaking up a large codebase into smaller, simpler, more loosely coupled parts improves maintainability, but how do we decide where and how to split the code into parts to achieve those desired properties? What rules do we use to know where one service ends and another one starts? Answering these fundamental questions is challenging. A lot of teams new to microservices stumble at them. Drawing the microservice boundaries incorrectly can significantly diminish the benefits of using microservices, or in some cases even derail the entire effort. It is then not surprising that the most frequent, most pressing question microservices practitioners ask is: how can a bigger application be properly sliced into a collection of microservices?

In this chapter, we look deep into the leading methodology for the effective analysis, modeling, and decomposition of large domains (Domain-Driven Design), explain the efficiency benefits of using Event Storming for domain analysis, and close by introducing the Universal Sizing Formula, a unique guidance for the effective sizing of microservices.

Why Boundaries Matter, When They Matter, and How to Find Them

Right in the title of the architectural pattern, we have the word *micro*—the architecture we are designing is that of "micro" services! But how "micro" should our services be? We are obviously not measuring the physical length of something and assuming that *micro* means one-millionth of a meter (i.e., of the base unit of length in the International System of Units). So what does *micro* mean for our purposes? How are we supposed to slice up our larger problem into smaller services to achieve the promised benefits of "micro" services? Maybe we could print our source code on paper, glue everything together, and measure the literal length of that? Or jokes aside, should we go by the number of lines in our source code—keeping that number small to ensure each of our microservices is also small enough? What is "enough," however? Maybe we just arbitrarily declare that each microservice must have no greater than 500 lines of code? We could also draw boundaries at the familiar, functional edges of our source code and say that each granular capability represented by a function in the source code of our system is a microservice. This way we could build our entire application with, say, serverless functions, declaring each such function to be a microservice. Clean and easy! Right? Maybe not.

In practice, each of these simplistic approaches has indeed been tried and they all have significant drawbacks. While source lines of code (SLOC) has historically enjoyed some usage as a measure of effort/complexity, it has since been widely acknowledged to be a poor measurement for determining the complexity or the true size of any code and one that can be easily manipulated. Therefore, even if our goal were to create "small" services with the hope of keeping them simple, lines of code would be a poor measurement.

Drawing boundaries at functional edges is even more tempting. And it has become even more tempting with the increase in popularity of serverless functions such as Amazon Web Services' Lambda functions. Building on top of the productivity and wide adoption of AWS Lambdas, many teams have rushed into declaring those functions "microservices." There are a number of significant problems if you go down this road, the most important of which are:

Drawing boundaries based on technical needs is an anti-pattern
> Per Lewis and Fowler (*https://oreil.ly/mRUrv*), microservices should be "organized around business capabilities," not technical needs. Similarly, Parnas (*https://oreil.ly/1AcI0*), in an article from 1972, recommends decomposing systems based on modular encapsulation of design changes over time. Neither approach necessarily aligns strongly with the boundaries of serverless functions.

Too much granularity, too soon
> An explosive level of granularity early in the microservices project life cycle can introduce crushing levels of complexity that will stop the microservices effort in its tracks, even before it has a chance to take off and succeed.

In Chapter 1 we stated the primary goal of a microservices architecture: it is primarily about minimization of coordination costs, in a complex, multiteam environment, to achieve harmony between speed and safety, at scale. Therefore, services should be designed in a way that minimizes coordination needs between the teams working on different microservices. However, if we break code up into functions in a way that does not necessarily lead to minimized coordination, we will end up with incorrectly sized microservices. Just assuming that any way of organizing code into serverless functions will reduce coordination is misguided.

Earlier we stated that an important reason for avoiding a size-based or functions-aligned approach when splitting an application into microservices is the danger of premature optimization—having too many services that are too small too early in your microservices journey. Early adopters of microservices, such as Netflix, Sound-Cloud, Amazon, and others, eventually found themselves having a lot of microservices (*https://oreil.ly/r5vYU*)! That, however, does not mean that these companies started with hundreds of very granular microservices on day one. Rather, a large number of microservices is what they optimized for after years of development, *after* having achieved the operational maturity capable of handling the level of complexity associated with the high granularity of microservices.

Avoid Creating Too Many Microservices Too Early

The sizing of services in a microservices architecture is most certainly a journey that should unfold in time. A sure way to sabotage the entire effort is to attempt designing an overly granular system early in that journey.

Whether you are working on a greenfield project or decomposing an existing monolith, the approach should absolutely be to start with only a handful of services and slowly increase the number of microservices over time. If this leads to some of your microservices initially being larger than in their target state, it is totally OK. You can split them up later.

Even if we are starting with just a few microservices, taking it slow, we need some reliable methodology to determine how to size microservices. Next, we will explore best practices successfully used in the industry.

Domain-Driven Design and Microservice Boundaries

At the onset of figuring out microservices design best practices, Sam Newman introduced some foundational ground rules in his book *Building Microservices* (O'Reilly). He suggested that when drawing service boundaries, we should strive for such a design that the resulting services are:

Loosely coupled

Services should be fairly unaware and independent of each other, so that a code modification in one of them doesn't result in ripple effects in others. We'll also probably want to limit the number of different types of runtime calls from one service to another since, beyond the potential performance problem, chatty communications can also lead to a tight coupling of components. Taking our "coordination minimization" approach, the benefit of the loose coupling of the services is quite obvious.

Highly cohesive

Features present in a service should be highly related, while unrelated features should be encapsulated elsewhere. This way, if you need to change a logical unit of functionality, you should be able to change it in one place, minimizing time to releasing that change (an important metric). In contrast, if we had to change the code in a number of services, we would have to release lots of different services at the same time to deliver that change. That would require significant levels of coordination, especially if those services are "owned" by multiple teams, and it would directly compromise our goal of minimizing coordination costs.

Aligned with business capabilities

Since most requests for the modification or extension of functionality are driven by business needs, if our boundaries are closely aligned with the boundaries of business capabilities, it would naturally follow that the first and second design requirements, above, are more easily satisfied. During the days of monolith architectures, software engineers often tried to standardize on "canonical data models." However, the practice demonstrated, over and over again, that detailed data models for modeling reality do not last for long—they change quite often and standardizing on them leads to frequent rework. Instead, what is more durable is a set of business capabilities that your subsystems provide. An accounting module will always be able to provide the desired set of capabilities to your larger system, regardless of how its inner workings may evolve over time.

These design principles have proven to be very useful and received wide adoption among microservices practitioners. However, they are fairly high-level, aspirational principles and arguably do not provide the specific service-sizing guidance needed by day-to-day practitioners. In search of a more practical methodology, many turned to Domain-Driven Design.

The software design methodology known as *Domain-Driven Design* (DDD) significantly predates microservices architecture. It was introduced by Eric Evans in 2003, in his seminal book of the same name, *Domain-Driven Design: Tackling Complexity in the Heart of Software* (Addison-Wesley). The main premise of the methodology is the assertion that, when analyzing complex systems, we should avoid seeking a single unified domain model representing the entire system. Rather, as Evans said in his book:

> Multiple models coexist on big projects, and this works fine in many cases. Different models apply in different contexts.

Once Evans established that a complex system is fundamentally a collection of multiple domain models, he made the critical additional step of introducing the notion of *bounded context*. Specifically, he stated that:

> A Bounded Context defines the range of applicability of each model.

Bounded contexts allow implementation and runtime execution of different parts of the larger system to occur without corrupting the independent domain models present in that system. After defining bounded contexts, Eric went on to also helpfully provide a formula for identifying the optimal edges of a bounded context by establishing the concept of *Ubiquitous Language*.

To understand the meaning of Ubiquitous Language, it is important to observe that a well-defined domain model first and foremost provides a common vocabulary of defined terms and notions, a common language for describing the domain, that subject-matter experts and engineers develop together in close collaboration, balancing the business requirements and implementation considerations. This common language, or shared vocabulary, is what in DDD we call Ubiquitous Language. The importance of this observation lies in acknowledging that same words may carry different meanings in different bounded contexts. A classic example of this is shown in Figure 4-1. The term *account* carries significantly different meaning in the identity and access management, customer management, and financial accounting contexts of an online reservation system.

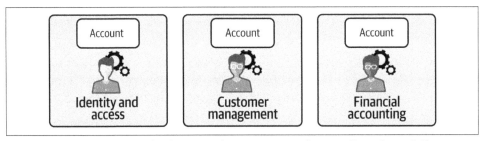

Figure 4-1. Depending on the domain where it appears, "account" can have different meanings

Indeed, for an identity and access management context, an account is a set of credentials used for authentication and authorization. For a customer management-bounded context, an account is a set of demographic and contact attributes, while for a financial accounting context, it's probably payment information and a list of past transactions. We can see that the same basic English word is used with significantly different meaning in different contexts, and it is OK because we only need to agree on the ubiquitous meaning of the terms (the Ubiquitous Language) within the bounded context of a specific domain model. According to DDD, by observing edges across which terms change their meaning, we can identify the boundaries of the contexts.

In DDD, not all terms that come to mind when discussing a domain model make into the corresponding Ubiquitous Language. Concepts in a bounded context that are core to the context's primary purpose are part of the team's Ubiquitous Language, all others should be left out. These core concepts can be discovered from the set of JTBDs that you create for the bounded context. As an example, let's look at Figure 4-2.

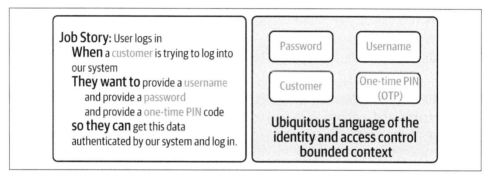

Figure 4-2. Using Job Story syntax to identify key terms of a Ubiquitous Language

In this example, we are using the Job Story format that we introduced in Chapter 3 and applying it to a job from the identity and access control bounded context. We can see that key nouns, highlighted in Figure 4-2, correspond to the terms in the related Ubiquitous Language. We highly recommend the technique of using key nouns from well-written Job Stories in the identification of the vocabulary terms relevant to your Ubiquitous Language.

Now that we have discussed some key concepts of DDD, let's also look at something that can be very useful in designing microservice interactions properly: context mapping. We will explore key aspects of context mapping in the next section.

Context Mapping

In DDD, we do not attempt to describe a complex system with a single domain model. Rather, we design multiple independent models that coexist in the system. These subdomains typically communicate with each other using published interface descriptions. The representation of various domains in a larger system and the way they collaborate with each other is called a *context map*. Consequently, the act of identifying and describing said collaborations is known as *context mapping*, as shown in Figure 4-3.

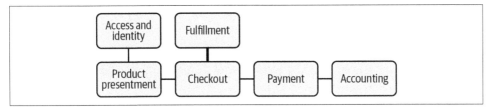

Figure 4-3. Context mapping

DDD identifies several major types of collaboration interactions when mapping bounded contexts. The most basic type is known as a *shared kernel*. It occurs when two domains are developed largely independently and, almost by accident, they end up overlapping on some subset of each other's domains (see Figure 4-4). Two parties may agree to collaborate on this shared kernel, which may also include shared code and data model, as well as the domain description.

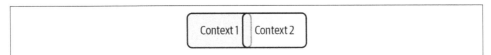

Figure 4-4. Shared kernel

While tempting on the surface of things (after all, the desire for collaboration is one of the most human of instincts), the shared kernel is a problematic pattern, especially when used for microservices architectures. By definition, a shared kernel immediately requires a high degree of coordination between two independent teams to even jump-start the relationship, and keeps requiring coordination for any further modifications. Sprinkling your microservices architecture with shared kernels will introduce many points of tight coordination. In cases when you do have to use a shared kernel in a microservices ecosystem, it's advised that one team is designated as the primary owner/curator, and everybody else is a contributor.

Alternatively, two bounded contexts can engage in what DDD calls an Upstream–Downstream kind of relationship. In this type of relationship, the Upstream acts as the provider of some capability, and the Downstream is the consumer of said capability. Since domain definitions and implementations do not overlap, this type of relationship is more loosely coupled than a shared kernel (see Figure 4-5).

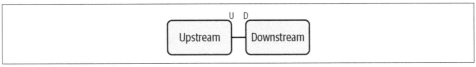

Figure 4-5. Upstream–Downstream relationship

Depending on the type of coordination and coupling, an Upstream–Downstream mapping can be introduced in several forms:

Customer–Supplier

In a customer–supplier scenario, Upstream (supplier) provides functionality to the Downstream (customer). As long as the provided functionality is valuable, everybody is happy; however, Upstream carries the overhead of backwards compatibility. When Upstream modifies their service, they need to ensure that they do not break anything for the customer. More dramatically, the Downstream (customer) carries the risk of the Upstream intentionally or unintentionally breaking something for it, or ignoring the customer's future needs.

Conformist

An extreme case of the risks for a customer–supplier relationship is the *conformist* relationship. It's a variation on Upstream–Downstream, when the Upstream explicitly does not or cannot care about the needs of its Downstream. It's a use at-your-own-risk kind of relationship. The Upstream provides some valuable capability that the Downstream is interested in using, but given that the Upstream will not cater to its needs, the Downstream needs to constantly conform to the changes in the Upstream.

Conformist relationships often occur in large organizations and systems when a much larger subsystem is used by a smaller one. Imagine developing a small, new capability inside an airline reservation system and needing to use, say, an enterprise payments system. Such a large enterprise system is unlikely to give the time of day to some small, new initiative, but you also cannot just reimplement a whole payments system on your own. Either you will have to become a conformist, or another viable solution may be to *separate ways*. The latter doesn't always mean that you will implement similar functionality yourself. Something like a payments system is complex enough that no small team should implement it as a side job of another goal, but you might be able go outside the confines of your enterprise and use a commercially available payments vendor instead, if your company allows it.

In addition to becoming a conformist or going separate ways, the Downstream has a few more DDD-sanctioned ways of protecting itself from the negligence of its Upstream: an anti-corruption layer and using Upstreams that provide open host interfaces.

Anti-corruption layer

In this scenario, the Downstream creates a translation layer called an *anti-corruption layer* (ACL) between its and the Upstream's Ubiquitous Languages, to guard itself from future breaking changes in the Upstream's interface. Creating an ACL is an effective, sometimes necessary, measure of protection, but teams should keep in mind that in the long term this can be quite expensive for the Downstream to maintain (see Figure 4-6).

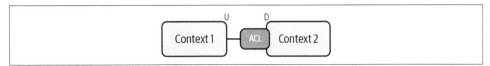

Figure 4-6. Anti-corruption layer

Open host service

When the Upstream knows that multiple Downstreams may be using its capabilities, instead of trying to coordinate the needs of its many current and future consumers, it should instead define and publish a standard interface, which all consumers will need to adopt. in DDD, such Upstreams are known as open host services. By providing an open, easy protocol for all authorized parties to integrate with, and maintaining said protocol's backwards compatibility or providing clear and safe versioning for it, the open host can scale its operations without much drama. Practically all public services (APIs) use this approach. For example, when you are using the APIs of a public cloud provider (AWS, Google, Azure, etc.), they usually don't know or cater to you specifically as they have millions of customers, but they are able to provide and evolve a useful service by operating as an open host (see Figure 4-7).

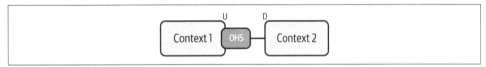

Figure 4-7. Open host service

In addition to relation types between domains, context mappings can also differentiate based on the integration types used between bounded contexts.

Synchronous Versus Asynchronous Integrations

Integration interfaces between bounded contexts can be synchronous or asynchronous, as shown in Figure 4-8. None of the integration patterns fundamentally assume one or the other style.

Common patterns for synchronous integrations between contexts are RESTful APIs deployed over HTTP, gRPC services using binary formats such as protobuf, and more recently services using GraphQL interfaces.

On the asynchronous side, publish–subscribe types of interactions lead the way. In this interaction pattern, the Upstream can generate events, and Downstream services have workers able and interested in processing those, as depicted in Figure 4-8.

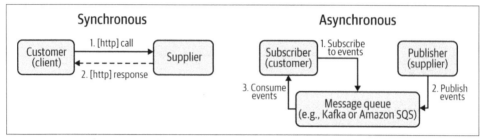

Figure 4-8. Synchronous and asynchronous integrations

Publish–subscribe interactions are more complex to implement and debug, but they can provide a superior level of scalability, resilience, and flexibility, in that: multiple receivers, even if implemented with heterogeneous tech stack, can subscribe to the same events using a uniform approach and implementation.

To wrap up the discussion of Domain-Driven Design's key concepts, we should explore the concept of an *aggregate*. We discuss it in the next section.

A DDD Aggregate

In DDD, an *aggregate* is a collection of related domain objects that can be viewed as a single unit by external consumers. Those external consumers only reference a single entity in the aggregate, and that entity is known in DDD as an *aggregate root*. Aggregates allow domains to hide internal complexities of a domain, and expose only information and capabilities (interface) that are "interesting" to an external consumer. For instance, in the Upstream–Downstream mappings that we discussed earlier, the Downstream does not have to, and typically will not want to, know about every single domain object within the Upstream. Instead, it will view the Upstream as an aggregate, or a collection of aggregates.

We will see the notion of an aggregate resurface, in the next section when we discuss Event Storming—a powerful methodology that can greatly streamline the process of domain-driven analysis and turn it into a much faster and more fun exercise.

Introduction to Event Storming

Domain-Driven Design is a powerful methodology for analyzing both the whole-system-level (called "strategic" in DDD) as well as the in-depth (called "tactical") composition of your large, complex systems. We have also seen that DDD analysis can help us identify fairly autonomous subcomponents, loosely coupled across bounded contexts of their respective domains.

It's very easy to jump to the conclusion that in order to fully learn how to properly size microservices, we just need to become really good in domain-driven analysis; if we make our entire company also learn and fall in love with it (because DDD is certainly a team sport), we'll be on our way to success!

In the early days of microservices architectures, DDD was so universally proclaimed as *the one true way* to size microservices that the rise of microservices gave a huge boost to the practice of DDD, as well—or at least more people became aware of it, and referenced it. Suddenly, many speakers were talking about DDD at all kinds of software conferences, and a lot of teams started claiming that they were employing it in their daily work. Alas, a close look easily uncovered that the reality was somewhat different and that DDD had become one of those "much-talked-about-less-practiced" things.

Don't get us wrong: there were people using DDD way before microservices, and there are plenty using it now as well, but speaking specifically of using it as a tool for sizing microservices, it was more hype and vaporware than reality.

There are two primary reasons why more people talked about DDD than practiced it in earnest: it is complex and it is expensive. Practicing DDD requires quite a lot of knowledge and experience. Eric Evans's original book on the subject is a hefty 520 pages long, and you would need to read at least a few more books to really get it, not to mention gain some experience actually implementing it on a number of projects. There simply were not enough people with the skills and experience and the learning curve was steep.

To exacerbate the problem, as we mentioned, DDD is a team sport, and a time-consuming one at that. It's not enough to have a handful of technologists well-versed in DDD; you also need to sell your business, product, design, etc., teams on participating in long and intense domain-design sessions, not to mention explain to them at least the basics of what you are trying to achieve. Now, in the grand scheme of things, is it worth it? Very likely, yes: especially for large, risky, expensive systems, DDD can have many benefits. However, if you are just looking to move quickly and size some microservices, and you have already cashed in your political capital at work, selling everybody on the new thing called microservices—good luck also asking a whole bunch of busy people to give you enough time to size your services right! It was just not happening—too expensive and too time-consuming.

And then suddenly a fellow by the name of Alberto Brandolini (*https://oreil.ly/ TiPOb*), who had invested decades in understanding better ways for teams to collaborate, found a shortcut! He proposed a fun, lightweight, and inexpensive process called Event Storming, which is heavily based and inspired by the concepts of DDD but can help you find bounded contexts in a matter of hours instead of weeks or months. The introduction of Event Storming was a breakthrough for inexpensive applicability of DDD specifically for the sake of service sizing. Of course, it's not a full replacement, and it won't give you *all* the benefits of formal DDD (otherwise it would be magic).

But as far as the discovery of bounded contexts goes, with good approximation—it is indeed magical!

Event Storming is a highly efficient exercise that helps identify bounded contexts of a domain in a streamlined, fun, and efficient manner, typically much faster than with more traditional, full DDD. It is a pragmatic approach that lowers the cost of DDD analysis enough to make it viable in situations in which DDD would not be affordable otherwise. Let's see how this "magic" of Event Storming is actually executed.

Key Decision: Use Event Storming Instead of Formal DDD

Use the more lightweight Event Storming process instead of formal DDD to discover the main aggregates in your subdomain and identify edges of the various bounded contexts present in your system.

The Event-Storming Process

The beauty of Event Storming is in its ingenious simplicity. In physical spaces (preferred, when possible), all you need to hold a session of Event Storming is a very long wall (the longer the better), a bunch of supplies, mostly stickies and Sharpies, and four to five hours of time from well-represented members of your team. For a successful Event Storming session, it is critical that participants are not only engineers. Broad participation from such groups as product, design, and business stakeholders makes a significant difference. You can also host virtual Event Storming sessions using digital collaboration tools that can mimic the physical process described here.

The process of hosting physical Event Storming sessions starts by purchasing the supplies. To make things easier, we've created an Amazon shopping list (*https://oreil.ly/T7Y0i*) that we use for Event Storming sessions (see Figure 4-9). It is comprised of:

- A large number of stickies of different colors, most importantly, orange and blue, and then several other colors for various object types. You need *a lot* of those. (Stores never had enough for me, so I got in the habit of buying online.)

- A roll of 1/2-inch white artist tape.

- A long roll of paper (e.g., IKEA Mala Drawing Paper) that we are going to hang on the wall using the artist tape. Go ahead and create multiple "lanes."

- At least as many Sharpies as the number of session participants. Everybody needs to have their own!

- Did we already mention a long, unobstructed wall that we can tape the roll of paper to?

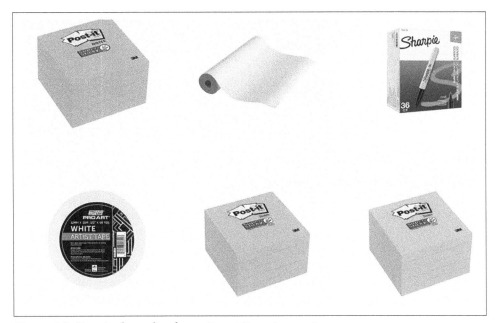

Figure 4-9. Required supplies for an Event Storming session

During Event Storming sessions, broad participation, e.g., from subject-matter experts, product owners, and interaction designers, is very valuable. Event Storming sessions are short enough (just several hours rather than analysis requiring days or weeks) that, considering the value of their outcomes, the clarity they bring for all represented groups and the time they save in the long term, they are time well-invested for all participants. An Event Storming session that is limited to just software engineers is mostly useless, since it happens in a bubble and cannot lead to the cross-functional conversations necessary for desired outcomes.

Once we have the supplies, the large room with a wide-open wall with a roll of paper we have taped to it, and all the required people, we (the facilitator) ask everybody to grab a bunch of orange stickies and a personal Sharpie. Then we give them a simple assignment: to write the key events of the domain being analyzed as orange sticky notes (one event per one note), expressed in a verb in the past tense, and place the notes along a timeline on the paper taped to the wall to create a "lane" of time, as shown in Figure 4-10.

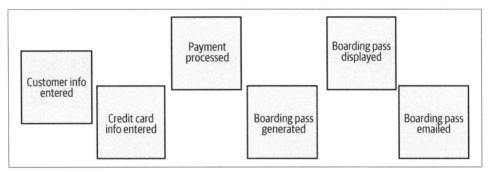

Figure 4-10. An event timeline with sticky notes

Participants should not obsess about the exact sequence of events, and at this stage there should be no coordination of events among participants. The only thing they are asked is to individually think of as many events as possible and put the events they think occur earlier in time to the left, and put the later events more to the right. It is not their job to weed out duplicates. At least, not yet. This phase of the assignment usually takes 30 minutes to an hour, depending on the size of the problem and the number of participants. Usually, you want to see at least 100 event sticky notes generated before you can call it a success.

In the second phase of the exercise, the group is asked to look at the resulting set of notes on the wall, and with the help of the facilitator, to start arranging them into a more coherent timeline, identifying and removing duplicates. Given enough time, it is very helpful for the participants to start creating a "storyline," walking through the events in an order that creates something like a "user journey." In this phase, the team may have some questions or confusion; we don't try to solve these issues, but rather capture them as "hotspots"—differently colored sticky notes (typically purple) that have the questions on them. Hotspots will need to be answered offline, in follow-ups. This phase can likewise take 30 to 60 minutes.

In the third stage, we create what in Event Storming is known as a *reverse narrative*. Basically, we walk the timeline backward, from the end to the start, and identify *commands*; things that caused the events. We use sticky notes of a different color (typically blue) for the commands. At this stage your storyboard may look something like Figure 4-11.

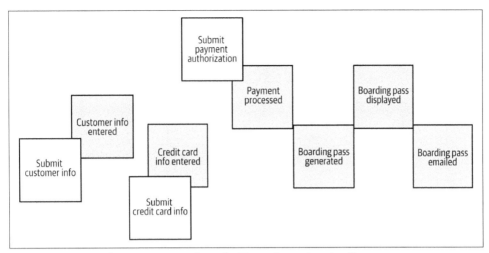

Figure 4-11. Introducing commands to the Event Storming timeline

Be aware that a lot of commands will have one-to-one relationship with an event. It will feel redundant, like the same thing worded in the past versus present. Indeed, if you look at the previous figure, the first two commands are like that. It often confuses people new to Event Storming. Just ignore it! We don't pass judgment during Event Storming, and while some commands may be 1:1 with events, some will not be. For example, the "Submit payment authorization" command triggers a whole bunch of events. Just capture what you know/think happens in real life and don't worry about making things "pretty" or "neat." The real world you are modeling is also usually messy.

In the next phase, we acknowledge that commands do not produce events directly. Rather, special types of domain entities accept commands and produce events. In Event Storming, these entities are called *aggregates* (yes, the name is inspired by the similar notion in DDD). What we do in this stage is rearrange our commands and events, breaking the timeline when needed, such that the commands that go to the same aggregate are grouped around that aggregate and the events "fired" by that aggregate are also moved to it. You can see an example of this stage of Event Storming in Figure 4-12.

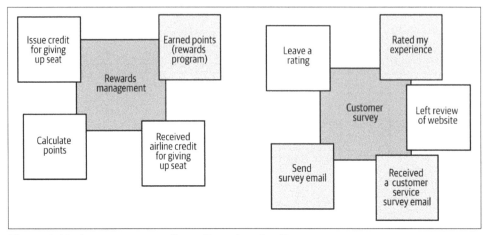

Figure 4-12. Aggregates on an Event Storming timeline

This phase of the exercise can take 15 to 25 minutes. Once we are done with it, you should discover that our wall now looks less like a timeline of events and more like a cluster of events and commands grouped around aggregates.

Guess what? These clusters are the bounded contexts we were looking for.

The only thing left is to classify various contexts by the level of their priority (similar to "root," "supportive," and "generic" in DDD). To do this, we create a matrix of bounded context/subdomains and rank them across two properties: difficulty and competitive edge. In each category, we use T-shirt sizes <S, M, or L> to rank accordingly. In the end, the decision making as to when to invest effort is based on the following guidelines:

1. Large competitive advantage/large effort: these are the contexts to design and implement in-house and spend most time on.
2. Small advantage/large effort: buy!
3. Small advantage/small effort: great assignments to trainees.
4. Other combinations are a coin toss and require a judgment call.

 This last phase, the "competitive analysis," is not part of Brandolini's original Event Storming process, and was proposed by Greg Young for prioritizing domains in DDD in general. We find it to be a useful and fun exercise when done with an adequate level of humor.

The entire process is very interactive, requires the involvement of all participants, and usually ends up being fun. It will require experienced facilitator to keep things moving smoothly, but the good news is that being a good facilitator doesn't take the same effort as becoming a rocket scientist (or DDD expert). After reading this book and facilitating some mock sessions for practice, you can easily become a world-class Event Storming facilitator!

As a facilitator, it is a good idea to watch the time and have a plan for your session. For a four-hour session rough allocation of time would look like:

- Phase 1 (~30 min): Discover domain events
- Phase 2 (~45 min): Enforce the timeline
- Phase 3 (~60 min): Reverse narrative and Command Identification
- Phase 4 (~30 min): Identify aggregates/bounded contexts
- Phase 5 (~15 min): Competitive analysis

And if you noticed that these times do not add up to 4 hours, keep in mind that you will want to give people some breaks in the middle, as well as leave yourself time to prepare the space and provide guidance in the beginning.

Introducing the Universal Sizing Formula

Bounded contexts are a fantastic starting point for rightsizing microservices. We have to be cautious, however, to not assume that microservice boundaries are synonymous with the bounded contexts from DDD or Event Storming. They are not. As a matter of fact, microservice boundaries cannot be assumed to be constant over time. They evolve over time and tend to follow an increasing granularity of microservices as the organizations and applications they are part of mature. For example, Adrian Cockroft (*https://oreil.ly/AzK4h*) noted that this was definitely a repeating trend that they had observed during his time at Netflix (*https://oreil.ly/LXK8F*).

Nobody Gets Microservice Boundaries Perfectly at the Outset

In successful cases of microservices adoption, teams do not start with hundreds of microservices. They start with a much smaller number, closely aligned with bounded contexts. As time goes by, teams split microservices when they run into coordination dependencies that they need to eliminate. This also means that teams are not expected to get service boundaries "right" out of the gate. Instead, boundaries evolve over time, with a general direction of increased granularity.

It is worth noting that it's typically easier to split a service than to merge several services back together, or to move a capability from one service to another. This is another reason why we recommend starting with a coarse-grained design and waiting until we learn more about the domain and have enough complexity before we split and increase service granularity.

We have found that there are three principles that work well together when thinking about the granularity of microservices. We call these principles the Universal Sizing Formula for microservices.

The Universal Sizing Formula

To achieve a reasonable sizing of microservices, you should:

- Start with just a few microservices, possibly using bounded contexts.
- Keep splitting as your application and services grow, being guided by the needs of coordination avoidance.
- Be on the right trajectory for decreasing coordination. This is vastly more important than the current state of how "perfectly" you get service sizing.

Summary

In this chapter we addressed a critical question of how to properly size microservices head-on. We looked at Domain-Driven Design, a popular methodology for modeling decomposition in complex systems; explained the process of conducting a highly efficient domain analysis with the Event Storming methodology, and introduced the Universal Sizing Formula, which offers unique guidance for effective sizing of microservices.

In the following chapters we will go deeper into implementation, showing how to manage data in a loosely coupled, componentized microservices environment. We also will walk you through a sample implementation for our demo project: an online reservation system.

## CHAPTER 5

Dealing with the Data

In this chapter, we'll cover why microservices need to "own their own data" and what it means for your architecture. We will discuss when and how to use the the most important patterns for microservices data management: delegates, data lakes, Sagas, Event Sourcing, and command query responsibility segregation (CQRS). While discussing these important topics, we will also try to demonstrate them on practical examples using our sample project.

When it comes to practical microservices development, one of the early challenges that almost everyone hits is dealing with the data. If it wasn't for the many challenges of data management in this space, turning complex, monolithic implementations into loosely coupled, "bite-sized," manageable microservices would be fairly easy.

The design considerations for logical and physical models in microservices implementation are not the same as for designing data tables for the conventional, N-tier, monolithic applications. In this chapter we will see why the differences arise, which patterns the microservices practitioners commonly use, and what techniques should be employed to tackle the additional complexities we face when implementing microservices systems.

Independent Deployability and Data Sharing

In Chapter 4, we mentioned that Sam Newman suggests microservices should generally be:

- Loosely coupled from each other; this also means independently deployable
- Highly cohesive vis-à-vis capabilities inside the microservices

When services are loosely coupled, a change to one service should not result in a change to another one. You may remember that the main benefit of a microservices architecture is increased speed, in harmony with safety and quality, at scale. And this benefit is achieved by eliminating, or at least decreasing, coordination needs between microservices. One critical, specific aspect of this loose coupling is what we call *independent deployability*—being able to make a change to one microservice, and deploy it, without the need to change or deploy any other parts of the system, any other microservices. This is really important and becomes vividly obvious if we visualize what a typical deployment pipeline looks like in a microservices architecture. In Figure 5-1, you can see a simplified graphic representation of deployment pipelines for multiple microservices going through several environments, on their way to production.

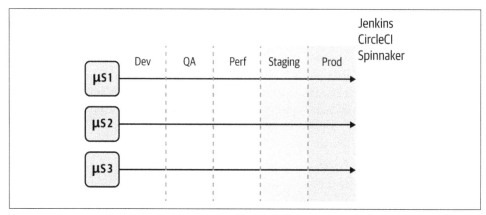

Figure 5-1. Example multi-environment release pipeline for microservices

The process of releasing code through a deployment pipeline becomes significantly more complex and fragile if a deployment of one microservice triggers ripple effects of having to also redeploy other parts of the application. Such interdependencies can compromise both the speed and safety of the entire system. Alternatively, if we can ensure that we can always deploy each microservice independently, without having to worry about the ripple effects, we can keep our deployments nimble and safe.

There can be a number of reasons why you may not be able to make a deployment of your microservices independent, but in the context of data management, the most common offender is co-ownership of a data space by multiple microservices. Such co-ownership can compromise their loose coupling and our ability to independently deploy code.

We will start exploring techniques for avoiding data co-ownership across microservices by discussing the notion of microservice-embedded data in the following sections.

Microservices Embed Their Data

In monolith architectures, sharing of data is a common practice. In typical legacy systems, even in the more modular, service-oriented architecture (SOA) ones, code components co-own data across multiple services as a regular practice. It is actually very much expected—shared data is a primary pattern of integrating various modularized parts of a larger system. Sometimes when we speak of a "monolith," people imagine that it has no modularization, that it is indeed just one big thing that is not divided into any kind of components. That is not true. Developers have long known that dividing a large codebase into smaller ones is highly beneficial for code organization and manageability. But a key shortcoming, before microservices, was that the modules that the monoliths were divided into were not independently deployable. That made them not loosely coupled, in relation to coordination costs! Case in point: it was primarily due to data coupling that SOA designs never achieved independent deployability and consequently the ability to both go fast and go safely at greater scale.

Let's look at an example of how a problem may occur. Say that multiple microservices share ownership of a customer table in a database, as depicted in Figure 5-2, in "Data Embedding and the Data Delegate Pattern" on page 79. By "ownership" we mean that different microservices read and modify data from the shared table.

Imagine that a flight-search microservice needs to change a field type of one of the columns in the shared table. If the developers of this microservice just go ahead and do it, let's say from integer to float or something like that, the change could break the reservations or flight-tracking microservices, since they also access the same table and may rely on that field to have values of a certain type. To avoid introducing bugs, when we change the data model because of the needs of the flight-search microservice, we will also need to accordingly change the code of the reservations microservice or potentially others as well. And we'll have to redeploy all of the changed microservices in one concerted effort. Ripple effects due to a changing data layer are very common when multiple components co-own data, and they can cause significant coupling of various services, which would be a problem for independent deployability.

Sharing data spaces is a primary killer of independent development and independent deployability, in monoliths. By contrast, in a microservices architecture, independent deployability is emphasized as a core value and consequently, data sharing is prohibited—microservices are never allowed co-own responsibility for a data space in a database. It should be very clear which microservice owns any dataset in the database, or as we commonly state the principle: microservices must own (embed) their data.

While embedding their own data is a universal rule for microservices, there are some important nuances to this principle that are critical to understand clearly. In the next section we will discuss one such consideration in greater detail.

Embedding Data Should Not Lead to an Explosion in the Number of Database Clusters

When building complex applications, we can often end up with different kinds of databases. Datasets in those databases (e.g., "tables" for relational databases) should never have multiple microservices as co-owners. When you build big systems, you could eventually have hundreds of microservices. Does it then mean that we have to deploy hundreds of distinct clusters of Cassandra, Postgres, Redis, or MySQL? Teams implementing microservices need clarity on how far they should take the notion of "microservices must embed their data." Databases are themselves complex software systems; they're not deployed on just one server, rather most databases are deployed on multiple servers for redundancy, reliability, and scalability—possibly dozens of servers across different geographic regions. When we introduce the concept of data embedding, teams will wonder if they need to create massive database clusters for each microservice they create.

This could turn into a major problem. If a massive number of database clusters (one or more per microservice) was required by a microservices architecture, then it would be the most expensive architectural style in our industry's history (or close to it). Fortunately, this is absolutely not the case. Data independence doesn't mean that each microservice has to deploy its own, distinct cluster of scalable, redundant, and complex database installations.

Key Decision: Microservices Can Share Physical Database Clusters

Microservices can and should share physical installations of database clusters. As long as services never share the same logical table space and never modify the same data, sharing physical installations is OK, in practice.

Independence of data management is more about not crossing the streams than anything else. It's about the ability to take your microservices and deploy with another database installation if you need to. But you don't have to deploy each service with a different database cluster out of the gate. Cost is an important consideration and so is simplicity. As long as multiple microservices are not accessing (most importantly: modifying) the same data space, the data independence requirement is intact.

Data Embedding and the Data Delegate Pattern

Let's look at an example in the context of our online reservation system. In the beginning we will look at the case in which the system is built with a conventional monolithic, N-tier architecture. Now, such an application would still be divided into different, smaller modules. These modules could even be deployed as networked services. And they could definitely be small enough to be called "micro." That does not necessarily mean they are microservices, however. They can only be considered microservices if these components were modularized with the elimination of coordination as the goal and, more specifically, if they are loosely coupled and independently deployable. If services are split arbitrarily and not loosely coupled, we can't call such a system an example of a microservices architecture.

In our scenario, depicted in Figure 5-2, we have three services all requiring data from the "flights" table: flight search, reservations management, and flight tracking.

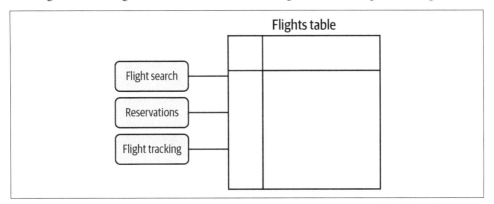

Figure 5-2. Example of a monolithic data management, characterized by data sharing

Clearly, based on our earlier analysis in this chapter, this data design is problematic for a microservices architecture, because three services are sharing the data space and thus are compromising independent deployability.

How can we fix this situation? This particular case is actually quite easy to resolve, and we can employ the simple technique of hiding shared data behind a delegate service, visualized in Figure 5-3.

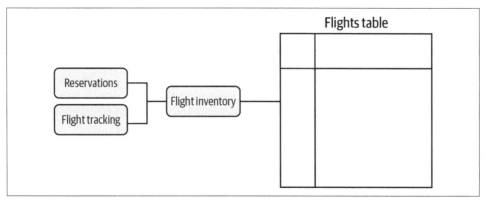

Figure 5-3. A simple graphic representation of data hiding via a delegate

Essentially, what we do here is declare the flight inventory service to be the authoritative service for all things related to flight information. Further, any service that requires information about flights or needs to update information about flights is required to invoke an appropriate endpoint in the flight inventory service. If we implement a sufficiently flexible flight lookup API call in the flight inventory service, the former flight search service just becomes part of the functionality of the new flight inventory service. More importantly, this allows us to stop accessing the flights table directly from the reservations and flight tracking services. Any information they need about a flight they can obtain through the flight inventory service, going forward.

For example, when the reservations system needs to know if there are enough seats left on a flight, it will send a corresponding query to the flight inventory service instead of querying the flights table directly in the database. Or when the flight tracking service needs to know or update the location of the plane in a flight, it will again do so via the flight inventory service, not by accessing and modifying the flights table directly. This way the flight inventory service can be the delegate that hides data behind itself, encapsulates the data, and wraps around the data. This will stop multiple services from sharing the same data table.

Please note that in this pattern, when several services need access to the same data, we don't have to necessarily convert one of them into a delegate. In the previous solution we converted the flight search service into an inventory service and made it encapsulate the flights table. We could have instead introduced a new service. For example, we could introduce a new service called flight inventory and have the flight search microservice refer to it, just like reservations and tracking services do.

The approach of introducing a delegate is very elegant and will work in many different cases. Unfortunately, not all data-sharing needs can be addressed this way. It would be extremely naive to think that the pattern we just discussed works for all scenarios. There are use cases where the required functionality legitimately needs to access or modify data across the boundaries of microservices. Examples of such needs are found in the analytics, data audit, and machine learning contexts, among others. Traditional approaches to database transactions also require locking in on shared data.

Fortunately, there are reasonable solutions for those other use cases as well, solutions that are also capable of avoiding data sharing. To understand the solutions in this space, let's first explore various data access patterns we commonly encounter.

Using Data Duplication to Solve for Independence

When we need read-only access to distributed data with no modification requirements, as in the contexts of enterprise analytics, machine learning, audits, etc., a common solution is to copy datasets from all concerned microservices into a shared space. The shared space is usually called a *data lake*. Please note that we are copying data, not moving it! Data lakes are read-only, query-able data sinks. Microservices still remain the authoritative sources of the corresponding datasets and act as the primary owners of the data. They just stream relevant data into the data lake where it accumulates and becomes ready for querying. For the sake of data integrity and clarity of data lineage, it's important that we *never* operationally update such data in an aggregate index like a data lake. Data lakes may never be treated as the databases of record. They are reference data stores. We can see a generic graphic representation of this setup in Figure 5-4.

Figure 5-4. Streaming data from microservices into data lakes

Once data is streamed from the system of record (SOR) data stores (such as microservices into data sinks), the aggregate data is indexed in a way that is optimized for query-ability. Streaming data from SORs into data lakes is usually done using a reliable messaging infrastructure. IBM MQ and RabbitMQ have been used for many years in this context; Kafka (*https://kafka.apache.org*) seems to be the current most popular solution, while Apache Pulsar (*https://pulsar.apache.org*) is probably the most prominent and interesting new entrant in the space.

Data lakes and shared data indexes can solve for many read-only use cases. But what should we do when distributed data is not read-only? In the next section we explore a solution for the cases when we need to modify data in a coordinated fashion across the datasets owned by multiple microservices. We will discuss how to implement distributed transactions in a microservices ecosystem.

Distributed Transactions and Surviving Failures

Let's consider an example from our online reservations sample project. Specifically, let's explore what happens when somebody books a seat on a flight and to fulfill the booking we need to execute a *distributed transaction*. This is a coordinated update across multiple microservices that are in charge of things like using loyalty miles for payment, securing a seat, and sending an itinerary to the customer's email. Such transactions span multiple microservices: payments (with loyalty points) processing, reservations, and notifications, to be specific. Most importantly, we would typically want all three steps to happen or none of them to happen. For instance, let's say we suddenly find out that the requested seat is no longer available. Perhaps when we started the process of deducting the miles for the payment, the seat was available, but by the time we finished the process, somebody had already reserved that seat. Obviously we can't reserve this seat twice, so we must consider what to do in that situation. In a busy-enough system, such race conditions and failures are inevitable, so when they do occur, we need to roll back the entire process. We clearly need to refund the loyalty points, at the very least. Let's understand how we would coordinate such a distributed transaction.

In conventional monolithic applications, a process like the one we described would be safely managed using database transactions. More specifically, this can be done with database transactions that are said to exhibit the ACID characteristics of safety, even in the event of failures. *ACID* stands for atomicity, consistency, isolation, and durability. These are defined as follows:

Atomicity
> The steps in a transaction are "all or nothing"; either all of them get executed, or none of them.

Consistency
> Any transaction should bring the system from one valid state into another valid state.

Isolation
> Parallel execution of various transactions should result in the same state as if the transactions were executed sequentially.

Durability
> Once a transaction is committed (fully executed), data won't be lost despite any possible failures.

Microservices simplify building systems safely at scale. It is critical to clarify, however, that this doesn't mean you can somehow prevent a failure from ever occurring. Completely avoiding failures, whether with microservices or by any other means, is an impossible task. Failures will always be present in a sufficiently complex system. What we need to do is account for them and create the means for auto-recovery. In conventional data management, ACID transactions (*https://oreil.ly/B1OTU*) are a great example of such thinking. Systems implementing ACID transactions assume that failures of all kinds happen all the time, so we design our data storage systems in a way to make them resilient to the failures.

Unfortunately, ACID transactions are not a viable solution for distributed systems in which functionality is spread across multiple microservices deployed across a network independently. ACID transactions typically rely on usage of exclusive locks. Given that microservices embed their data and do not allow code to manipulate data in another microservice, such locks would be either impossible or very expensive for a microservices system to implement. Instead, we need to use patterns that work better in distributed architectures. In the next section we introduce a popular solution of this type called saga transactions.

Distributed transactions with sagas

Sagas were first described by Hector Garcia-Molina (*https://oreil.ly/bIRr3*) in 1987, long before modern distributed systems were a thing, and were later popularized by Clement Vasters's 2012 blog post (*https://oreil.ly/f5cLI*) as an effective solution for distributed systems.

With sagas, every step of a transaction not only performs the required action for that step, but it also defines a compensating action that should execute if we need to roll back the transaction due to a later failure. A pointer (e.g., discovery information on a queue) to this compensating action is registered on a *routing slip* and passed along to the next step. If one of the later steps fails, it kicks off execution of all compensating actions on the routing slip, thus "undoing" the modifications and bringing the system to a reasonably compensated state.

> **Sagas Are Not Directly Equivalent to ACID Transactions**
>
> Sagas do not promise that when a distributed transaction is rolled back, the system will necessarily get back to the initial state. Rather, the system should get to a reasonable state that reflects an acceptable level of undoing of the partially completed transaction.

To understand what we mean by "reasonable state," let's look at our initial example of a seat reservation, as depicted in Figure 5-5.

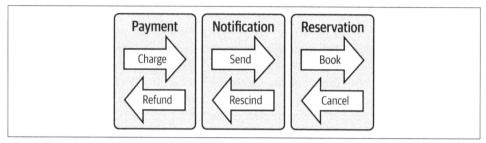

Figure 5-5. A transaction distributed across multiple microservices

If a reservation booking attempt fails, for whatever reason, it will be cancelled, but we will also invoke the compensating action of the previous steps: notification and payment. The compensating action of a payment refunds money to the customer. Depending on the type of payment, a refund may not get processed immediately; so the system may not return to its initial state immediately, but eventually the customer will get all their money. That said, it will be visible that two payment actions cancelled (compensated) each other, rather than the customer not noticing any trace of transaction reversal at all, which would have been the goal with ACID transactions.

In case of a notification things can become even messier. We may not be able to literally recall an email or a text message that was sent, so the compensating transaction may involve sending a new message notifying the customer that the previous message should be disregarded and booking was actually unsuccessful. In some circumstances, it can be a reasonable solution (if not, we will see later in the chapter how to avoid it with proper sequencing), but doesn't bring the system back to the initial state: a customer will see two messages, instead of not seeing any.

These two examples hopefully gave a clear understanding of some of the ways in which compensating transactions, in sagas, are different from the conventional ACID transactions.

The Sequence of Events in a Saga Is Meaningful

Note that the sequence of events in a saga does matter and should be constructed carefully. It usually pays off to move steps that are harder to compensate for toward the end of the transaction. For instance, if business rules allow it, moving a notification to the very end of the process may save us from having to send a lot of correction messages. This way, by the time the transaction gets to sending alerts, we will know that the previous steps have succeeded.

Delegate services, data lakes, and sagas are powerful patterns. They can solve many data isolation challenges in microservices architectures, but not all of them. In the next section we will discuss a powerful duo of design patterns: Event Sourcing and CQRS. These can pretty much address everything else remaining, providing a complete toolset for data management in a microservices environment.

Event Sourcing and CQRS

Up to this point we have discussed some ways to avoid data sharing when using traditional, relational data modeling. We showed how you can solve some of the data-sharing challenges, but eventually, for advanced scenarios, we will run into cases where relational modeling itself falls short of allowing the desired levels of data isolation and loose coupling. A very common example is when teams need to create a "join" across datasets owned by different microservices. At its core, relational data modeling is rooted in such foundational principles as data normalization, data reuse, and cross-referencing common data elements; i.e., it is fundamentally biased toward favoring data sharing.

Event Sourcing

Sometimes, rather than trying to go around the predisposition for relational modeling, we should switch to a completely different way of modeling data. A data modeling approach that allows avoidance of data sharing, and thus has become popular in microservices, is known as Event Sourcing.

One of the earliest known mentions of Event Sourcing is in Martin Fowler's 2005 article (*https://oreil.ly/BHKl9*). In 2014, Greg Young gave a seminal conference talk[1] about Event Sourcing that jump-started a new, strong wave of popularity for the design pattern. Greg has been an important voice and one of the key advocates in this space. We owe him a lot of gratitude for the advancement of Event Sourcing (and its relationship with CQRS, another important pattern that we will discuss later in this chapter). In Greg's own words, Event Sourcing is an approach to data modeling that is all about storing events rather than the states of the domain objects of a system:

> Event Sourcing is all about storing facts and any time you have "state" (structural models)—they are first-level derivative off of your facts. And they are transient.

---

1 Greg Young, "CQRS and Event Sourcing," Code on the Beach 2014, *https://oreil.ly/5-d5u*.

In this context, by "facts," Young means the representative values of event occurrences. An example could be "the price of an economy seat on the LAX–IAD flight increased by $200."

Event Sourcing in accounting and chess

Unless you have prior experience with Event Sourcing, this may feel odd. Most people who haven't worked on systems dealing with high-frequency trading platforms or haven't had a ton of advanced experience with microservices probably do not have any experience with Event Sourcing. That said, we can easily find examples of Event-Sourcing systems in real life. If you've ever seen an accounting journal, it is a classic event store. Accountants record individual transactions, and the balance is a result of summing up all transactions. Accountants are not allowed to record "state"; i.e., they just write down the resulting balance after each transaction, without capturing the transactions themselves. Similarly, if you have played chess and have recorded a chess game, you would not write down the position of each piece on the board after each move. Instead you are recording moves individually, and after each move the state of the board is a result of the sum of all moves that have happened.

For instance, consider the record of the first seven moves of the historical game 6 between many-times world chess champion Gary Kasparov and the IBM supercomputer Deep Blue, in 1997. Represented in algebraic notation (*https://oreil.ly/txpy7*), looks like the following:

1. e4 c6
2. d4 d5
3. Nc3 dxe4
4. Nxe4 Nd7
5. Ng5 Ngf6
6. Bd3 e6
7. N1f3 h6

The corresponding state after the initial seven moves is depicted in Figure 5-6.

We can completely re-create the state of a chess game, such as that between Kasparov and Deep Blue, if we have the event log of all moves. This is an analog equivalent of Event Sourcing from real life.

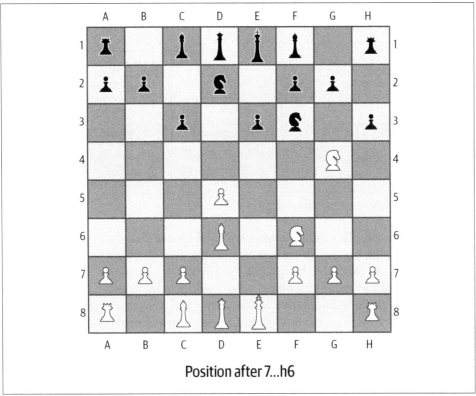

Position after 7...h6

Figure 5-6. Deep Blue versus Kasparov (source: Wikipedia (https://oreil.ly/-chbm))

Event Sourcing versus relational modeling

In conventional data systems such as relational databases, or even the more contemporary NoSQL and document databases, we usually store a state of something; for instance, the current price of an economy seat on a flight. In Event Sourcing, we operate with a completely different approach. In Event Sourcing we do not store current state, rather we store *facts*; the incremental changes of the data. The current state of the system is a derivative, a value that is calculated from the sequence of changes (events).

Let's look at an example. A relational data model describing the customer management system for a flight reservations system may look like the diagram in Figure 5-7.

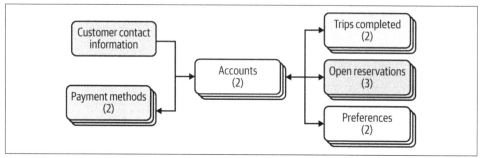

Figure 5-7. Example of a relational data model

We can see that the data model could consist of a table storing customers' contact information, which has one-to-many relationships with customer accounts and payment methods. In turn, each customer account (e.g., business versus personal accounts) record can point to multiple completed trips, open reservations, and preferences related to the account. While the details may vary, this is the kind of data model most software engineers would design using conventional databases.

Using Event Sourcing, we can design the same data model as a sequence of events, shown in Figure 5-8. Here you can see a representation of events that led to the same state of the system as described in the state-oriented model earlier: first, the customer contact information was collected, then a personal account was opened, which was followed by entering a personal payment method. After several reservations, and completed trips, this customer apparently decided to also open a business account; they added payment information and started booking trips with this new account. Along the way several preferences were also added and updated, bringing the system to the same state as in Figure 5-7, except here we can see the exact sequence of "facts" that led to the current state, as opposed to just looking at the result in the state-oriented representation.

So the sequence of events on the diagram gives you the same state that we had in the relational data model. It is equivalent to what we had there, except this looks very, very different. For instance, you may notice it looks much more uniform. There are significantly fewer opinionated decisions to be made about the various entity types and their relationships with each other. Event Sourcing in some ways is much simpler in that you just have a variety of business events that happen and then you can calculate the current state as a derivative of these events.

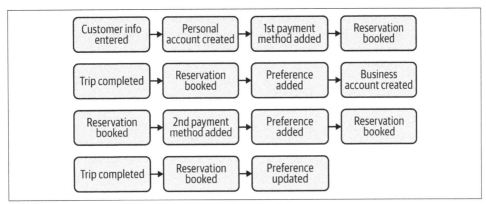

Figure 5-8. Example of an event-sourced data model

Not only is Event Sourcing more straightforward andpredictable, in Event Sourcing there are no referential relationships between various entities. If we wanted to do a brute force data segregation here, all we would need to do is say each type of event is owned by a different microservice, and voila, we could do that and avoid data sharing. For instance, we could have a microservice that is a customer demographics microservice and "customer info entered" would be an event that very naturally belongs to that system of record.

What does an event look like?

Now that we hopefully have a good intuition about Event Sourcing and how it works, let's dig a little bit deeper into what data modeling and data management looks like in Event Sourcing. It's an approach of capturing the sequence of events. The state is just something you calculate off of these events—a state is a function of events. OK, this sounds a bit mathematical, but what does an event even look like? Well, events are very simple. If we look at the "shape" of an event data structure, all it needs to have are three parts.

First, the event needs some kind of unique identifier. You could for instance use a universally unique identifier (UUID), since they are globally unique, and this uniqueness obviously helps in distributed systems. It also needs to have an event type, so we don't mistake different event types. And then there's just data, whatever data is relevant for that event type:

```
{
  "eventId" : "afb2d89d-2789-451f-857d-80442c8cd9a1",
  "eventType" : "priceIncreased",
  "data" : {
    "amount" : 120.99,
    "currency" : "USD"
  }
}
```

Design decisions of a technical nature are fairly straightforward when working with events. Most work goes into properly describing domain-relevant fields of the events, based on the business logic. There's much less of the kind of subjective, technical table-shape and relationship crafting that we engage in with the relational approach.

Calculating current state with projections

What happens when we actually need to calculate the point-in-time (e.g., current) state of something? We run what in Event Sourcing is called *projections*. Projections give us state based on events, and they're also fairly simple. To run a projection, we need a projection function. A projection function takes the current state and a new event to calculate the new state.

For instance, a `priceUp` projection function, for an airline ticket price, may look like the following:

```
function priceUp(state, event) {
  state.increasePrice(event.amount)
}
```

It would be equivalent to an `UPDATE prices SET price=…` SQL query in a relational model. If we also had a corresponding price decrease projection function and we wanted to calculate price (state) at some point, we could run a projection by calling the projection functions for all relevant events, like the following:

```
function priceUp(state, event) {
  state.increasePrice(event.amount)
}

function priceDown(state, event) {
  state.decreasePrice(event.amount)
}

let price = priceUp(priceUp(priceDown(s,e),e),e);
```

If you have ever worked with functional programming, you may notice that the current state is the *left fold* of the events that occurred until the current time. Note that through using Event Sourcing you can calculate not just the current state but the state as of any point in time. This capability opens up endless possibilities for sophisticated analytics, where you can ask questions like, "OK, I know what the state of the entity is *now*, but what was the state at a date in the past that I am interested in?" This flexibility can become one of the powerful benefits of using Event Sourcing, if you frequently need to answer such questions.

Improving Performance with Rolling Snapshots

One thing to note here is that projections can be computationally expensive. If a value is a current state and it's the result of a sequence of thousands of state changes, like a bank account balance, whenever you need the value of a current balance, would you want to calculate it from scratch? You could argue that such an approach is slow and it can waste time and computational resources. It also cannot be as instantaneous as just retrieving the current state. You would be correct in that; however, we can optimize for speed and it doesn't necessarily require a change in the approach. Instead of recalculating everything from the beginning—for example, the opening of a bank account—we can keep saving intermediary values, along the way, and later we can quickly calculate the state from the last snapshot. That would significantly speed up calculations.

Depending on the event store implementation, it is common to snapshot intermediary values at various time points. How to choose the appropriate moment of snapshotting may depend on your application's domain. For instance, in a banking system, you may snapshot account balances on the last day of every month, so that if you need the balance on January 15, 2020, you will already have it from December 31, 2019, and will just need to calculate the projection for two weeks, rather than the entire life of the bank account.

In Event Sourcing, the saved projections are usually called *rolling snapshots*. The specifics of how you implement rolling snapshots and projections may depend on the context of your application. For instance, when we used monthly rolling snapshots for the banking application example earlier, it made a lot of sense because this approach closely aligns with what happens in real life anyway. Banks calculate various types of balances at the end of the month, quarter, and year; this is known as "closing the books." You should always try to find *natural time points* in your own domains and align your snapshots with them.

Later in this chapter we will see that with a pattern called Command Query Responsibility Segregation (CQRS), we can do much more than just cache states in rolling snapshots.

Having acquired an understanding and appreciation of Event Sourcing, let's learn more about how to implement it. What would the event store itself look like? And how would we go about implementing one? We will answer these questions in the next section.

Event Store

Event stores can be relatively simple systems. You can use a variety of data storage systems to implement one. Simple files on the filesystem, Amazon Simple Storage Service (S3) buckets, or any database storage that can reliably store a sequence of data entries can all do the job. The interface of an event store needs to support three basic functions:

- The ability to store new events and assign the correct sequence so we can retrieve events in the order they were saved
- The capability to notify event subscribers who are building projections about new events they care about and enable the Competing Consumers pattern (*https://oreil.ly/WZ9Ss*)
- The ability to get N number of events after event X for a specific event type, for reconciliation flows; i.e., recalculation in case projection is lost, compromised, or doubted

So, at its essence, the basic interface of an event store is comprised of just two functions:

```
save(x)
getNAfterX()
```

In addition, there is a kind of robust notification system that allows consumers to subscribe to events. By "robust" we mean conformation to the Competing Consumers pattern. This pattern is important because whatever system is building a projection off of your events will likely want to have multiple instances of a client "listening" to the events, both for redundancy and scalability's sake. Our notifier must reasonably accommodate only-once delivery to a single instance of a listener, to avoid accidental event duplication leading to data corruption. There are two approaches you can employ here:

1. Use a message queue implementation that already provides such guarantees to its consumers; e.g., Apache Kafka (*https://kafka.apache.org*).
2. Allow consumers to register HTTP endpoints as callbacks. Invoke the callback endpoint for each new event and let a load balancer on the consumer side handle the distribution of work.

Neither approach is inherently better. One is push-based and the other is pull-based, and depending on what you are doing, you may prefer one over the other.

Check Out a Sample Implementation

During the writing of this book, we published an opinionated reference implementation (*https://oreil.ly/LPD8y*) of a skeleton event store on GitHub that you can check out, take for a test drive, or contribute to.

To implement robust projections, Event Sourcing systems often use a complementary pattern known as CQRS. In the next section we will explore the ideas behind it and try to understand its essence.

Command Query Responsibility Segregation

Projections for advanced event-sourced systems are typically built using the Command Query Responsibility Segregation (CQRS) pattern. The idea of CQRS is that the way we query systems and the way we store data do not have to be the same. When we were talking about the event store and how simple it can be, one thing we skipped over was that the simple interface of `save(x)` and `getNAfterX()` functions is not going to allow us to run elaborate queries over that data. For instance, it won't allow us to run queries asking for all reservations in which a passenger has updated their seat in the last 24 hours. Those kind of queries are not implemented against the event store, to keep the event store simple and focused. Event Sourcing should only solve the problem of authoritatively and reliably storing an event log. For advanced queries, every time an event occurs, we let another system, subscribed to the event store, know about it and that system can then start building the indices that are optimized for querying the data any way they need. The idea behind CQRS is that you should not try to solve data storage, data ownership, and data queryability issues with the same system. These concerns should be solved for independently.

The big win with using Event Sourcing and CQRS is that they allow us to design very granular, loosely coupled components. With Event Sourcing, we can create microservices so tiny that they just manage one type of event or run a single report. Targeted use of Event Sourcing and CQRS can take us to the next level of autonomous granularity in microservices architectures. As such, they play a crucial role in the architectural style.

Event Sourcing and CQRS Should Not Be Abused as a Cure-All Solution

Be careful not to overuse Event Sourcing and CQRS. You should only use them when necessary, since they can complicate your implementation. They should not be used as the one and only data modeling approach for your entire system. There are still many use cases in which the conventional, relational model is much simpler and should be utilized.

Event Sourcing and CQRS can help you avoid data sharing between microservices in sophisticated cases where you require data joins across service boundaries, but they come with a cost of complexity. Always consider other, simpler approaches, such as the delegate service we described in this chapter, before you resort to Event Sourcing, for a particular microservice.

Now that we have acquired a solid, foundational understanding of Event Sourcing and CQRS, let's also address where else these patterns can and should be used, beyond just helping with loose data coupling for the data-embedding needs of microservices.

Event Sourcing and CQRS Beyond Microservices

Event Sourcing and CQRS can certainly be invaluable in avoiding data sharing and achieving loose coupling of microservices. Their benefit is not limited to loose coupling or even microservices architectures, however. Event Sourcing and CQRS are powerful data modeling tools that can benefit a variety of systems.

Consider Event Sourcing and CQRS in relation to the consistency, availability, and partition tolerance (CAP) theorem. This theorem was famously formulated as a conjecture by Eric Brewer in his 2000 keynote (*https://oreil.ly/hiQMB*) at the Symposium on Principles of Distributed Computing. The theorem, in its original form, stated that any distributed shared-data system can only have two out of three desirable properties:

Consistency
    Having a single view of the latest state of the data

Availability
    Ability to always read or update data

Partition tolerance
    Getting accurate data even in the face of network partitions

Over time, it was clarified that not all combinations of CAP are valid.[2] For a distributed system we have to account for partition tolerance because network partitions cannot be avoided, and the choice becomes a sacrifice between consistency or availability. But what do we do if we really need both? It sounds childish to insist on wanting everything if a mathematically proven theorem (which CAP became eventually) tells you that you cannot have it all.

---

2 Eric Brewer, "CAP Twelve Years Later," InfoQ, 2012, *https://oreil.ly/Pg1pO*, and Coda Hale, "You Can't Sacrifice Partition," 2010, *https://oreil.ly/nHBoN*.

But there is a catch! The CAP theorem tells us that a single system, with data sharing cannot violate the theorem. However, what if, using CQRS, we employ multiple systems and minimize data sharing? In such a case, we can prioritize consistency in the event store and prioritize availability in the query indices. Certainly, that means whatever system we use for query indices may get consistency wrong, but they are not authoritative sources, so we can always re-index from the event store, if need be. In a way, this allows us to, indeed, have the best of both worlds.

The second major benefit of the Event Sourcing and CQRS approach is related to auditability. When we use a relational data model, we do in-place updates. For instance, if we decide that the customer's address or phone number is wrong we will update it in the corresponding table. But what happens if the customer later disputes their record? With a relational model, we may have lost the history and find ourselves helpless. With Event Sourcing, we have a perfect history of every change safely preserved and we can see what the value of customer data was at any time in the past, as well as how and when it got updated.

Some readers may point out that even when they use relational modeling, it doesn't necessarily mean that they lose the history of data. They may be logging every change in some file, or systems like Splunk (*https://oreil.ly/C3oY-*) or ELK (*https://oreil.ly/80teW*). So, how is logging different from Event Sourcing? Are we just talking about good old logging here, branding it with some new buzz name? The answer is absolutely not. It all comes down to: which system is the source of truth in our architecture? Who do I "trust" if my log disagrees with my current state? In Event Sourcing, the "state" is calculated from the events, so the answer is self-evident. For Splunk logs that is not the case, so your source of truth is most likely your relational model, even if you occasionally double-check it from the logs to hunt down some bugs. When your reliable log of events is your source of truth, you are using Event Sourcing as your data modeling approach. Otherwise, you are not, no matter how many logs you may be generating.

Summary

In this chapter we discussed a fundamental concept of microservices architectures: data isolation and the principle of embedding data into corresponding microservices. We also explored how this principle, while necessary for loose coupling and independent deployability, can lead us to significant data management challenges if we approach them with conventional data modeling solutions, the ones designed for monolithic N-tier applications. Further, we looked into a complete toolset of solutions to the described challenges in the form of powerful, tried-and-true patterns that address those challenges head-on. Last but not least, we introduced a new approach to data modeling, which is distinctly different from conventional, relational modeling. We explained the benefits and appropriate usage contexts of Event Sourcing and CQRS, even beyond microservices needs.

Armed with this powerful, foundational knowledge, we can now dive deep into the implementation of our sample project. We will first start by setting up an automated, containerized infrastructure and deployment pipelines for the project. This step is crucial for tackling the operational complexities of a microservices-based project. Then we will share detailed guidance on creating a productive and repeatable developer workspace—a critical foundation for creating an enjoyable developer experience in a heterogeneous environment. Finally, we will try to implement code for a couple of microservices of our sample project, leveraging all of the insights we have learned so far.

## CHAPTER 6

Building an Infrastructure Pipeline

In this chapter, we'll establish the foundation for our infrastructure work. We'll start by setting up an Amazon Web Services (AWS) account. Following that, we'll set up a tool called a continuous integration and continuous delivery (CI/CD) pipeline to automate infrastructure changes. With these tools, we'll be able to define and provision microservices infrastructures throughout the book.

Earlier, in Chapter 2, we established a platform team responsible for delivering the microservices infrastructure. We decided that this team would offer the infrastructure as a service. That meant that other teams should be able to use the infrastructure in a self-service manner, without having to coordinate heavily with the platform team. Enabling the "as a service" model requires some up-front investment. That's what the tools in this chapter will help address.

In order to reduce the work that our microservices teams need to do, we'll need to make it easy for teams to move their code from local workstations onto a hosted infrastructure. So we'll need to lower the barrier for teams to be able to provision environments and deploy their services into a hosted system. We'll need to make it cheap and easy to create a new environment and provide the right kit to make releases safe and easy.

In practice, achieving those goals is difficult if you don't have a good way of improving the way you make changes to the infrastructure itself. If we can reduce the effort cost of building and changing the infrastructure, we'll be able to deliver new environments more easily and put more focus on improving the infrastructure to meet our system goals.

Thankfully, we don't have to invent a solution for infrastructure changes by ourselves. We have the luxury of being able to draw on the principles and philosophies of DevOps. In particular, using the DevOps practices of infrastructure as code (IaC), CI, and CD will help us achieve our objectives. We'll be able to make infrastructure changes faster, cheaper, and safe, and scale the work of building environments across our microservices teams.

DevOps and Microservices

The goal of DevOps is the pursuit of improvements to the way that software is developed, released, and supported. Working towards that goal can span the domains of organizational design, culture, process, and tooling. The microservices style of architecture shares a similar overall goal, but adds the additional characteristic of bounded services and independent deployment and management. Microservices and DevOps go hand in hand—in fact, it would be extremely challenging to build applications in the microservices style without adopting DevOps practices.

Adopting DevOps practices means that we get to take advantage of a bountiful ecosystem of tools for code management, build management, and releases. Using these tools will greatly reduce the time it takes to get our infrastructure solution up and running. By the end of this chapter, we'll have set up a cloud-based toolchain that we can use to build a microservices infrastructure. We'll have an IaC repository, a starter file for the infrastructure code, a pipeline for testing and building (see Figure 6-1), and a cloud foundation that we can build environments within.

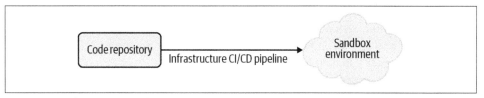

Figure 6-1. The target pipeline

But before we start building the pipeline, let's take a look at the DevOps-based principles and practices we've used to inform the design.

DevOps Principles and Practices

Building software in the DevOps way helps you reduce the time it takes to make changes to your applications, without introducing additional risk. When you do it right, it gives you both change speed and change safety at the same time.

That's exactly the benefit we want to provide with our infrastructure toolchain. If we can improve the speed and safety of infrastructure changes, we can do more of them. We'll also be able to make more improvements more often and offer a better platform service to our microservices teams.

To make this happen, we'll use three concepts from the DevOps world in our infrastructure platform:

- Immutable infrastructure
- IaC
- CI and CD

Let's take a look at each of these ideas in more detail to understand how they'll help us, starting with the principle of immutable infrastructure.

Immutable Infrastructure

An object is immutable if it can't be changed after it's created. The only way to update an immutable object is to destroy it and create a new one. Things that are immutable contain behavior and structures that are easier to predict and reproduce because they don't change. For example, in programming, an immutable data type would let you assign a value when it's created but never let you change it. If you created a data type called x with a value of 10, you could be sure that it will always be 10 forever more. This predictability can make activities like testing and replication of these objects easier.

The immutable infrastructure principle is an application of this immutability property on infrastructure components. Suppose we were to set up and install a network load balancer with a set of defined routes. If we apply the immutability principle, the network routes we've defined can't be changed without destroying the load balancer and making a new one.

The main advantage of applying immutability here is to create predictable and easily reproducible infrastructures. In traditional systems, human operators need to do a lot of manual work to get things running. They patch systems, alter configurations, and stop and start processes. Servers and devices are kept continually running and the operator shapes the environment so that the application can run. When there are multiple environments and servers, the operator needs to shape them all.

But, over time, as more changes are applied (often inconsistently), the state of these systems drift. It becomes increasingly difficult to keep all of the servers running in the same state. Introducing new servers or making changes to environment states becomes a problem because of this variability and unpredictability. This unpredictability means that more expertise and manual effort is required, which slows down delivery and makes it difficult to offer the infrastructure platform in a self-service tool as we outlined in our operating model.

That's where immutable infrastructure comes in. By adopting the principle of immutability, we can create an infrastructure that is highly predictable and easy to replicate.

This lends itself very well to the model we're targeting. So, let's make that our first key decision for our infrastructure foundation.

Key Decision: Apply the Principle of Immutable Infrastructure

Infrastructure components must not be changed after they've been created. Changes must be made by re-creating the component (and any dependent components) with the new or altered properties.

The decision we've just made comes with a trade-off: the cost of destroying and re-creating configurations. So we'll need to make some additional decisions to make this process easier. Otherwise, we'll end up never making infrastructure changes because it will be too difficult and too costly. The first decision we'll make is one we've alluded to earlier in the book. We'll build our platform in the cloud.

Key Decision: Implement the Infrastructure in the Cloud

Infrastructure components will be deployed and managed in a cloud platform.

This decision to build our microservices infrastructure in the cloud is an important enabler for our immutable infrastructure. Without it, the cost of physical hardware acquisition, server management, and software procurement would bury us in complexity and cost. But in the cloud, the infrastructure components are virtual. With virtuality, we can treat the infrastructure the same way we treat software. It gives us the freedom to create and destroy servers and devices in the same way as we might do with a software component or an object in a object-oriented system.

Immutable infrastructure will help us avoid server drift and improve our ability to replicate and instantiate new environments with a production-like state. However, we'll still need a way of defining all of our infrastructure with a manageable set of configurations. That's where the principle of IaC can help.

Infrastructure as Code

IaC is based on a single powerful constraint: all infrastructure changes must be represented as a set of machine-readable files (or code). Teams that apply this contraint can point to a group of files that define the target state for their infrastructure, and can re-create an environment by reapplying the code that created it. Managing the infrastructure code becomes a way of managing the infrastructure state. Ultimately adopting the principle of IaC means we can manage changes to our environments by managing the way we write, test and deploy our infrastructure code.

IaC is also very important for enabling our immutable infrastructure. Immutability requires us to manage definitions for objects so they can be changed through re-creation. There are plenty of ways to do that, but IaC lets us treat infrastructure the way we treat applications. With IaC, creating and changing components is similar to running a program. We'll get to apply our know-how from the application development world to the infrastructure.

IaC is a good fit for the system we're trying to build, so let's formalize this decision with an ADR.

Key Decision: Adopt IaC

All infrastructure changes should be made in managed code files. Changes should not be made manually by human operators outside of the code.

To get going with an IaC approach, we'll need a tool that will allow us to define the changes we want to make as machine-readable code files. That tool will also need to interpret our IaC files and apply them to a target environment. Years ago, we might have had to build this tooling ourselves, but now there are lots of tools available that can do this work for us. For our example project, we're going to use HashiCorp's Terraform to define our changes and apply them to our cloud-based environment.

An introduction to Terraform

Terraform is a popular tool for teams that are employing IaC principles and managing their infrastructure in an automated, repeatable way. We've had success using Terraform in our own projects and our straw poll of practitioners showed that it's a popular choice among other implementers as well. In this model, we've chosen to use Terraform as the tool for infrastructure changes, so let's start by documenting that decision.

Key Decision: Use Terraform for Infrastructure Changes

We'll use HashiCorp's Terraform tool to manage and apply changes to the platform infrastructure.

Terraform isn't the only tool that can help us with infrastructure changes and there are plenty of popular alternatives available for use. We've chosen to use Terraform because it applies a declarative approach to infrastructure management. So we get to declare a target state for the infrastructure and Terraform will do the hard work of making it happen. That's quite different from traditional configuration management approaches where we need to instruct the tool with step-by-step imperatives.

Terraform also embraces the principle of immutable infrastructure that we decided to adopt earlier. In practice, this enables us to write Terraform code that describes a desired state for an infrastructure component. When we apply our code, Terraform will do the hard work of destroying it and re-creating it in its new form. That includes dealing with any dependent objects and destroying and re-creating those as well.

To make that magic happen, Terraform needs to keep track of states. It needs to track the current state of the environment so that it can come up with a plan to produce the end state that we've defined. That state needs to be managed carefully and needs to be shared by everyone using the tool. Effective management of a Terraform solution means managing the state, configuration files, and quality, safety, and maintainability of the entire solution (just like we would for a software application).

 If you want to learn more about Terraform, a good place to start is their documentation (*https://oreil.ly/qaMM5*).

Continuous Integration and Continuous Delivery

Immutability and IaC make our infrastructure changes more predictable. But, those predictable changes may not always be safe. For example, what happens if a small change to a network inadvertently brings down a load balancer in production? Or what if a change intended only for the development environment accidentally makes its way to production and causes an outage?

One way to mitigate these risks is to do a lot of checking (and double-checking) for every change. But the problem with this approach is that it slows down our rate of change because of all the validation work we'd need to do. It can also lead to the late discovery of problems that we should have found a lot earlier in our infrastructure design and development work. We end up spending a lot of time in a testing phase where we need to fix a large batch of problems that could fundamentally alter our infrastructure plan.

A more efficient approach is to apply the DevOps software practices of continuous integration and continuous delivery (CI/CD). Instead of scheduling a big testing effort right before making a production change, we'll *continuously* integrate our changes into our repository. We'll also continuously test that our changes work and automatically deliver them. The goal is to get into a rhythm of releasing small, testable changes instead of a big batch.

Understanding CI/CD

If you want to understand CI/CD and learn how to implement it effectively, we recommend the books *Continuous Integration* by Paul M. Duvall, and *Continuous Delivery* by Jez Humble and David Farley (both Addison-Wesley).

CI/CD practices rely heavily on tooling. Tools allows teams to run higher volumes of tests against their code in a more efficient way. There's usually lots of different tools required to automate the integrateion and testing of software and infrastructure. That's why we'll be using a special kind of tool called a *pipeline*. A pipeline tool lets you define and manage the steps of a CI/CD process. That way, any code changes that we make can automatically be integrated and delivered in the same way, every time. Let's formalize our decision to use a CI/CD pipeline in this project.

Key Decision: Apply System Changes with a CI/CD Pipeline

All changes *must* be applied through an automated pipeline and/or tool. There should be no changes introduced through instructions in command line or operator consoles.

We'll be using a pipeline for all changes—not just infrastructure ones. In this chapter, we'll focus on the pipeline for our infrastructure changes. Later, in Chapter 10, we'll define a CI/CD pipeline for the microservices. There are plenty of pipeline tool options available, so we have another decision to make on tool choice. For our model, we've decided to use GitHub Actions as our CI/CD pipeline tool.

Key Decision: Use GitHub Actions for CI/CD Pipelines

Teams should use GitHub Actions to implement CI/CD pipelines for infrastructure and microservices.

At the time of this writing, GitHub Actions is a relatively new product and is not as feature rich as more established options like Jenkins and GitLab. We chose GitHub Actions because we plan to use GitHub to manage our code. Being able to use a single tool for code management and CI/CD is attractive. That's doubly true for this book, where we're constrained by the limits of the printed page.

By the end of this chapter, we will have built a CI/CD pipeline in GitHub Actions. We'll also configure the pipeline to handle Terraform code and make changes to a cloud-hosted environment. In Chapter 7, we will use our pipeline to provision a microservices infrastructure. But the first step is to install some tools and set up a working environment.

Setting Up the IaC Environment

When you write application code, you need a development environment with tools that let you write, manage, test, and run your code. The same is true for infrastructure code. In this section, we'll set up both a local environment and a cloud-hosted environment. We'll be using these environments to write, test, and publish infrastructure code.

Set Up GitHub

The first thing we'll need is a way to manage and release our code. We'll be using Git for code management and GitHub as a host. There are plenty of great options available for Git hosting, GitLab being one of the most popular alternatives. We've chosen to use GitHub for our model because it's become a very popular place to share code. That's useful for our implementation, because we'll be sharing a lot of code and configuration with you as we build our example application.

Key Decision: Use GitHub for Code Management

All code will be managed using the Git version control system and hosted in GitHub.

In order to work with our examples, you'll need to register for a GitHub account and you'll also need a local copy of a Git client. Git is an incredibly popular source control tool, so chances are that you already have it installed in your machine and you are familiar with how to use it. If you don't already have the Git client installed, visit the Git downloads page (*https://oreil.ly/5Vlcy*) and follow the instructions to download the appropriate version.

 If Git is new to you, we recommend that you start with the "Git Basics" chapter in Scott Chacon and Ben Straub's *Pro Git* (*https://oreil.ly/CK29D*), which they've graciously made available for free online. You can also visit GitHub's "Git Handbook" (*https://oreil.ly/raKSF*) if you're just looking for a quick overview of what Git is and why it's useful.

In addition to the Git client, you'll need a GitHub account so you can manage your code and configure your own CI/CD pipelines. If you don't have a GitHub account already, you can register for a free account (*https://oreil.ly/WcXv-*).

We'll be using Git and GitHub to manage our microservices code. But, applying our principle of IaC, we'll also be using these tools to manage infrastructure code. That code will be written in a special language called HCL that Terraform will be able to understand. Let's move on to installing the Terraform client.

Install Terraform

As we mentioned earlier, we'll be using Terraform to manage and apply our infrastructure code declaratively. Our plan is to automatically run the Terraform client in an automated CI/CD pipeline. Since that pipeline will be hosted in GitHub, you don't actually need to install Terraform on your workstation. However, in our experience you'll need a local installation to test code before you commit it to the pipeline. So, it's worthwhile installing Terraform in your local environment.

At the time of writing, Terraform is available to run on the following platforms:

- OS/X
- FreeBSD
- Linux
- OpenBSD
- Solaris
- Windows

Visit the Terraform site (*https://www.terraform.io*) to download the client of your choice and install it on your machine. We used version 0.12.20 for all of the examples in this book. We'll leave it to you to follow the instructions for the platform you've chosen.

Once you have completed the installation, run the following command to make sure Terraform is set up correctly:

```
$ terraform version
```

You should get back something that looks like the following, depending on the version you've installed:

```
Terraform v0.12.20
```

We'll be using Terraform to manage infrastructure resources in a cloud platform. In our model, those resources will be hosted in AWS. Let's take a look at how and why we'll be using AWS and what we need to do to get started with it.

Configuring Amazon Web Services

Earlier, we made a decision to use a cloud-hosted infrastructure. But we didn't decide on which cloud platform to use. Today, there are three cloud platforms that most microservices practitioners use: Microsoft Azure, Google Cloud Platform (GCP), and AWS. We've had success using all of these with our own implementations and have even worked with companies who've embraced all three.

For our model and sample application we've decided to build for a single cloud provider. That will make our implementation simpler and faster to implement. In that vein, we've decided to use AWS and its services for our examples, primarily because it had the biggest userbase at the time of writing. However, all of the big three cloud vendors offer similar services, so you'll be able to adapt our model to all of them with a bit of work.

Key Decision: Host Microservices in AWS

We'll use AWS as the cloud platform for microservices.

Since we've decided to use AWS, you will need to have an AWS account to follow along with our examples. If you don't have one already, you can register (*https://aws.amazon.com*). Keep in mind that you'll need a credit card to activate your account.

Keep an Eye on Your Billing

Although AWS offers a free account tier, the examples in this book use resources that aren't included in the scope of free services. We'll give you instructions for tearing down any resources that we create, but it will be up to you to make sure those resources are destroyed.

In addition to setting up an initial account, you'll also need to set up an "operator" account so that the tools we're setting up will have access to your AWS instance.

Setting Up an AWS Operations Account

By the end of this chapter, we'll have a pipeline that can deploy infrastructure into AWS automatically. Sticking to our principles of infeastructure as code and immutability, we should never have to manage our AWS infrastructure by making changes directly through the browser. But, to start off with, we'll need to perform a few steps manually to get our system up and running. The first step will be to configure a set of credentials and permissions to allow our tools to work with our AWS objects.

In AWS, users, groups, and permissions are all managed within the Identity and Access Management (IAM) service. We'll need to create a special user that represents our tooling and define a set of permissions for what our tools can do. We'll use this user identity whenever we are making calls from our CI/CD pipeline platform. As we mentioned earlier, we'll be using Terraform as our primary IaC tool. Follow the steps in this section to create a Terraform user in AWS that will allow us to make the kinds of changes we'll need for our microservices environment.

Log in to your AWS management console (*https://oreil.ly/8LpnE*) with your root user credentials. Once you've logged in, you should be presented with a list of AWS services. Find and select the IAM service—it's usually found in the Security, Identity & Compliance section (see Figure 6-2).

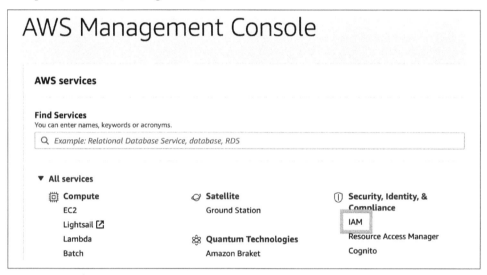

Figure 6-2. Select IAM

Select the Users link from the IAM navigation menu on the lefthand side of the screen. Click the Add user button to start the IAM user creation process, as shown in Figure 6-3.

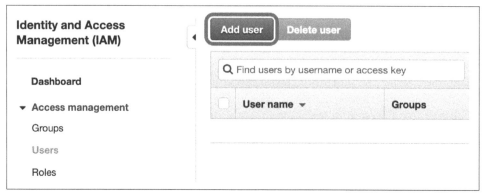

Figure 6-3. Add user button

Enter ops-account in the User name field. We also want to use this account to acccess the CLI and API, so select "Programmatic acccss" as the AWS "Access type," as in Figure 6-4.

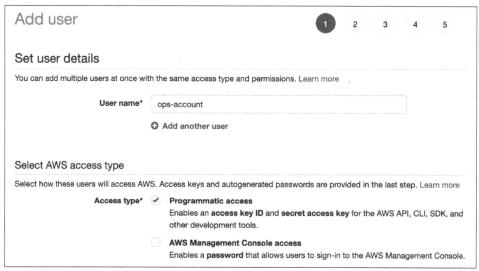

Figure 6-4. Enter user details

When you've done that, click the Next: Permissions button.

Our operator account will need a lot of permissions to do work in AWS on our behalf. For now, however, we're only going to attach a single set of permissions, packaged together in an AWS policy called IAMFullAccess.

To add this policy, select "Attach existing policies directly" from the set of options at the top. Search for a policy called IAMFullAccess and select it by ticking its checkbox, as shown in Figure 6-5.

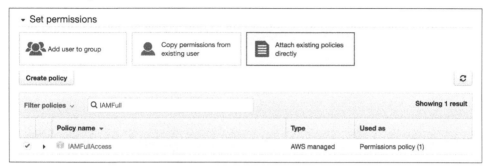

Figure 6-5. Attach the IAMFullAccess policy

When that's done, click the Next: Tags button. We won't be creating any tags, so click the Next: Review button to review our user's details (see Figure 6-6).

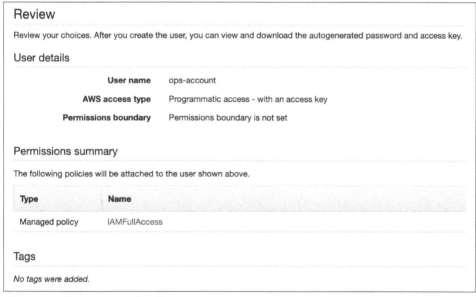

Figure 6-6. Review user details

If everything looks OK to you, click the Create user button. You should now see a screen that looks something like Figure 6-7.

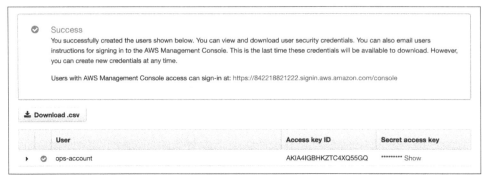

Figure 6-7. User created

Before we do anything else, we'll need to make a note of our new user's keys. Click the Show link and copy and paste both the "Access key ID" and the "Secret access key" into a temporary file. We'll use both of these later in this section with our automated pipeline. Be careful with this key material as it will give whoever has it an opportunity to create resources in your AWS environment—at your expense.

Make sure you take note of the access key ID and the secret access key that were generated before you leave this screen. You'll need them later in this chapter.

We have now created a user called `ops-account` with permission to make IAM changes. That gives us all that we need to transition from using the browser-based console over to the AWS CLI application that we installed earlier. The first thing we'll need to do is configure the CLI to use the ops user we've just created.

Configure the AWS CLI

There are three ways to manage major cloud provider configurations: a web browser, web-based APIs, and a CLI. We've already used a web browser to create our operator account and later we'll be using Terraform to configure changes via the AWS APIs. But, we'll need to make some more changes before Terraform can make AWS API calls on our behalf. For that we'll use the AWS CLI.

Using the CLI makes it a lot easier for us to describe the changes you need to make. It's also less prone to the changes that user interfaces (UIs) go through. But to use the CLI, the first thing we'll need to do is install it into our local working environment.

Navigate to the AWS CLI download page (*https://aws.amazon.com/cli*) and follow the instructions there to install the CLI onto your local system.

Once it's ready, the first thing we'll do is configure the CLI so it can access our instance. Run the `aws configure` command as shown in Example 6-1. You can replace the default region name with an AWS region that is closer to you; a full list of AWS regions is available at AWS (*https://oreil.ly/UrX_t*).

Example 6-1. Configure the AWS CLI

```
$ aws configure
AWS Access Key ID [****************AMCK]: AMIB3IIUDHKPENIBWUVGR
AWS Secret Access Key [****************t+ND]: /xd5QWmsqRsM1Lj4ISUmKoqV7/...
Default region name [None]: eu-west-2
Default output format [None]: json
```

You can test that you've configured the CLI correctly by listing the user accounts that have been created. Run the `iam list-users` command to test your setup:

```
$ aws iam list-users
{
    "Users": [
        {
            "Path": "/",
            "UserName": "admin",
            "UserId": "AYURIGDYE7PXW3QCYYEWM",
            "Arn": "arn:aws:iam::842218941332:user/admin",
            "CreateDate": "2019-03-21T14:01:03+00:00"
        },
        {
            "Path": "/",
            "UserName": "ops-account",
            "UserId": "AYUR4IGBHKZTE3YVBO2OB",
            "Arn": "arn:aws:iam::842218941332:user/ops-account",
            "CreateDate": "2020-07-06T15:15:31+00:00"
        }
    ]
}
```

If you've done everything correctly, you should see a list of your AWS user accounts. That indicates that AWS CLI is working properly and has access to your instance. Now, we can set up the permissions our operations account will need.

Setting Up AWS Permissions

When we created our ops-account user we attached an IAM policy to it that only gives it permission to modify IAM settings. But our ops account will need a lot more permissions than that to manage the AWS resources we'll need for our infrastructure build. In this section, we'll use the AWS command-line tool to create and attach additional permission policies to the ops account.

The first thing we'll do is make the ops-account user part of a new group called Ops-Accounts. That way we'll be able to assign new users to the group if we want them to have the same permissions. Use the following command to create a new group called Ops-Accounts:

```
$ aws iam create-group --group-name Ops-Accounts
```

If this is successful, the AWS CLI will display the group that has been created:

```
{

    "Group": {
        "Path": "/",
        "GroupName": "Ops-Accounts",
        "GroupId": "AGPA4IGBHKZTGWGQWW67X",
        "Arn": "arn:aws:iam::842218941332:group/Ops-Accounts",
        "CreateDate": "2020-07-06T15:29:14+00:00"
    }
}
```

Now, we just need to add our user to the new group. Use the following command to do that:

```
$ aws iam add-user-to-group --user-name ops-account --group-name Ops-Accounts
```

If it works, you'll get no response from the CLI. In this case, no news is good news.

Next, we need to attach a set of permissions to our Ops-Account group. Those permissions will automatically be applied to our operations users, since we've made it part of the group. The permissions we'll be attaching will let our user create and change AWS resources. In practice, you'd likely need to change the permissions for your Ops user as you go through the process of designing your infrastructure. In this book, we've already done the design work ahead of time, so we know exactly which policies need to be attached.

Run the following command to attach all the policies we'll need to the Ops-Accounts group:

```
$ aws iam attach-group-policy --group-name Ops-Accounts\
  --policy-arn arn:aws:iam::aws:policy/IAMFullAccess &&\
aws iam attach-group-policy --group-name Ops-Accounts\
  --policy-arn arn:aws:iam::aws:policy/AmazonEC2FullAccess &&\
aws iam attach-group-policy --group-name Ops-Accounts\
```

```
 --policy-arn arn:aws:iam::aws:policy/AmazonEC2ContainerRegistryFullAccess &&\
aws iam attach-group-policy --group-name Ops-Accounts\
 --policy-arn arn:aws:iam::aws:policy/AmazonEKSClusterPolicy &&\
aws iam attach-group-policy --group-name Ops-Accounts\
 --policy-arn arn:aws:iam::aws:policy/AmazonEKSServicePolicy &&\
aws iam attach-group-policy --group-name Ops-Accounts\
 --policy-arn arn:aws:iam::aws:policy/AmazonVPCFullAccess &&\
aws iam attach-group-policy --group-name Ops-Accounts\
 --policy-arn arn:aws:iam::aws:policy/AmazonRoute53FullAccess &&\
aws iam attach-group-policy --group-name Ops-Accounts\
 --policy-arn arn:aws:iam::aws:policy/AmazonS3FullAccess
```

> A scripted copy of this command is available at this book's GitHub
> site (*https://oreil.ly/Microservices_UpandRunning_scripted*).

In addition to the out-of-the-box policies that AWS provides, we'll also need some special permissions to work with the AWS Elastic Kubernetes Service (EKS). We'll be introducing EKS properly in the next chapter, but for now we need to get the permissions sorted out. There isn't an existing policy that we can attach for the permissions we need, so we'll need to create our own custom policy and attach it to our user group.

To do this, create a file called *custom-eks-policy.json* and populate it with the code in Example 6-2. We have also made a copy of this JSON file available in this book's GitHub repository (*https://oreil.ly/Microservices_UpandRunning_json*).

Example 6-2. Custom JSON policy for EKS

```
{
  "Version": "2012-10-17",
  "Statement": [
    {
      "Effect": "Allow",
      "Action": [
        "eks:DescribeNodegroup",
        "eks:DeleteNodegroup",
        "eks:ListClusters",
        "eks:CreateCluster"
      ],
      "Resource": "*"
    },
    {
      "Effect": "Allow",
      "Action": "eks:*",
      "Resource": "arn:aws:eks:*:*:cluster/*"
    }
```

```
    ]
}
```

Now, run the following command to create a new policy named EKS-Management
based on the JSON we've just created:

```
$ aws iam create-policy --policy-name EKS-Management\
  --policy-document file://custom-eks-policy.json
```

If the command was successful, you'll see a JSON representation of the new policy:

```
{
    "Policy": {
        "PolicyName": "EKS-Management",
        "PolicyId": "ANPA4IGBHKZTP3CFK4FAW",
        "Arn": "arn:aws:iam::[some_number]:policy/EKS-Management",
        "Path": "/",
        "DefaultVersionId": "v1",
        "AttachmentCount": 0,
        "PermissionsBoundaryUsageCount": 0,
        "IsAttachable": true,
        "CreateDate": "2020-07-06T15:50:26+00:00",
        "UpdateDate": "2020-07-06T15:50:26+00:00"
    }
}
```

In AWS, every resource has a unique identifier called an Amazon
Resource Name (ARN). The string of digits in the ARN of the policy you've just created will be unique to you and your AWS
instance. You'll need to make note of your policy's ARN string so
that you can reference it in the following steps.

With the new policy created, all that's left is to attach it to our user group. Run the
following command, replacing the token we've called *{YOUR_POLICY_ARN}* with the
ARN from your policy:

```
$ aws iam attach-group-policy --group-name Ops-Accounts \
  --policy-arn {YOUR_POLICY_ARN}
```

You now have an ops-account user that has the permissions needed to automatically
create AWS infrastructure resources for us. We'll be using this user account when we
write our Terraform code and when we configure the infrastructure pipeline. Make
sure you keep the access key and secret somewhere handy (and safe) as we'll need it
later.

We have one last bit of setup to take care of before we can get to work building the
pipeline: the creation of an AWS S3 storage bucket for Terraform to store state.

Creating an S3 Backend for Terraform

Terraform is powerful because it allows us to declare what an infrastructure should look like, rather than defining the specific steps needed to reach that state. Terraform works its magic by making the right changes to an environment to make it look the way we've described. But, in order to do that, Terraform needs to keep track of what the environment looks like and the last operations it's performed. Terraform keeps track of all that information in a JSON-based state file that is read and updated every time it is run.

By default, Terraform will keep this state file in your local filesystem. In practice, storing the state file locally is problematic. State often needs to be shared across machines and users so that an environment can be managed in multiple places. However, local state files are difficult to share and you can easily find yourself dealing with state conflicts and synchronization issues.

Instead, we'll use the AWS S3 service to store the Terraform state file. Terraform comes with out-of-the-box support for using S3 as a state backend. All we'll need to do is create a new "bucket" for the data and make sure we have the correct permissions set for our ops user account.

> Like most cloud providers, AWS provides lots of different data storage options. Amazon's *Simple Storage Service* (S3) lets you create data objects that can be referenced by a key. The data objects are just blobs to Amazon and can be in any format you like. In this case, Terraform will be storing environment state as JSON objects.

To create a bucket, you'll need to give it a unique name and pick the region that it should reside in. You should have already selected a default region when you configured the AWS CLI and we suggest that you use the same region for the S3 bucket. You can find more information about S3 bucket regions in the AWS documentation (*https://oreil.ly/5Frfk*).

S3 Bucket Names Must Be Unique

Amazon S3 buckets can be referenced by their names. So the name you pick must be unique across the entire AWS region that you select. There is a good chance you won't be able to use a generic name like "test" or "microservices." Instead, you'll need to come up with something unique. Usually, appending your name to the bucket name works. Throughout this book, whenever we refer to this S3 bucket, we'll use the token *{YOUR_S3_BUCKET_NAME}* and leave it to you to replace it with your bucket name.

If you are hosting your bucket in the us-east-1 region, use the following command:

 S3 requires special handling if you're not in the us-east-1 region. We've listed the default us-east-1 and nondefault versions of the command in the following examples. We've also split up the command lines using the bash multiline operator "\" for readability.

```
$ aws s3api create-bucket --bucket {YOUR_S3_BUCKET_NAME} \
> --region us-east-1
```

If you are hosting the s3 bucket in a region *other* than us-east-1, use the following command:

```
$ aws s3api create-bucket --bucket {YOUR_S3_BUCKET_NAME} \
> --region {YOUR_AWS_REGION} --create-bucket-configuration \
> LocationConstraint={YOUR_AWS_REGION}
```

If everything has gone well, you should see a JSON object with the location of your bucket. It will look something like this example for a bucket named my-msur-test:

```
{
    "Location": "http://my-msur-test.s3.amazonaws.com/"
}
```

This indicates that the bucket has been successfully created and has been assigned its own unique URL. By default, S3 buckets aren't publicly accessible. That's a good thing because we don't want just anyone to be able to see and change our Terraform state file. However, we've already given our ops account user full permissions to the S3 service, so it is ready for use.

With this final step complete, we now have an AWS user called ops-account configured to create, edit, and delete resources in AWS. We've also given it permissions to store objects in a special S3 bucket we've created just for managing Terraform state. This should be the last time we make manual operator changes to our AWS instance; from here on out we'll only make changes through code and with an automated pipeline!

Building an IaC Pipeline

With the accounts, permissions, and tools ready to go, we can now get on with the real focus of this chapter. By the end of this section, we'll have an IaC pipeline implemented and ready to use. Remember, the infrastructure pipeline is incredibly important because it gives us a safe and easy way to provision environments quickly. Without a pipeline, we'd end up with lots of manual steps and microservices environments that have drifted apart in the way they work.

Instead, we'll have a stable declarative definition of the infrastructure for our services. Our development and operations teams will be able to use those definitions to create their own environments to perform testing, make changes, and release services into production. We won't be implementing any of the actual AWS infrastructure in this chapter, but we will be implementing a foundation that we'll use in the next chapter. In this section we'll build the following components:

- A GitHub-hosted Git repository for a sandbox testing environment
- A Terraform root module that defines the sandbox
- A GitHub Actions CI/CD pipeline that can create a sandbox environment

The sandbox testing environment we're building is just a test environment that will give us a chance to try out our IaC modules and pipelines. We'll build it out in the next chapter and then throw it away when we're happy that everything works. Later, we'll use all of these assets to build a test environment for the microservices that we'll be designing and building.

But our first step will be to establish a repository for the code and pipeline, so let's get started with creating the repository.

Creating the Sandbox Repository

We've already mentioned in the beginning of this chapter that we'll be using Git and GitHub to manage our infrastructure code. If you've been following along, you'll already have a local copy of Git installed and a GitHub account ready to be used. We're going to use both of those tools to create a new repository for our sandbox environment.

In our model, we've decided to give each environment its own repository with the code and pipeline bundled within it. We like this approach because it gives teams more independence in how they manage the environments they want to create, while still keeping the pipeline configuration and code together for easier management.

> ### Key Decision: One Repository per Environment
>
> Each environment's code and pipeline will be managed independently in its own code repository.

We'll use GitHub's browser-based interface to create the sandbox repository. Although there is a GitHub CLI application available, it will be quicker and easier to use the web-based interface to create our new repository. Later, we'll also be using GitHub's browser interface to run and monitor the pipeline.

Some practitioners like to keep all of the environment configurations together in a single "monorepo." This makes it easier to share libraries, components, and actions between all the environments and helps keep things consistent. Most practitioners also use specialized CI/CD tooling (Jenkins being one of the most popular), rather than building inside GitHub. This is an important decision, so you'll need to consider the trade-offs when you build your next microservices architecture based on the observations you make from the one we're building together.

To create the repository, open your browser and navigate to the GitHub sign-in page (*https://github.com/new*). If you haven't already logged in to your GitHub account, you'll be prompted to enter your login credentials. Once that is done, you'll be presented with a form to create a new repository. Give your new repository the name env-sandbox and select Private from the access options. You should also tick the Add .gitignore checkbox and choose Terraform from the drop-down, as shown in Figure 6-8.

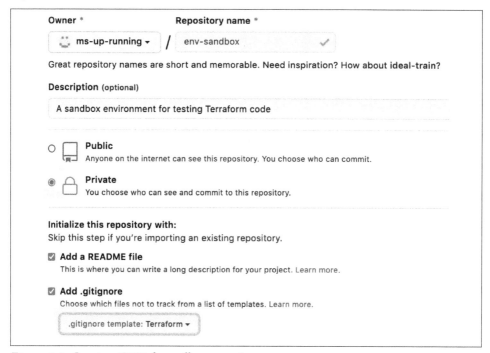

Figure 6-8. Create a GitHub sandbox repository

It's important that we ask GitHub to add a *.gitignore* for Terraform to the module because it will make sure we don't accidentally commit Terraform's hidden working files to our module. If you've missed this step you can always add this file later by copying the source from this GitHub site (*https://oreil.ly/VZ0Xk*).

It's possible to write code using GitHub's browser-based text editor, but it's not very practical for doing real work. Instead, we'll clone this repository into a local development environment so we can use our own tools. We'll leave it to you to create a clone of your env-sandbox repository in your local development environment.

 If you've never worked with Git and GitHub before, you can find helpful instructions on how to clone a GitHub repository in the official GitHub documentation (*https://oreil.ly/tZXaG*).

That's all we need to do with GitHub for now. We'll come back to the browser-based GitHub interface later when we work on the pipeline. But with the local clone created, we can begin work on the Terraform code.

Understanding Terraform

We mentioned earlier that we'll be using Terraform as our tool of choice for declaratively coding our infrastructure foundation. Terraform does a lot of complicated work to make changes that match a declared state. That said, it's surprisingly easy to get started with and the language it uses is fairly intuitive. That makes it a great fit for our architecture and our goal of getting a system running as quickly as possible.

Terraform files are configured in a data format called HCL, which was invented by HashiCorp (the company that created Terraform). HCL is similar to JSON, with a few adaptations and improvements. If you're used to JSON, the biggest difference you'll notice is that HCL doesn't use a ":" delimiter between key and value pairs. Instead, keys and values are just separated by a white space or an "=" depending on the context. There are some other minor improvements, such as comments and multiline strings. In our experience, it's an easy language with a very low learning curve if you've used JSON or YAML in the past.

In addition to understanding HCL, it's useful to understand four of the key Terraform concepts—backends, providers, resources, and modules:

Backends
> Terraform needs to maintain a state file so that it knows what kinds of changes to make to the infrastructure environment. A backend is the location of that state file. By default this is located in the local filesystem. We'll be using an AWS S3 bucket that we configured earlier.

Resources

A resource is an object that represents a thing for which you are declaring a state. Terraform does the work of making the changes to bring the resource to that state.

Providers

A Terraform provider is a packaged library of resources that you can use in your code. We'll be using Terraform's AWS provider for most of our work. The nice thing about Terraform is that you can use it for lots of different cloud platforms and infrastructure environments—you just need to specify the provider you plan to use.

Modules

Terraform modules are similar to functions or procedures in a regular programming language. They give you a nice way of encapsulating your HCL code in a reusable, modular way.

There's a lot more to Terraform that what we've described here, but this is enough knowledge for us to get started with our environment build work. If you want to go deeper, the Terraform documentation (*https://oreil.ly/07b_c*) is a great place to start.

Our next step is to write some Terraform code that will help us build a sandbox environment.

Writing the Code for the Sandbox Environment

Our goal in this chapter is to set up the tooling and infrastructure for our environment build, so we won't be writing a complete Terraform file that defines our infrastructure until the next chapter. For now, we'll need to create a simple starter file to test our Terraform-based tool chain.

The Terraform CLI tool works by looking for files it recognizes in the working directory where it's run. In particular, it looks for a file called *main.tf* and will parse that file and apply changes based on its contents. You can only have one *main.tf* file in a single directory, so we'll need to have a directory dedicated to our sandbox environment and we'll need to create a Terraform *main.tf* file that will describe its target state.

We've already created a Git repository called `env-sandox` for the sandbox environment, so that's the directory we'll use for the Terraform code. Let's get started by creating a new file called *main.tf* in the local sandbox Git repository. Populate it with the HCL code in Example 6-3.

You'll need to replace the tokens *{YOUR_S3_BUCKET_NAME}* and *{YOUR_AWS_REGION}* with the S3 bucket name you created earlier and the AWS region you've been using.

Example 6-3. env-sandbox/main.tf

```
terraform {
  backend "s3" {
    bucket = "{YOUR_S3_BUCKET_NAME}"
    key    = "terraform/backend"
    region = "{YOUR_AWS_REGION}"
  }
}

locals {
  env_name         = "sandbox"
  aws_region       = "{YOUR_AWS_REGION}"
  k8s_cluster_name = "ms-cluster"
}

# Network Configuration

# EKS Configuration

# GitOps Configuration
```

The S3 bucket name should just be the name of your bucket, not the full URL (for example, my-bucket).

The HCL snippet you've just written lets Terraform know that we are using an S3 bucket to store our backend state. It also defines a set of local variables using a Terraform construct called locals. Finally, it has a few Terraform comments at the end, indicating where we'll be adding details for the infrastructure. We'll be using the local variables and filling in the rest of the configuration in the next chapter. For now, we just want to test the scaffolding of our Terraform file.

With our first Terraform code file written, we're ready to try running some Terraform commands to make sure it works as expected. The Terraform CLI tool includes a lot of helpful features to improve the quality and safety of your infrastructure code. You can use it to format (or *lint*) the HCL that you've written, validate the syntax, and do a dry run of the changes that Terraform would run against your provider.

If you've followed the instructions earlier in this chapter, you should have a local copy of Terraform available in your working environment. Make sure you are in the same working directory as your *main.tf* file and try running the `fmt` command to format your code:

```
env-sandbox msur$ terraform fmt main.tf
```

The `fmt` command is a formatter that will examine your HCL file and make changes to improve its consistency and readability. If any changes were made it will output the name of the file that it changed.

Next, we'll validate that the syntax of the HCL we've written is valid. But, before we do that we'll need to install the providers we're using; otherwise Terraform will complain that it can't do the syntax check. Run the following command to install the providers:

```
env-sandbox msur$ terraform init

Successfully configured the backend "s3"! Terraform will automatically
use this backend unless the backend configuration changes.

Terraform has been successfully initialized!

You may now begin working with Terraform. Try running "terraform plan" to see
any changes that are required for your infrastructure. All Terraform commands
should now work.

If you ever set or change modules or backend configuration for Terraform,
rerun this command to reinitialize your working directory. If you forget, other
commands will detect it and remind you to do so if necessary.
```

 If you get an error related to AWS credentials, make sure you've followed the instructions at the beginning of this chapter to configure access to an AWS environment first.

Now we can run a validate command to ensure that we haven't introduced any syntax errors:

```
env-sandbox msur$ terraform validate
Success! The configuration is valid.
```

Finally, we can run a command called `plan` to see what changes Terraform would make to create the environment we've specified. This performs the same steps that will be run when the code is applied, but it doesn't actually make any changes. Think of it as a dry run that allows Terraform to show you its plan for getting the infrastructure to the state you've asked for. Use the following command to run a `plan`:

```
$ terraform plan

Refreshing Terraform state in-memory prior to plan...
The refreshed state will be used to calculate this plan, but will not be
persisted to local or remote state storage.

No changes. Infrastructure is up-to-date.
```

This means that Terraform did not detect any differences between your configuration and the real physical resources. As a result, no actions need to be performed.

Notice that our plan result isn't very interesting: "No changes." That's because we haven't actually defined any resources to create. The good news is that we now have a syntactically valid Terraform file to start building our sandbox environment. This is a good time to commit and push the file into the GitHub repository so that the file is available for use:

```
$ git add .
$ git commit -m "The sandbox starter file"
$ git push origin
```

With our Terraform file working and ready to be used, we can shift our focus over to the pipeline that we'll use to automatically apply it.

Building the Pipeline

In this section we'll set up an automated CI/CD pipeline that will automatically apply the Terraform file that we've just created. To configure the pipeline activities, we'll be using GitHub's built-in DevOps tool, GitHub Actions. The nice thing about using GitHub Actions is that we can put our pipeline configuration in the same place as our infrastructure code.

The easiest way to use GitHub Actions is to configure it through the browser interface. So go back to your browser and navigate to the sandbox repository you created earlier in GitHub.

Our plan is to create resources in the AWS account that we created earlier in this chapter. Thus, we'll need to make sure that GitHub is able to use the AWS access key and secret that we provisioned when we created the operator account. There are lots of ways to manage secrets in a microservices architecture, but for our DevOps tooling, we'll just use GitHub's built-in secrets storage function.

Setting up secrets

Navigate to the GitHub secrets storage area by selecting Settings from the top navigation of your repository. Select Secrets from the menu of settings options on the left-hand side of the screen, as shown in Figure 6-9.

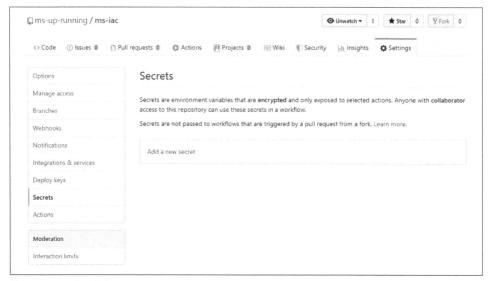

Figure 6-9. GitHub secrets

Select "Add a new secret" and create a secret called AWS_ACCESS_KEY_ID. Enter the access key ID that you tucked away earlier in this chapter when you created your operator user. Repeat the process and create a secret named AWS_SECRET_ACCESS_KEY with the secret access key you generated earlier. When you are done, you should have something that looks like Figure 6-10.

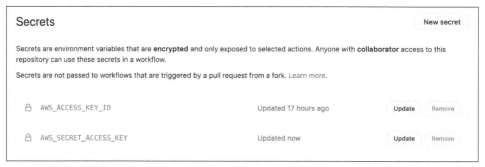

Figure 6-10. Add your AWS ID and key

Now that the secrets have been added, we can get started on the workflow for the pipeline.

Creating the workflow

A workflow is the set of steps that we want to run whenever a pipeline is triggered. For our microservices infrastructure pipeline, we'll want a workflow that validates Terraform files and then applies them to our sandbox environment. But in addition to testing and applying infrastructure changes, we'll need to add a few steps before and after applying our Terraform files.

The workflow will need to start with a trigger that lets GitHub know when the workflow should start. GitHub Actions gives us a few different options for triggers, but we'll use Git's `tag` mechanism as the trigger for our infrastructure builds. A *tag* is a way of giving a name to or labeling a particular point in a Git repository history. Using tagging as a trigger gives us a nice versioning history for the changes we are making to the environment. It also gives us a way of committing files to the repository without triggering a build.

When our pipeline workflow is triggered it will need to operate on the Terraform files that we've committed to the repository. But, we'll need some setup steps to prepare the build environment. First, we'll install Terraform and AWS just like we did in our local environment. Although we are running this in GitHub Actions, the actual build takes place in a virtual machine, so we'll also need to grab a copy of the code from our code repository.

Finally, when the changes are applied to our sandbox environment, we'll have a chance to do any cleanup or post-provisioning activities. In our case, we'll be making a special configuration file available for download so that we can connect to the AWS-based microservices environment from a local machine. When it's complete, the pipeline will look like Figure 6-11.

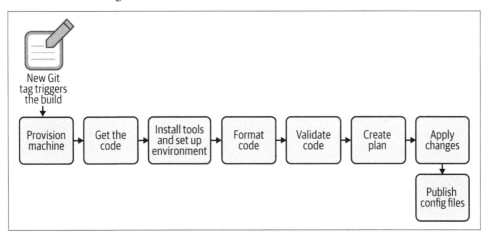

Figure 6-11. Infrastructure pipeline steps

We'll be defining the steps of the pipeline using the YAML language and the set of workflow commands in GitHub Actions. You can refer to the full GitHub Actions documentation (*https://oreil.ly/Kk7-J*). Let's dig into the YAML configuration by navigating to the GitHub Actions page for your repository. You should be able to do this by selecting Actions from the top navigation bar in your sandbox's GitHub repository page. When you get there, you should see a screen that looks similar to Figure 6-12.

Figure 6-12. Create a GitHub Actions workflow

GitHub Actions provides you with templates you can use to quickly get started with a workflow. However, we're going to ignore the templates and set up a workflow ourselves from scratch. Click the Set up a workflow yourself button in the top-right corner of the screen (or wherever it is in the latest version of the interface).

You'll now find yourself editing a newly created YAML file for your workflow. GitHub keeps the Actions files in a hidden directory called */.github/workflows*. When you clone a GitHub repository, you can edit these files in whatever editor you like, or create new YAML files to define new GitHub Action workflows. But the advantage of editing Actions on the GitHub website is that you can search for plug-ins from the marketplace. So we'll stick to the browser-based editor for our initial workflow editing.

The first thing we'll do is configure a trigger for the workflow and set up a container environment to do the infrastructure build.

To help you understand what is happening, we're going to explore the workflow file as individual parts. We'll explain each part as we go along, but the actual workflow is all contained in a single file. You can see an example of the completed workflow file at this book's GitHub site (*https://oreil.ly/Microservices_UpandRunning_env_sandbox*).

Configuring the trigger and setup

One of the most important steps in our workflow is the trigger step that initiates it. As we mentioned earlier, we'll use a simple trigger based on Git's tagging mechanism. We'll configure our pipeline so that it runs whenever infrastructure is tagged with a label that starts with a *v*. That way we can keep a version history of the infrastructure that we've built. For example, our first infrastructure build could be tagged with "v1.0."

Replace the YAML in your workflow editor with the code in Example 6-4 to get started.

Example 6-4. Workflow trigger and job setup

```
name: Sandbox Environment Build

on:
  create:
    tags:
      - v*
jobs:
  build:
    runs-on: ubuntu-latest
    env:
        AWS_ACCESS_KEY_ID: ${{ secrets.AWS_ACCESS_KEY_ID }}
        AWS_SECRET_ACCESS_KEY: ${{ secrets.AWS_SECRET_ACCESS_KEY }}

    steps:
    - uses: actions/checkout@v2

    # Install Dependencies
```

 # Install Dependencies in Example 6-4 is a comment. We'll use comments in the YAML to describe what is happening, but also to indicate where we'll be adding additional YAML in later steps.

In the preceding snippet, on is a GitHub Actions command that specifies the trigger for the workflow. We've configured our workflow to run when a new tag that matches the pattern v* is created. In addition, we've added a jobs collection that specifies the work that GitHub should do when it is triggered. Jobs need to be run in a machine or a container. The runs-on property indicates that we want to run this build in an Ubuntu Linux Virtual Machine. We're also adding the AWS secrets that we configured earlier in the build environment.

The steps collection indicates the specific workflow steps that the workflow will perform within the environment we have set up. But before we do anything else we need to get the code. So the first step we've defined is to check out our Terraform code from Git using the GitHub `actions/checkout@v2` action. This creates a copy of the code inside of the Ubuntu build environment for the rest of the job steps to act upon.

 Actions are modularized libraries of code that can be called from a GitHub Actions workflow. Actions are the heart of the GitHub Actions system and give it a richness of features and integration. There is a large catalog of actions available in the GitHub Actions marketplace that you can use in your workflow files. But, be selective when choosing them as anyone can create and publish new actions, so support, security, and quality are not guaranteed.

We have enough in our workflow to be able to run it, but it would not be able to do anything useful beyond grabbing a copy of our code. What we really want to do is start working with Terraform, but before we can do that we need to get the environment set up so that our tooling can be run. That means we need to add some dependency installation instructions.

Installing dependencies

When we set up our local infrastructure development environment, we needed to install the Git, AWS, and Terraform command-line tools. We'll need to do something similar in our build environment, but since we know the specific operations we'll be running, we can set up a slightly leaner set of dependencies.

The good news is that we get Git for free when we use GitHub Actions, so we won't need to worry about installing it. Also, HashiCorp provides a ready-to-go GitHub Action for Terraform, so we won't need to worry about installing the Terraform client. The only thing that's left to deal with is our AWS configuration.

Earlier in this chapter we used the AWS CLI to make changes to our AWS account. In our pipeline environment, however, we want to use Terraform to make changes. In fact, we don't want to make any changes to the environment beyond what we've specified in our Terraform code. So we won't need to install the AWS CLI.

All of this tells us that we don't need to install any dependencies to make a pipeline that can create AWS resources for us. But as we start building out our infrastructure in the next chapter, we'll find out that our infrastructure needs some special dependencies to deal with some of the complexities of installing a Kubernetes-based microservices architecture.

Because this is a book, we've identified the dependencies you'll need for the pipeline before you know you need them. That's because books are easier to read when they are linear, so we've done the work to give you a linear set of instructions to follow. In practice, you'll go through several iterations of editing your pipeline actions as you test, and learn and develop your infrastructure and microservices pipelines.

Specifically, we'll be installing an AWS authenticator tool and an installer for the Istio service mesh. The AWS authenticator is a command-line tool that other tools can use to authenticate and access an AWS environment. This will come in handy later, when we are working with Kubernetes and need to configure access to an AWS-hosted Kubernetes cluster. Istio is a service mesh tool. We'll introduce Istio in the next chapter; for now we just need to make sure we've installed the CLI tool.

Add the code in Example 6-5 to your workflow file to set up those dependencies in the build environment. These steps need to be added after the `# Install Dependen cies` comment we added earlier. Be careful with the indenting and make sure you are lined up with the `-uses` step from earlier as YAML is very particular about spacing.

Example 6-5. Installing dependencies

```
[...]

    # Install Dependencies

    - name: Install aws-iam-authenticator
      run: |
        echo Installing aws-iam-authenticator...
        mkdir ~/aws
        curl -o ~/aws/aws-iam-authenticator \
        "https://amazon-eks.s3.us-west-2.amazonaws.com/\
        1.16.8/2020-04-16/bin/linux/amd64/aws-iam-authenticator"
        chmod +x ~/aws/aws-iam-authenticator
        sudo cp ~/aws/aws-iam-authenticator /usr/local/bin/aws-iam-authenticator

  # Apply Terraform
```

The `run` commands in the YAML you've just added will run shell commands in the Ubuntu build environment. We've added instructions to install the AWS IAM Authenticator based on the AWS documentation as well as the Istio CLI tool.

The virtual machine (VM) defined in our GitHub Actions workflow will be created at the start of every pipeline run and destroyed at completion. That means our tools will be installed every time we trigger our pipeline job and no state will be retained between runs.

The last part of our YAML code uses HashiCorp's Terraform setup action. As you can see, this is much cleaner and easier to read and understand than the command-line installations we included for the AWS authenticator and Istio. GitHub Actions is better when you have actions to use, so it's a good idea to take advantage of them when they fit your needs.

With our dependencies set up and Terraform ready to go, we can now add some Terraform handling steps to our workflow.

Applying Terraform files

In "Writing the Code for the Sandbox Environment" on page 120, we used Terraform commands to format and validate the HCL code we wrote in *main.tf*. We want to do something similar in our pipeline, but we want these activities to happen automatically. The goal is for the Terraform code to be automatically formatted, validated, and planned. We'll also add an automatic "apply" step that will apply the plan and implement changes.

Add the YAML code in Example 6-6 to the end of your workflow YAML, after the `# Apply Terraform` comment.

Example 6-6. Terraform workflow

```
# Apply Terraform

    - uses: hashicorp/setup-terraform@v1
  with:
    terraform_version: 0.12.19

  - name: Terraform fmt
    run: terraform fmt

  - name: Terraform Init
    run: terraform init

  - name: Terraform Validate
    run: terraform validate -no-color

  - name: Terraform Plan
    run: terraform plan -no-color

  - name: Terraform Apply
    run: terraform apply -no-color -auto-approve

  # Publish Assets
```

As you can see from your YAML, we're using the run action to call the Terraform CLI from the Ubuntu shell. This is largely the same as what you did in your local environment with the addition of the apply step at the end that will make real changes in the AWS infrastructure. Notice that we've added the -auto-approve flag to the apply command so that there won't be any need for human interaction.

We're almost done with the pipeline. The final step is to publish any files that we want to keep from our run.

Publishing assets and committing changes

When a GitHub Actions workflow completes, the VM that we used for our build is destroyed. But sometimes we want to keep some of the state, files, or results for later use. To help with that, GitHub provides an upload-artifact action that gives us an easy way to make files available for us to download later.

In the next chapter, we'll be setting up a Kubernetes cluster on AWS. When you work with Kubernetes, it's useful to connect to the cluster from your remote machine. To do that, you need a lot of connection and authentication details, which we'll make easier by introducing a final step that provisions a Kubernetes configuration file that can be downloaded to connect to the cluster once it is created.

Add the code in Example 6-7 to the end of the workflow file to implement the final step of our job.

Example 6-7. Upload kubeconfig

```
# Publish Assets
- name: Upload kubeconfig file
  uses: actions/upload-artifact@v2
  with:
    name: kubeconfig
    path: kubeconfig
```

This action uploads a file called *kubeconfig* from the local working directory of the build environment to your GitHub Actions repository. It assumes that the file exists, so we'll need to create that file in the next chapter when we get into the details of buildling our sandbox infrastructure.

With this final addition, you now have a complete infrastructure pipeline for your sandbox environment. GitHub manages the workflow files the same way it manages code. So, we'll need to commit our changes to save them. Click the Start commit button, give the commit a description, and click the Commit new file button to finish commiting the change (see Figure 6-13).

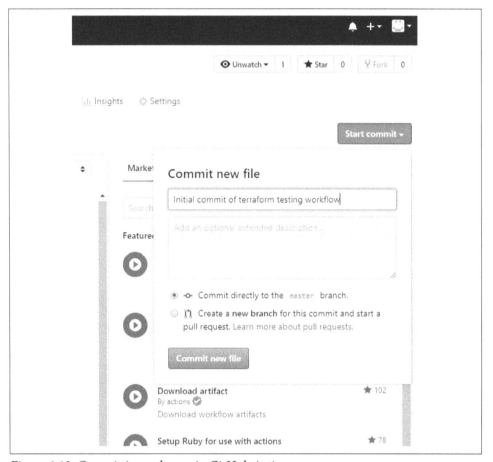

Figure 6-13. Committing a change in GitHub Actions

Taking Your Pipeline Further

We couldn't fit all of the things that a production CI/CD IaC pipeline would have in this chapter. In particular, we had to omit integration testing from our pipeline activities. But we highly recommend that you investigate and implement an integration-test step for your Terraform code. The Go-based tool Terratest (*https://oreil.ly/UKvMQ*) from Gruntworks.io is worth looking at when you start introducing this kind of functionality.

All that's left is to try out our workflow to make sure that it runs correctly.

Testing the Pipeline

To test the pipeline that we've created, we'll need to fire the trigger for the job we defined. In our case, we need to create a Git tag in our repository with a label that starts with the letter *v*. We could do this in the browser-based UI by using GitHub's *Releases* feature. But since we'll be doing most of our work outside GitHub on our local workstation, we'll create the tag there instead.

The first thing we need to do is get the local clone of the repository up to date with the changes we've made. To do that, open a shell in your workstation and run the command `git pull` in your env-sandbox directory. You should get a result that looks something like Example 6-8 indicating that we've pulled the new *.github/workflows/main.yml* file into the local repository.

Example 6-8. Pull changes into the local repository

```
env-sandbox msur$ git pull
remote: Enumerating objects: 6, done.
remote: Counting objects: 100% (6/6), done.
remote: Compressing objects: 100% (3/3), done.
remote: Total 5 (delta 0), reused 0 (delta 0), pack-reused 0
Unpacking objects: 100% (5/5), done.
From https://github.com/msur/env-sandbox
   a6b706f..9923863  master      -> origin/master
Updating a6b706f..9923863
Fast-forward
 .github/workflows/main.yml | 54 ++++++++++++++++++++++++++++++++++++++++++++++++++
 1 file changed, 54 insertions(+)
 create mode 100644 .github/workflows/main.yml
```

Now that we are up to date with the GitHub-hosted repository, we can create a tag. Since this is just a test, we'll label our release "v0.1." Use the `git tag` command as shown in Example 6-9 to create the new tag with a label.

Example 6-9. Create a v0.1 tag

```
env-sandbox msur$ git tag -a v0.1 -m "workflow test"
```

Although we've created a tag, it only exists locally in our workstation clone of the repository. In order to trigger our workflow, we'll need to push this tag to our GitHub-hosted repository. Use the `git push` command with the name of the tag to do this, as shown in Example 6-10.

Example 6-10. Push the tag to GitHub

```
env-sandbox testuser$ git push origin v0.1
Enumerating objects: 1, done.
Counting objects: 100% (1/1), done.
Writing objects: 100% (1/1), 165 bytes | 165.00 KiB/s, done.
Total 1 (delta 0), reused 0 (delta 0)
To https://github.com/mitraman/env-sandbox.git
 * [new tag]        v0.1 -> v0.1
```

We'll be doing this sequence of tagging and pushing a tag whenever we want the pipeline to run. Pushing the tag should have triggered the workflow we've created in GitHub Actions, so all we need to do now is check to make sure it has run successfully.

To see the status of the run, go back to the browser-based GitHub interface and navigate to Actions just like we did before. You should see something like Figure 6-14, indicating that our workflow job has completed successfully.

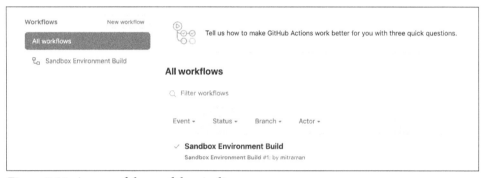

Figure 6-14. A successful run of the pipeline

You can also see more details of the job that has been run. This can be useful if your job hasn't run as expected and you need to do some troubleshooting. To see job details, select the workflow you want more details on (ours is called `Sandbox Environment Build`), then select the job (in our case the job is called `build`). In the detail screen you'll be able to see what happened at each step of the job when the pipeline ran (see Figure 6-15).

GitHub Actions is a relatively new product and GitHub changes the UI frequently, so the exact steps you need to take to reach this screen may have changed by the time you read this. If you are having trouble getting to the steps for your job, refer to the GitHub documentation (*https://oreil.ly/LPieV*).

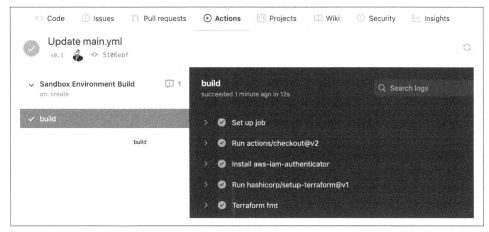

Figure 6-15. Details of a job

With our pipeline successfully tested, we've finished setting up the tooling we need to declaratively build our infrastructure.

Summary

In this chapter we set up a simple but powerful IaC pipeline based on some important DevOps principles and practices. We installed and used Terraform as our tool for implementing the principles of IaC and immutable infrastructure. We set up a GitHub-based code repository to manage that code. Finally, we created a GitHub Actions workflow as a CI/CD pipeline with automated testing to improve the safety and speed of our infrastructure changes.

We didn't actually create any infrastructure resources, but we did walk through the steps of making an infrastructure change. We created and edited a Terraform file, tested and ran it locally, committed it to the repository, and tagged it to kick off a build and apply pipeline process. This sequence of steps is going to be our method for immutable infrastructure development and we'll be using it often in the next chapter where we design and build our microservices infrastructure.

## CHAPTER 7

Building a Microservices Infrastructure

In the previous chapter we built a CI/CD pipeline for infrastructure changes. The infrastructure for our microservices system will be defined in code and we'll be able to use the pipeline to automate the testing and implementation of that code. With our automated pipeline in place, we can start writing the code that will define the infrastructure for our microservices-based application. That's what we'll focus on in this chapter.

Setting up the right infrastructure is vital to getting the most out of your microservices system. Microservices give us a nice way of breaking the parts of our application into bite-sized pieces. But we'll need a lot of supporting infrastructure to make all those bite-sized services work together properly. Before we can tackle the challenges of designing and engineering the services themselves, we'll need to spend some time establishing a network architecture and a deployment architecture for the services to use.

By the end of this chapter, you'll have built a cloud-based infrastructure designed to host the microservices we'll be building in the next chapter. We'll start by introducing the infrastructure and its components.

Infrastructure Components

The infrastructure is the set of components that will allow us to deploy, manage, and support a microservices-based application. An infrastructure can include a lot of parts: hardware, software, networks, and tools. So the scope of components we'll need to set up is quite large and getting all of those parts up and running is a big task.

Thankfully, as microservices approaches have matured, there's been an explosion in tools and services that make this work easier. In our model, we'll use tools like these as much as we can. We'll also focus on getting the infrastructure to work with a single cloud platform (AWS) rather than building a cloud-agnostic application that can be "lifted and shifted" to other hosts. These decisions will make it possible for us to define a feature-rich infrastructure in the small space of this single chapter.

But it's still quite a challenge! We'll be covering a lot of topics in a small number of pages. That means we'll need to make some trade-offs. For example, we won't be able to cover security, operations controls, or event logging and support. Instead we'll focus on designing and writing Terraform code to create a working network, an AWS managed Kubernetes service, and a declarative GitOps server. These three components will give us the foundation we need to deploy our example microservices.

 Network design and Kubernetes are deep and complex topics that require much more discussion than we can afford to give them. The good news is, you don't need to be a network or Kubernetes expert to set up your first microservices environment. If these are new domains for you, you can follow the instructions we've provided to get those parts of the system up and running as a first step to learning more about them.

Let's kick things off by taking a quick tour of our main components, starting with the network.

The Network

Microservices need to be run on a network. So we'll need to make sure we have a suitable one set up. Since we've made the decision to host our services on an AWS cloud, we'll need to tailor our network design accordingly, and create a virtual network instead of a physical one. We won't need to worry about the details of physical routers, cables, or network devices. Instead, we'll need to learn to use the language of AWS network resources and configure those accordingly.

We're going to keep our network design as simple as we can. We'll build just enough to get our system up and running. But, we'll still need to build and configure a few basic resources to support the running of our future microservices:

A virtual private cloud
> In AWS, a *virtual private cloud* (VPC) is the parent object for a virtual network. We'll be creating and configuring a VPC as part of our network design.

Subnets
> A VPC can be partitioned into multiple smaller networks called subnets. Subnets give us a way of organizing network traffic and controlling access to resources. We'll be creating a total of four subnets as part of our network configuration.

Routing and security

> In addition to creating the VPC and subnet objects, we'll be defining objects that dictate how traffic can flow in and out of them. For example, we'll be defining two "private" subnets that will only accept traffic from inside our VPC.

As you can see, our network has a bit of complexity that we'll need to deal with, including managing four "subnets" and connecting them. The main driver for this complexity comes from the needs of the Kubernetes service running on top of it. So, let's take a look at that next.

The Kubernetes Service

Throughout this book, we've emphasized that reducing coordination costs is an important success factor for the system. We've also mentioned containers and containerization a few times in earlier chapters. That's because containers are a great way of helping our teams get more done with less coordination costs. Containers give us the advantages of running applications in a predictable, isolated system configuration without the overhead and heavy lifting that comes with a VM deployment. Microservices and containers are a natural fit.

 If you need help understanding containers and containerization, Docker's website has a nice introductory explanation of containers (*https://oreil.ly/tC7aZ*).

Containers make it easy for us to build microservices that run predictably across environments as a self-contained unit. But, containers don't know how to start themselves, scale themselves, or heal themselves when they break. Containers work great in isolation, but a lot of operations work is required to manage them in production-like environments. That's where Kubernetes comes in.

Kubernetes is a container orchestration tool developed by Google. It solves the problems of working with containers at scale. Kubernetes provides a tool-based solution for deploying, scaling, observing, and managing container-based applications. It can help you roll out and roll back container deployments, automatically deploy or destroy container deployments based on demand patterns, mount storage systems, manage secrets, and help with load balancing and traffic management. Kubernetes can do a lot of complicated and complex work, and has quickly become an essential part of a microservices infrastructure stack.

Kubernetes is also pretty complicated itself, however. Because of this, we won't be diving into the details of how Kubernetes works in this book. But we will be able to put together a working Kubernetes infrastructure hosted on AWS.

If you want to learn about Kubernetes, a great introduction is provided by *Kubernetes: Up and Running* by Brendan Burns, Joe Beda, and Kelsey Hightower (O'Reilly).

If you're new to Kubernetes, it's worth understanding the big moving parts in a Kubernetes system, so you'll be able to follow along as we set one up:

Kubernetes cluster
> The cluster is the parent object in a Kubernetes system. When you install Kubernetes, you are installing a cluster. A cluster contains a control plane and a set of nodes.

Control plane
> In Kubernetes, the control plane is the "brains" of the cluster. It manages the system by making decisions about starting, stopping, and replicating containers. The control plane also provides an API that we can use to administrate the cluster.

Nodes
> The runtime work happens in the nodes. Each node is a physical or virtual machine that runs the container-based workload. In Kubernetes, nodes run *pods*. Each pod contains one or more containers. Every cluster has at least one node.

In our implementation, we'll be using an AWS managed service for Kubernetes called Elastic Kubernetes Service (EKS). We're using EKS because it handles for us a lot of Kubernetes' complexity. It will help us provision the cluster and give us a control plane to use as a managed service. All we'll need to do is configure the number and types of nodes we want and provision a suitable network.

Key Decision: Use a Managed Kubernetes Service

We will use AWS EKS as a managed service for our Kubernetes cluster.

The last piece of our infrastructure is the GitOps deployment server. Let's find out more about what that is and how it will help us.

The GitOps Deployment Server

In Chapter 2, we introduced the release team. This is the team that will be responsible for deploying microservices into production. We expect our microservices teams to use a CI/CD pipeline to integrate, test, build, and deliver their services. But in our operating model they don't own the actual deployment of the service into the system. We made that decision because in our experience, production deployments are fairly complex and require special attention. To facilitate the deployment work of the release team, we're introducing a special tool in our platform service offering: a GitOps deployment server.

Continuous Delivery Versus Continuous Deployment

One of the confusing things about CI/CD is that the "CD" part can mean either Continuous Delivery or Continuous Deployment, depending on who you ask. In our model, Continuous Delivery (CD) of microservices happens when our teams are able to automatically and continually ship their finished microservices as containers. Deployment happens when these containers are released into the production environment by our release team.

The name *GitOps*, created by a company called WeaveWorks, describes a way of working that uses Git as a "source of truth." That means that whatever is in Git should be the target state for the system. Like Terraform, GitOps prescribes a declarative approach. GitOps tools need to do the work of synchronizing system configurations to look like the state described in the Git repository. They also need to alert operations teams if the real world has drifted from the state defined in Git.

Argo CD is a GitOps tool that facilitates the work of deploying Kubernetes applications. We've decided to use Argo CD for our release process because we like the declarative GitOps approach. If we didn't use Argo CD we'd need to automate a series of Kubernetes calls to deploy an application. Instead, with the GitOps approach, we only need to point Argo CD at a Git source and let it do the work of keeping our environment up to date.

For example, once we have Argo CD set up, we'll be able to have it watch a microservice code repository. When new changes are comitted and tested, Argo CD will be able to automatically deploy the new version of the service into the environment. This declarative, continuous deployment capability makes Argo CD a great product for our release teams to use.

Key Decision: Deploy Microservices Using a GitOps Deployment Tool

Our release teams will use Argo CD to manage microservice deployment into production and production-like environments.

By the end of this chapter, we'll have created a sandbox environment with an Argo CD server installed on top of an AWS managed Kubernetes cluster, running on an AWS VPC network. It will take a lot of Terraform code to make that happen, so prepare to roll up your sleeves. We'll dive into the build in the next section.

Implementing the Infrastructure

In Chapter 6 we established a decision to use Terraform to write the code that defines our infrastructure and GitHub Actions to test and apply our infrastructure changes. In this section, we'll break our infrastructure design into discrete Terraform modules and call them from the sandbox environment we started building in the previous chapter. We'll start by setting up the tools you'll need in your infrastructure development workspace.

Installing kubectl

If you've followed along with the instructions in Chapter 6, you'll already have an environment ready for the infrastructure build. So you'll have:

- An AWS instance and a configured operator account
- Git, Terraform, and AWS CLI tools installed in your workstation
- A GitHub Actions pipeline for the infrastructure

If you haven't yet set up your GitHub Actions pipeline, or you had trouble getting it to work the way we've described, you can create a fork of a basic sandbox environment by following the instructions in this book's GitHub repository (*https://oreil.ly/Microservices_UpandRunning_env_starter*).

In addition to the setup we've done in the previous chapter, you'll need to do one more installation step to get ready for this chapter: installing kubectl. When we're installing the Kubernetes service, we'll need a way to test and interact with the Kubernetes system. To do that, we'll use the command-line application kubectl to interact with a Kubernetes server.

Follow the instructions in the Kubernetes documentation (*https://oreil.ly/sji9x*) to install kubectl in your local system. We'll leave it to you to pick the flavor that's appropriate to your operating system.

With the workspace set up and ready to go, we can move on to writing the Terraform modules that will define the infrastructure.

Setting Up the Module Repositories

When you write professional software, it's important to write clean, professional code. When code is too difficult to understand, to maintain, or to change, the project becomes costly to operate and maintain. All of that is true for our infrastructure code as well.

Since we're taking the IaC approach, we'll need to apply good code practices to our infrastructure project. The good news is that we have lots of existing guidance in our industry on how to write code that is easier to learn, understand, and extend. The bad news is that not every principle and practice from traditional software development is going to be easy to implement in the IaC domain. That's partly because the tooling and languages for IaC are still evolving and partly because the context of changing a live, physical device is a different model from the traditional software development model.

But with Terraform we'll be able to apply three essential coding practices that will help us write clean, easier-to-maintain code:

Use modules
Writing small functions that do one thing well

Encapsulate
Hiding internal data structures and implementation details

Avoid repetition
Don't repeat yourself (DRY), implementing code once in only one location

Terraform's built-in support for modules of infrastructure code will help us in using all three of these practices. We'll be able to maintain our infrastructure code as a set of reusable, encapsulated modules. We'll build modules for each of the architecturally significant parts of our system: networks, the API gateway, and the managed Amazon Kubernetes service (EKS). Once we have our reusable modules in place, we'll be able to implement another set of Terraform files that use them. We'll be able to have a different Terraform file for each environment that we want to create without repeating the same infrastructure declarations in each one (see Figure 7-1).

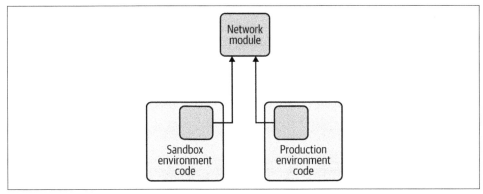

Figure 7-1. Reusing a network module

This approach allows us to easily spin up new environments by creating new Terraform files that reuse the modules we've developed. It also lets us make changes in just one place when we want to change an infrastructure configuration across all environments. We can start by creating a simple module that defines a basic network and an environment file that uses it.

The infrastructure code we are writing in this chapter uses Terraform's module structure. Each module will have its own directory and contain *variables.tf*, *main.tf*, and *output.tf* files. The advantage of this approach is that you can define a module once and use it in a parameterized way to build multiple environments. You can learn more about these modules in the Terraform documentation (*https://oreil.ly/87ahC*).

We're going to create two modules for our microservices infrastructure. First, we'll create an AWS networking module that contains a declarative configuration of our software-defined network. We'll also create a Kubernetes module that defines an AWS-based managed Kubernetes configuration for our environments. We'll be able to use both of these modules to create our sandbox environment.

Don't Use Our Configuration Files in Your Production Environment!

We've done our best to design an infrastructure that mirrors production environments that large organizations use for microservices. But space constraints prevent us from giving you a comprehensive set of configurations that will work for your specific environment, security needs, and constraints. You can use this chapter as a quick starter and guide to the tools you'll need, but we advise that you spend time designing your own production-grade infrastructure, configuration, and architecture.

In Chapter 6, we created a GitHub code repository for the sandbox environment code and its CI/CD pipeline. We'll be using that code repository in this chapter, but we'll also create a new repository for each module we write. Terraform has built-in support for importing modules that are managed as GitHub repositories, so it will be easy to pull them in when we want to use them.

To get started, let's create the repositories for all the modules we'll be writing in this chapter. Go ahead and create three new public GitHub-hosted repositories with the names described in Table 7-1.

Table 7-1. Infrastructure module names

Repository name	Visibility	Description
module-aws-network	Public	A Terraform module that creates the network
module-aws-kubernetes	Public	A Terraform module that sets up EKS
module-argo-cd	Public	A Terraform module that installs Argo CD into a cluster

If you aren't sure how to create a GitHub repository, you can follow the GitHub instructions (*https://oreil.ly/wNY0P*).

We recommend that you make these repositories public so that they are easier to import into your Terraform environment definition. You can use private repositories if you prefer—you'll just have to add some authentication information to your import command so that Terraform can get to the files correctly. You should also add a *.gitignore* file to these repositories so you don't end up with a lot of Terraform working files pushed to your GitHub server. You can do that by choosing a Terraform *.gitignore* in the GitHub web GUI, or save the contents as a *.gitignore* file in the root directory of your code repository, as outlined on this GitHub site (*https://oreil.ly/7AUJl*).

With our three GitHub module repositories created and ready to be populated, we can dive into the work of actually writing the actual infrastructure definitions—starting with the network.

The Network Module

The virtual network is a foundational part of our infrastructure, so it makes sense for us to start by defining the network module. In this section, we'll write an AWS network module that will support a specific Kubernetes and microservices architecture and workload. Because it's a module, we'll be writing input, main, and output code—just like we'd write inputs, logic, and return values for an application function. When we're done, we'll be able to use this module to easily provision a network environment by specifying just a few input values.

We'll be writing the network infrastructure code in the `module-aws-network` GitHub repository that you created earlier. We'll be creating and editing Terraform files in the root directory of this module. If you haven't already done so, clone the repository into your local environment and get your favorite text editor ready.

A completed listing for this AWS network module is available in this book's GitHub repository (*https://oreil.ly/Microservices_Upan dRunning_mod_aws_netw*).

Network module outputs

Let's start by defining the resources that we expect the networking module to produce. We'll do this by creating a Terraform file called *output.tf* in the root directory of module-aws-network, as in Example 7-1.

Example 7-1. module-aws-network/output.tf

```
output "vpc_id" {
  value = aws_vpc.main.id
}

output "subnet_ids" {
  value = [
    aws_subnet.public-subnet-a.id,
    aws_subnet.public-subnet-b.id,
    aws_subnet.private-subnet-a.id,
    aws_subnet.private-subnet-b.id]
}

output "public_subnet_ids" {
  value = [aws_subnet.public-subnet-a.id, aws_subnet.public-subnet-b.id]
}

output "private_subnet_ids" {
  value = [aws_subnet.private-subnet-a.id, aws_subnet.private-subnet-b.id]
}
```

Based on the Terraform module output file, we can see that the network module creates a VPC resource that represents the software-defined network for our system. Within that network, our module will also create four logical subnets—these are the bounded parts of our network (or subnetworks). Two of these subnets will be public, meaning that they will be accessible over the internet. Later, we'll use all four subnets for our Kubernetes cluster setup and eventually we'll deploy our microservices into them.

Network module main configuration

With the output of our module defined, we can start putting together the declarative code that builds it and creates the outputs we are expecting. In a Terraform module, we'll be creating and editing a file named *main.tf* in the root directory of the module-aws-network repository.

Getting the Source Code

To help you understand the network implementation, we've broken the *main.tf* source code file into smaller parts. You can find the complete source code listing for this module at this book's GitHub site (*https://oreil.ly/Microservices_UpandRunning_maintf*).

We'll start our module implementation by creating an AWS VPC resource. Terraform provides us with a special resource for defining AWS VPCs, so we'll just need to fill in a few parameters to create our definition. When we create a resource in Terraform,

---

we define the parameters and configuration details for it in the Terraform syntax. When we apply these changes, Terraform will make an AWS API call and create the resource if it doesn't exist already.

 You can find all the Terraform documentation for the AWS provider on the Terraform site (*https://oreil.ly/pvWJS*). You can also consult this documentation if you're building a similar implementation in GCP or Azure.

Create a file called *main.tf* in the root of your network module's repository and add the Terraform code in Example 7-2 to the *main.tf* file to define a new AWS VPC resource.

Example 7-2. modules-aws-network/main.tf

```
provider "aws" {
  region = var.aws_region
}

locals {
  vpc_name = "${var.env_name} ${var.vpc_name}"
  cluster_name = "${var.cluster_name}-${var.env_name}"
}


## AWS VPC definition
resource "aws_vpc" "main" {
  cidr_block = var.main_vpc_cidr
  tags = {
    "Name"                                 = local.vpc_name,
    "kubernetes.io/cluster/${local.cluster_name}" = "shared",
  }
}
```

The network module starts with a declaration that it is using the AWS *provider*. This is a special instruction that lets Terraform know that it needs to download and install the libraries it will need in order to communicate with the AWS API and create resources on our behalf. When we validate or apply this file in Terraform, it will attempt to connect to the AWS API using the credentials we've configured in the system as environment variables. We're also specifying an AWS region here so that Terraform knows which region it should be working in.

We've also specified two local variables using a Terraform `locals` block. These variables define a naming standard that will help us differentiate environment resources in the AWS console. This is especially important if we plan to create multiple environments in the same AWS account space as it will help us avoid naming collisions.

After the local variable declaration, you'll find the code for creating a new AWS VPC. As you can see, there isn't much to it, but it does define two important things: a CIDR block and a set of descriptive tags.

Classless inter-domain routing (CIDR) is a standard way of describing an IP address range for the network. It's a shorthand string that defines which IP addresses are allowed inside a network or a subnet. For example, a CIDR value of `10.0.0.0/16` would mean that you could bind to any IP address between 10.0.0.0 and 10.0.255.255 inside the VPC. We'll be defining a pretty standard CIDR range for you when we build the sandbox environment, but for more details on how CIDRs work and why they exist, you can read about them in the RFC (*https://oreil.ly/PtHmq*).

We've also added some tag values to the VPC. Resource tags are useful because they give us a way of easily identifying groups of resources when we need to administrate them. Tags are also useful for automated tasks and for identifying resources that should be managed in specific ways. In our definition, we have defined a "Name" tag to make our VPC easier to identify. We've also defined a Kubernetes tag that identifies this cluster as a target for our Kubernetes cluster (which we'll define in "Defining the EKS cluster" on page 162).

Also, notice that in a few cases we've referenced a variable instead of an actual value in our configuration. For example, our CIDR block is defined as `var.main_vpc_cidr` and it has a Name tag with the value `local.vpc_name`. These are Terraform variables, and we'll define their values later when we use this module as part of our sandbox environment. The variables are what makes the modules reusable—by changing the variable values we can change the types of environments that we create.

With our main VPC defined, we can move on to configuring the subnets for the network. As we mentioned earlier in this chapter, we'll be using Amazon's managed Kubernetes service (EKS) to run our workload. In order for EKS to function properly, we'll need to have subnets defined in two different "availability zones." In AWS, an availability zone represents a separate physical data center. It's a useful construct, because even though the AWS resources are virtual, they're still running on a computer plugged into an outlet somewhere. By using two availability zones for our deployment, we ensure that our services will still work even if one of the data centers goes down.

In addition to configuring two availability zones, Amazon also recommends a VPC configuration with both public and private subnets. So our network will have public subnets that allow traffic from the internet and private subnets that will only allow traffic from inside the VPC. When EKS is running, it will deploy load balancers in the public subnet to manage inbound traffic, which will be routed to our containerized microservices deployed in the private subnets.

To meet those requirements, we'll define a total of four subnets. Two of them will be designated as public subnets, so they'll be accessible over the web. The other two subnets will be private. We'll also split our public and private subnets up so that they are deployed in separate availability zones. When we're done, we'll have a network that looks like Figure 7-2.

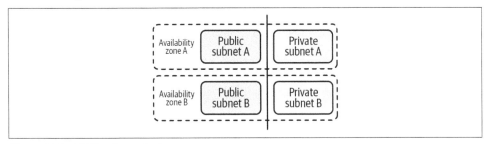

Figure 7-2. AWS subnet design

We've already specified a CIDR for the IP range in our VPC. Now we'll need to split up those IP addresses for the subnets to use. Since the subnets are inside of the VPC, they'll need to have a CIDR that is within the boundaries of the VPC IP range. We won't actually be defining those IP addresses in our module though. Instead, we'll use variables just like we did for the VPC.

In addition to the CIDR blocks, we'll specify the availability zones for our subnets as a parameter. Rather than hardcoding the name of the availability zone, we'll use a special Terraform type called `data` that will let us dynamically choose the zone name. In this case, we'll put `public-subnet-a` and `private-subnet-a` in `data.aws.availabil ity_zones.available.names[0]` and `public-subnet-b` and `private-subnet-b` in `data.aws.availability_zones.available.names[1]`. Using dynamic data like this makes it easier for us to spin up this infrastructure in different regions.

Finally, we'll add a name tag so that we can easily find our network resources through the admin and ops consoles. We'll also need to add some EKS tags to the subnet resources so that our AWS Kubernetes service will know which subnets we are using and what they are for. We'll tag our public subnets with an `elb` role so that EKS knows it can use these subnets to create and deploy an elastic load balancer. We'll tag the private subnets with an `internal-elb` role to indicate that our workloads will be deployed into them and can be load balanced. For more details on how AWS EKS uses load balancer tags, consult the AWS documentation (*https://oreil.ly/WlqQh*).

Add the Terraform code in Example 7-3 to the end of your *main.tf* file in order to declare the subnet configuration.

Example 7-3. modules-aws-network/main.tf (subnets)

```
# subnet definition

data "aws_availability_zones" "available" {
  state = "available"
}

resource "aws_subnet" "public-subnet-a" {
  vpc_id            = aws_vpc.main.id
  cidr_block        = var.public_subnet_a_cidr
  availability_zone = data.aws_availability_zones.available.names[0]

  tags = {
    "Name"                                       = (
      "${local.vpc_name}-public-subnet-a"
    )
    "kubernetes.io/cluster/${local.cluster_name}" = "shared"
    "kubernetes.io/role/elb"                      = "1"
  }
}

resource "aws_subnet" "public-subnet-b" {
  vpc_id            = aws_vpc.main.id
  cidr_block        = var.public_subnet_b_cidr
  availability_zone = data.aws_availability_zones.available.names[1]

  tags = {
    "Name"                                       = (
      "${local.vpc_name}-public-subnet-b"
    )
    "kubernetes.io/cluster/${local.cluster_name}" = "shared"
    "kubernetes.io/role/elb"                      = "1"
  }
}

resource "aws_subnet" "private-subnet-a" {
  vpc_id            = aws_vpc.main.id
  cidr_block        = var.private_subnet_a_cidr
  availability_zone = data.aws_availability_zones.available.names[0]

  tags = {
    "Name"                                       = (
      "${local.vpc_name}-private-subnet-a"
    )
    "kubernetes.io/cluster/${local.cluster_name}" = "shared"
    "kubernetes.io/role/internal-elb"             = "1"
  }
}

resource "aws_subnet" "private-subnet-b" {
  vpc_id            = aws_vpc.main.id
```

```
cidr_block        = var.private_subnet_b_cidr
availability_zone = data.aws_availability_zones.available.names[1]

tags = {
  "Name"                                       = (
    "${local.vpc_name}-private-subnet-b"
  )
  "kubernetes.io/cluster/${local.cluster_name}" = "shared"
  "kubernetes.io/role/internal-elb"             = "1"
}
}
```

 In Terraform, a `data` element is a way of querying the provider for information. In the network module, we're using the `aws_availa bility_zones` data element to ask AWS for availability zone IDs in the region we've specified. This is a nice way to avoid hardcoding values into the module.

Although we've configured four subnets and their IP ranges, we haven't yet defined the network rules that AWS will need to manage traffic through them. To finish our network design, we'll need to implement a set of routing tables that define what traffic sources we will allow into our subnets. For example, we'll need to establish how traffic will be routed through our public subnets and how each of the subnets will be allowed to communicate with each other.

We'll start by defining the routing rules for our two public subnets: `public-subnet-a` and `public-subnet-b`. To make these subnets accessible on the internet, we'll need to add a special resource to our VPC called an *internet gateway*. This is an AWS network component that connects our private cloud to the public internet. Terraform gives us a resource definition for the gateway, so we'll use that and tie it to our VPC with the `vpc_id` configuration parameter.

Once we've added the internet gateway, we'll need to define routing rules that let AWS know how to route traffic from the gateway into our subnets. To do that, we'll create an `aws_route_table` resource that allows all traffic from the internet (which we'll identify with CIDR block 0.0.0.0/0) through the gateway. Then we just need to create associations between our two public subnets and the table we've defined.

Add the Terraform code in Example 7-4 to *main.tf* to define routing instructions for our network.

Example 7-4. modules-aws-network/main.tf (public routes)

```
# Internet gateway and routing tables for public subnets
resource "aws_internet_gateway" "igw" {
  vpc_id = aws_vpc.main.id

  tags = {
    Name = "${local.vpc_name}-igw"
  }
}

resource "aws_route_table" "public-route" {
  vpc_id = aws_vpc.main.id

  route {
    cidr_block = "0.0.0.0/0"
    gateway_id = aws_internet_gateway.igw.id
  }

  tags = {
    "Name" = "${local.vpc_name}-public-route"
  }
}

resource "aws_route_table_association" "public-a-association" {
  subnet_id      = aws_subnet.public-subnet-a.id
  route_table_id = aws_route_table.public-route.id
}

resource "aws_route_table_association" "public-b-association" {
  subnet_id      = aws_subnet.public-subnet-b.id
  route_table_id = aws_route_table.public-route.id
}
```

With the routes for our public subnets defined, we can dive into the setup for our two private subnets. The route configuration for the private subnets will be a bit more complicated than what we've done so far. That's because we'll need to define a route from our private subnet out to the internet to allow our Kubernetes Pods to talk to the EKS service.

For that kind of route to work, we'll need a way for nodes in our private subnet to talk to the internet gateway we've deployed in the public subnets. In AWS, we'll need to create a network address translation (NAT) gateway resource that gives us a path out. When we create the NAT, we'll also need to assign it a special kind of IP address called an *elastic IP address* (or EIP). Because this is an AWS construct, the IP is a real internet-accessible network address, unlike all the other addresses in our network, which are virtual and exist inside AWS alone. Since real IP addresses aren't unlimited, AWS limits the amount of these available. Unfortunately, we can't create an NAT without one, so we'll have to use two of them—one for each NAT we are creating.

Add the Terraform code in Example 7-5 to implement an NAT gateway in our network.

Example 7-5. modules-aws-network/main.tf (NAT gateway)

```
resource "aws_eip" "nat-a" {
  vpc = true
  tags = {
    "Name" = "${local.vpc_name}-NAT-a"
  }
}

resource "aws_eip" "nat-b" {
  vpc = true
  tags = {
    "Name" = "${local.vpc_name}-NAT-b"
  }
}

resource "aws_nat_gateway" "nat-gw-a" {
  allocation_id = aws_eip.nat-a.id
  subnet_id     = aws_subnet.public-subnet-a.id
  depends_on    = [aws_internet_gateway.igw]

  tags = {
    "Name" = "${local.vpc_name}-NAT-gw-a"
  }
}

resource "aws_nat_gateway" "nat-gw-b" {
  allocation_id = aws_eip.nat-b.id
  subnet_id     = aws_subnet.public-subnet-b.id
  depends_on    = [aws_internet_gateway.igw]

  tags = {
    "Name" = "${local.vpc_name}-NAT-gw-b"
  }
}
```

In addition to the NAT gateway we've created, we'll need to define routes for our private subnets. Add the Terraform code in Example 7-6 to *main.tf* to complete the definition of our network routes.

Example 7-6. modules/network/main.tf (private routes)

```
resource "aws_route_table" "private-route-a" {
  vpc_id = aws_vpc.main.id
  route {
    cidr_block     = "0.0.0.0/0"
    nat_gateway_id = aws_nat_gateway.nat-gw-a.id
```

```
  }

  tags = {
    "Name" = "${local.vpc_name}-private-route-a"
  }
}

resource "aws_route_table" "private-route-b" {
  vpc_id = aws_vpc.main.id
  route {
    cidr_block     = "0.0.0.0/0"
    nat_gateway_id = aws_nat_gateway.nat-gw-b.id
  }

  tags = {
    "Name" = "${local.vpc_name}-private-route-b"
  }
}

resource "aws_route_table_association" "private-a-association" {
  subnet_id      = aws_subnet.private-subnet-a.id
  route_table_id = aws_route_table.private-route-a.id
}

resource "aws_route_table_association" "private-b-association" {
  subnet_id      = aws_subnet.private-subnet-b.id
  route_table_id = aws_route_table.private-route-b.id
}
```

That's it for our main network definition. When we eventually run this Terraform file, we'll have an AWS software-defined network that is ready for Kubernetes and our microservices. But, before we can use it, we'll need to define all of the input variables that this module needs. Although we've referenced a lot of var values in our code, Terraform modules require us to identify all of the input variables we'll be using in a specific file called *variables.tf*. If we don't do that, we won't be able to pass variable values into our module.

Network module variables

Create a file in the root folder of the network module called *variables.tf*. Add the Terraform code in Example 7-7 to *variables.tf* to define the inputs for the module.

Example 7-7. modules/network/variables.tf

```
variable "env_name" {
  type = string
}

variable "aws_region" {
  type = string
}

variable "vpc_name" {
  type    = string
  default = "ms-up-running"
}

variable "main_vpc_cidr" {
  type = string
}

variable "public_subnet_a_cidr" {
  type = string
}

variable "public_subnet_b_cidr" {
  type = string
}

variable "private_subnet_a_cidr" {
  type = string
}

variable "private_subnet_b_cidr" {
  type = string
}

variable "cluster_name" {
  type = string
}
```

As you can see, the variable definitions are fairly self-explanatory. They describe a name, optional description, and type value. In our module we're only using string values. In some cases, we've also provided a default value so that those inputs don't always have to be defined for every environment. We'll give the module values for those variables when we use it to create an environment.

It's good practice to include a description attribute for every variable in your Terraform module. This improves the maintainability and usability of your modules and becomes increasingly important over time. We've done this for the Terraform files we've published in GitHub, but we've removed the descriptions in all our examples to save space in the book.

The Terraform code for our network module is now complete. At this point, you should have a list of files that looks something like this in your module directory:

```
drwxr-xr-x   3 msur   staff    96 14 Jun 09:57 ..
drwxr-xr-x   7 msur   staff   224 14 Jun 09:58 .
-rw-r--r--   1 msur   staff    23 14 Jun 09:57 README.md
drwxr-xr-x  13 msur   staff   416 14 Jun 09:57 .git
-rw-r--r--   1 msur   staff     0 14 Jun 09:58 main.tf
-rw-r--r--   1 msur   staff   612 14 Jun 09:58 variables.tf
-rw-r--r--   1 msur   staff    72 14 Jun 09:58 outputs.tf
```

With the code written, we'll be testing the network module by creating a sandbox environment network, but before we use the module we should make sure we haven't made any syntax errors. The Terraform command-line application includes some handy features to format and validate code. If you haven't already installed the Terraform client in your local system, you can find a binary for your operating system on the Terraform site (*https://oreil.ly/pFDq8*).

Use the following Terraform command while you are in your module's working directory to format the module's code:

```
module-aws-network$ terraform fmt
```

The fmt command will *lint*, or format, all the Terraform code in the working directory and ensure that it conforms to a set of built-in style guidelines. It will automatically make those changes for you and will list any files that have been updated.

Next, run terraform init so that Terraform can install the AWS provider libraries. We need to do this so that we can validate the code. Note that you'll need to have AWS credentials defined for this to work. If you haven't done that yet, follow the instructions in the previous chapter:

```
module-aws-network$ terraform init
```

If you run into any problems, try to fix those before you continue; the Terraform documentation has a helpful section on troubleshooting (*https://oreil.ly/oh_Wn*). Finally, you can run the validate command to make sure that our module is syntactically correct:

```
module-aws-network$ terraform validate
Success! The configuration is valid.
```

If you need to debug your Terraform code, you can set the environment variable TF_LOG to INFO or DEBUG. That will instruct Terraform to emit logging info to standard output.

When you are satisfied that the code is formatted and valid, you can commit your changes to the GitHub repository. If you've been working in a local repository, you can use the following command to push your changes to the main repository:

```
module-aws-network$ git add .
module-aws-network$ git commit -m "network module created"
[master ddb7e41] network module created
 3 files changed, 226 insertions(+)
module-aws-network$ git push
```

Our Terraform-based network module is now complete and available for use. It has a *variables.tf* file that describes the required and optional input variables to use it. It has a *main.tf* file that declaratively defines the resources for our network design. Finally, it has an *outputs.tf* file that defines the significant resources that we've created in the module. Now we can use the module to create a real network in our sandbox environment.

Create a sandbox network

The nice thing about using Terraform modules is that we can create our environments easily in a repeatable way. Outside of the specific values we've defined in the *variables.tf* file, any environment that we create with the module we've defined will operate with a network infrastructure that we know and understand. That means we can expect our microservices to work in a predictable way as we move them through testing and release environments since we have reduced the level of variation.

But to apply the module we've defined and create a new environment, we'll need to call it from a Terraform file that defines values for the module's variables. To do that, we'll create a sandbox environment that demonstrates a practical example of using a Terraform module. If you followed the steps in Chapter 6, you'll already have a code repository for your sandbox environment with a single *main.tf* file in it.

In order to use the network module that we've created, we'll use a special Terraform resource called module. It allows us to reference a Terraform module that we've created and pass in values for the variables that we've defined. Terraform expects a property called source to exist in the module that indicates where it can find the code.

In our case, we want Terraform to retrieve the network module from a GitHub repository. To do this, we need to use a source property that starts with the string "git hub.com" and contains the path of our repository. That lets Terraform know it needs to pull the source from GitHub.

For example, a source value of `"github.com/implementing-microservices/module-aws-network"` references our example network module. You can find the path for your module's repository by copying the path from its GitHub URL (see Table 7-2).

Table 7-2. Sandbox environment network variable

Name	Description	Example
YOUR_NETWORK_MOD ULE_REPO_PATH	The path to your module's repository in GitHub	github.com/implementing-microservices/module-aws-network

When you have the path for your network module ready, open the *main.tf* file for the sandbox environment you created in Chapter 6. Add the Terraform code in Example 7-8 after the `# Network Configuration` comment. Don't forget to replace the source value with the path of your network module's GitHub repository.

Example 7-8. env-sandbox/main.tf (network)

```
...

# Network Configuration
module "aws-network" {
  source = "github.com/{YOUR_NETWORK_MODULE_REPO_PATH}"

  env_name             = local.env_name
  vpc_name             = "msur-VPC"
  cluster_name         = local.k8s_cluster_name
  aws_region           = local.aws_region
  main_vpc_cidr        = "10.10.0.0/16"
  public_subnet_a_cidr  = "10.10.0.0/18"
  public_subnet_b_cidr  = "10.10.64.0/18"
  private_subnet_a_cidr = "10.10.128.0/18"
  private_subnet_b_cidr = "10.10.192.0/18"
}

# EKS Configuration

# GitOps Configuration
```

 Amazon's S3 bucket names must be globally unique, so you'll need to change the value of `bucket` to something that is unique and meaningful for you. Refer to "Creating an S3 Backend for Terraform" on page 115 for instructions on how to set up the backend. If you want to do a quick and dirty test, omit the backend definition and Terraform will store state locally in your filesystem.

Our infrastructure pipeline will apply Terraform changes, but before we kick it off we need to check to make sure that the Terraform code we've written will work. A good first step is to format and validate the code locally:

```
$ terraform fmt
[...]
$ terraform init
[...]
$ terraform validate
Success! The configuration is valid.
```

If you need to debug the networking module and end up making code changes, you may need to run the following command in your sandbox environment directory:

```
$ terraform get -update
```

This will instruct Terraform to pull the latest version of the network module from GitHub.

If the code is valid, we can get a plan to validate the changes that Terraform will make when they are applied. It's always a good idea to do a dry run and examine the changes that will be made before you actually change the environment, so make this step a part of your workflow. To get the Terraform plan, run this command:

```
$ terraform plan
```

Terraform will provide you with a list of the resources that will be created, deleted, and updated. If Terraform and AWS are new to you, the plan might be difficult to evaluate and understand in detail. But, you should still be able to get a general sense of what is going to happen. Since this is the first update, the plan should list a lot of new resources that Terraform will create. When you're ready, you can push the code to the GitHub repository and tag it for release:

```
$ git add .
$ git commit -m "initial network release"
$ git push origin
$ git tag -a v1.0 -m "network build"
$ git push origin v1.0
```

There are two git push commands that we need to run. The first one pushes the code changes we've made and the second only pushes the tag.

With the code tagged and pushed, our GitHub Actions pipeline should take over and start building the network for our sandbox environment. You'll need to log in to GitHub and check the Actions tab in your sandbox environment repository to make sure that everything goes according to plan. If you don't remember how to do that, you'll find instructions in Chapter 6.

You can test that the VPC has been successfully created by making an AWS CLI call. Run the following command to list the VPCs with a CIDR block that matches the one that we've defined:

```
$ aws ec2 describe-vpcs --filters Name=cidr,Values=10.10.0.0/16
```

You should get a JSON body back describing the VPC that we created. If that has happened, it indicates that you now have an AWS network running and ready to use. It's now time to start writing the module for the Kubernetes service.

The Kubernetes Module

One of the most important parts of our microservices infrastructure is the Kubernetes layer that orchestrates our container-based services. If we set it up correctly, Kubernetes will give us an automated solution for resiliency, scaling, and fault tolerance. It will also give us a great foundation for deploying our services in a dependable way. On top of that, an Istio service mesh gives us a powerful way of managing traffic and improving the way our microservices communicate.

To build our Kubernetes module, we'll follow the same steps that we did to build our network module. We'll start by defining a set of output variables that define what the module will produce, then we'll write the code that declaratively defines the configuration that Terraform will create. Finally, we'll define the inputs. As we mentioned earlier in this chapter, we are managing each of infrastructure modules in it's own GitHub code repository. So make sure you start by creating a new GitHub repository for our Kubernetes module if you haven't done so already.

Implementing Kubernetes can get very complicated. So, to get our system up and running as quickly as possible, we'll use a managed service that will hide some of the setup and management complexity for us. Since we are running on AWS in our examples, we'll use the EKS bundled in Amazon's cloud offering.

The configuration for managed Kubernetes services tends to be very vendor specific, so the examples we provide here will likely take some reworking if you want to use them in Google Cloud, Azure, or another hosted service.

An EKS cluster contains two parts: a control plane that hosts the Kubernetes system software and a node group that hosts the VMs that our microservices will run on. In order to configure EKS, we'll need to provide parameters for both of these areas. When the module is finished running, we can return an EKS cluster identifier so that we have the option of inspecting or adding to the cluster with other modules.

With all that in mind, let's dive into the code that will make it come to life. We'll be working in the `module-aws-kubernetes` GitHub repository that you created earlier, so make sure you start by cloning it to your local machine. When you've done that, we can begin by editing the Terraform outputs file.

 A completed listing for this Kubernetes module is available in this book's GitHub repository (*https://oreil.ly/Microservices_UpandRunning_Kmod*).

Kubernetes module outputs

We'll start by declaring the outputs that our module provides. Create a Terraform file called *outputs.tf* in the root directory of the `module-aws-kubernets` repository and add to it the code in Example 7-9.

Example 7-9. module-aws-kubernetes/outputs.tf

```
output "eks_cluster_id" {
  value = aws_eks_cluster.ms-up-running.id
}

output "eks_cluster_name" {
  value = aws_eks_cluster.ms-up-running.name
}

output "eks_cluster_certificate_data" {
  value = aws_eks_cluster.ms-up-running.certificate_authority.0.data
}

output "eks_cluster_endpoint" {
  value = aws_eks_cluster.ms-up-running.endpoint
}

output "eks_cluster_nodegroup_id" {
  value = aws_eks_node_group.ms-node-group.id
}
```

The main value we're returning is the identifier for the EKS cluster that we'll be creating in this module. The rest of the values need to be returned so that we can access the cluster from other modules once the cluster is ready and operational. For example, we'll need the endpoint and certificate data when we install the Argo CD server into this EKS cluster at the end of the chapter.

While the output of our module is pretty simple, the work of getting our EKS-based Kubernetes system set up is going to be a bit more complicated. Just like we did before, we'll build the module's main Terraform file in parts before we test it and apply it.

Defining the EKS cluster

To start, create a Terraform file called *main.tf* in the root directory of your Kubernetes module and add an AWS provider definition, as in Example 7-10.

Example 7-10. module-aws-kubernetes/main.tf

```
provider "aws" {
  region = var.aws_region
}
```

Remember that we'll be using the Terraform naming convention of `var` to indicate values that can be replaced by variables when our module is invoked.

As we mentioned earlier, we're going to use Amazon's EKS to create and manage our Kubernetes installation. But EKS will need to create and modify AWS resources on our behalf in order to run. So we'll need to set up permissions in our AWS account so that it can do the work it needs to do. We'll need to define policies and security rules at the overall cluster level and also for the VMs or nodes that EKS will be spinning up for us to run microservices on.

We'll start by focusing on the rules and policies for the entire EKS cluster. Add the Terraform code in Example 7-11 to your *main.tf* file to define a new cluster access management policy.

Example 7-11. module-aws-kubernetes/main.tf (cluster access management)

```
locals {
  cluster_name = "${var.cluster_name}-${var.env_name}"
}

resource "aws_iam_role" "ms-cluster" {
  name = local.cluster_name

  assume_role_policy = <<POLICY
{
  "Version": "2012-10-17",
  "Statement": [
    {
      "Effect": "Allow",
      "Principal": {
        "Service": "eks.amazonaws.com"
      },
      "Action": "sts:AssumeRole"
    }
```

```
  ]
}
POLICY
}

resource "aws_iam_role_policy_attachment" "ms-cluster-AmazonEKSClusterPolicy" {
  policy_arn = "arn:aws:iam::aws:policy/AmazonEKSClusterPolicy"
  role       = aws_iam_role.ms-cluster.name
}
```

The snippet here establishes a trust policy that allows the AWS EKS service to act on your behalf. It defines a new identity and access management role for our EKS service and attaches a policy called `AmazonEKSClusterPolicy` to it. This policy has been defined by AWS for us and gives the EKS the permissions it needs to create VMs and make network changes as part of its Kubernetes management work. Notice that we are also defining and using a local variable for the name of the cluster. We'll use that variable throughout the module.

Now that the cluster service's role and policy are defined, add the code in Example 7-12 to your module's *main.tf* file to define a network security policy for the cluster.

Example 7-12. module-aws-kubernetes/main.tf (network security policy)

```
resource "aws_security_group" "ms-cluster" {
  name       = local.cluster
  vpc_id     = var.vpc_id

  egress {
    from_port   = 0
    to_port     = 0
    protocol    = "-1"
    cidr_blocks = ["0.0.0.0/0"]
  }

  tags = {
    Name = "ms-up-running"
  }
}
```

A VPC security group restricts the kind of traffic that can go into and out of the network. The Terraform code we've just written defines an egress rule that allows unrestricted outbound traffic, but doesn't allow any inbound traffic, because there is no ingress rule defined. Notice that we are applying this security group to a VPC that will be defined by an input variable. When we use this module, we can give it the ID of the VPC that our networking module has created.

With these policies and a security group defined for the EKS cluster, we can now add the declaration for the cluster itself to the *main.tf* Terraform file (see Example 7-13).

Example 7-13. module-aws-kubernetes/main.tf (cluster definition)

```
resource "aws_eks_cluster" "ms-up-running" {
  name     = local.cluster_name
  role_arn = aws_iam_role.ms-cluster.arn

  vpc_config {
    security_group_ids = [aws_security_group.ms-cluster.id]
    subnet_ids         = var.cluster_subnet_ids
  }

  depends_on = [
    aws_iam_role_policy_attachment.ms-cluster-AmazonEKSClusterPolicy
  ]
}
```

The EKS cluster definition we've just created is pretty simple. It simply references the name, role, policy, and security group values we defined earlier. It also references a set of subnets that the cluster will be managing. These subnets will be the ones that we created earlier in the networking module, and we'll be able to pass them into this Kubernetes module as a variable.

When AWS creates an EKS cluster, it automatically sets up all of the management components that we need to run our Kubernetes cluster. This is called the *control plane* because it's the brain of our Kubernetes system. But in addition to the control plane, our microservices need a place where they can run. In Kubernetes, that means we need to set up nodes—the physical or VMs that containerized workloads can run on.

One of the advantages of using a managed Kubernetes service like EKS is that we can offload some of the work of managing the creation, removal, and updating of Kubernetes nodes. For our configuration, we'll define a managed EKS node group and let AWS provision resources and interact with the Kubernetes system for us. But to get a managed node group running, we'll still need to define a few important configuration values.

Defining the EKS node group

Just like we did for our cluster, we'll begin the node configuration by defining a role and some security policies. Add the node group IAM definitions in Example 7-14 to the Kubernetes module's *main.tf* file.

Example 7-14. module-aws-kubernetes/main.tf (node group IAM)

```
# Node Role
resource "aws_iam_role" "ms-node" {
  name = "${local.cluster_name}.node"

  assume_role_policy = <<POLICY
{
  "Version": "2012-10-17",
  "Statement": [
    {
      "Effect": "Allow",
      "Principal": {
        "Service": "ec2.amazonaws.com"
      },
      "Action": "sts:AssumeRole"
    }
  ]
}
POLICY
}

# Node Policy
resource "aws_iam_role_policy_attachment" "ms-node-AmazonEKSWorkerNodePolicy" {
  policy_arn = "arn:aws:iam::aws:policy/AmazonEKSWorkerNodePolicy"
  role       = aws_iam_role.ms-node.name
}

resource "aws_iam_role_policy_attachment" "ms-node-AmazonEKS_CNI_Policy" {
  policy_arn = "arn:aws:iam::aws:policy/AmazonEKS_CNI_Policy"
  role       = aws_iam_role.ms-node.name
}

[...]
resource "aws_iam_role_policy_attachment" "ms-node-ContainerRegistryReadOnly" {
[...]
  policy_arn = "arn:aws:iam::aws:policy/AmazonEC2ContainerRegistryReadOnly"
  role       = aws_iam_role.ms-node.name
}
```

The role and policies in this Terraform snippet will allow any nodes that are created to communicate with Amazon's container registries and VM services. We need these policies because the nodes in our Kubernetes system will need to be able to provision computing resources and access containers in order to run services. For more details on the IAM role for EKS worker nodes, check out the AWS EKS documentation (*https://oreil.ly/fm75j*).

Now that we have our node's role and policy resources defined, we can write the declaration for a node group that uses them. In EKS, a managed node group needs to specify the types of compute and storage resources it will use along with some defined limits for the number of individual nodes or VMs that can be created automatically. This is important because we are letting EKS automatically provision and scale our nodes. We don't want to inadvertently consume massive amounts of AWS resources and end up with a correspondingly massive bill.

We could hardcode all of these parameters in our module, but instead we'll use input variables as values for the size limits, disk size, and CPU types. That way we'll be able to use the same Kubernetes module to create different kinds of environments. For example, a development environment can be set up to use minimal resources, while a production environment can be more robust.

Add the Terraform code in Example 7-15 to the end of the module's *main.tf* file to define our EKS node group.

Example 7-15. module-aws-kubernetes/main.tf (node group)

```
resource "aws_eks_node_group" "ms-node-group" {
  cluster_name     = aws_eks_cluster.ms-up-running.name
  node_group_name  = "microservices"
  node_role_arn    = aws_iam_role.ms-node.arn
  subnet_ids       = var.nodegroup_subnet_ids

  scaling_config {
    desired_size = var.nodegroup_desired_size
    max_size     = var.nodegroup_max_size
    min_size     = var.nodegroup_min_size
  }

  disk_size      = var.nodegroup_disk_size
  instance_types = var.nodegroup_instance_types

  depends_on = [
    aws_iam_role_policy_attachment.ms-node-AmazonEKSWorkerNodePolicy,
    aws_iam_role_policy_attachment.ms-node-AmazonEKS_CNI_Policy,
    aws_iam_role_policy_attachment.ms-node-AmazonEC2ContainerRegistryReadOnly,
  ]
}
```

The node group declaration is the last part of our EKS configuration. We have enough here to be able to call this module from our sandbox environment and instantiate a running Kubernetes cluster on the AWS EKS service. Our module's outputs will return the values that are needed to connect to the node group once it's running. But it's also useful to provide those connection details in a configuration file for the kubectl CLI that most operators use for Kubernetes management.

Our last step is to generate a *kubeconfig* file that we'll be able to use to connect to the cluster. Append the code in Example 7-16 to your module's *main.tf* file.

Example 7-16. module-aws-kubernetes/main.tf (generate kubeconfig)

```
# Create a kubeconfig file based on the cluster that has been created
resource "local_file" "kubeconfig" {
  content  = <<KUBECONFIG_END
apiVersion: v1
clusters:
- cluster:
    "certificate-authority-data: >
   ${aws_eks_cluster.ms-up-running.certificate_authority.0.data}"
    server: ${aws_eks_cluster.ms-up-running.endpoint}
  name: ${aws_eks_cluster.ms-up-running.arn}
contexts:
- context:
    cluster: ${aws_eks_cluster.ms-up-running.arn}
    user: ${aws_eks_cluster.ms-up-running.arn}
  name: ${aws_eks_cluster.ms-up-running.arn}
current-context: ${aws_eks_cluster.ms-up-running.arn}
kind: Config
preferences: {}
users:
- name: ${aws_eks_cluster.ms-up-running.arn}
  user:
    exec:
      apiVersion: client.authentication.k8s.io/v1alpha1
      command: aws-iam-authenticator
      args:
        - "token"
        - "-i"
        - "${aws_eks_cluster.ms-up-running.name}"
    KUBECONFIG_END
  filename = "kubeconfig"
}
```

This code looks complicated, but it's actually fairly simple. We are using a special Terraform resource called `local_file` to create a file named *kubeconfig*. We are then populating *kubeconfig* with YAML content that defines the connection parameters for our Kubernetes cluster. Notice that we are getting the values for the YAML file from the EKS resources that we created in the module.

When Terraform runs this block of code, it will create a *kubeconfig* file in a local directory. We'll be able to use that file to connect to the Kubernetes environment from CLI tools. We made a special provision for this file when we built our pipeline in Chapter 6. When you run the infrastructure pipeline, you'll be able to download this populated configuration file and use it to connect to the cluster. This configuration file will make it a lot easier for you to connect to the cluster from your machine.

We're almost done writing our Kubernetes service module; all that's left is to define the variables.

Kubernetes module variables

To declare the variables for our Kubernetes module, create a file called *variables.tf* in your module-aws-kubernetes repository and add the code in Example 7-17.

Example 7-17. module-aws-kubernetes/variables.tf

```
variable "aws_region" {
  type      = string
  default   = "eu-west-2"
}

variable "env_name" {
  type = string
}

variable "cluster_name" {
  type = string
}

variable "ms_namespace" {
  type    = string
  default = "microservices"
}

variable "vpc_id" {
  type = string
}

variable "cluster_subnet_ids" {
  type = list(string)
}

variable "nodegroup_subnet_ids" {
  type = list(string)
}

variable "nodegroup_desired_size" {
  type    = number
  default = 1
}

variable "nodegroup_min_size" {
  type    = number
  default = 1
}

variable "nodegroup_max_size" {
  type    = number
  default = 5
}
```

```
variable "nodegroup_disk_size" {
  type = string
}

variable "nodegroup_instance_types" {
  type = list(string)
}
```

Our AWS Kubernetes module is now fully written. As we did for our network module, we'll take a moment to clean up the formatting and validate the syntax of the code by running the following Terraform commands:

```
module-aws-kubernetes$ terraform fmt
[...]
module-aws-kubernetes$ terraform init
[...]
module-aws-kubernetes$ terraform validate
Success! The configuration is valid.
```

When you are satisfied that the code is valid, commit your changes and push them to GitHub, so that we can use this module in the sandbox environment:

```
$ git add .
$ git commit -m "kubernetes module complete"
$ git push origin
```

With the EKS module ready to go, we can go back to our sandbox Terraform file and use it.

Create a sandbox Kubernetes cluster

Now that our complex Kubernetes system is wrapped up in a simple module, the work of setting it up in our sandbox environment is pretty simple. All we'll need to do is call our module with the input parameters that we want. Remember that our sandbox environment is defined in its own code repository and has its own Terraform file called *main.tf* which we've used to set up the network. We'll be editing that file again, but this time we'll add a call to the Terraform module.

If you recall, we gave some of our input variables default values. To keep things simple, we'll just use those default values in our sandbox environment. We'll also need to pass some of the output variables from our network module into this Kubernetes module so that it installs the cluster on the network we've just created. But beyond those inputs, you'll need to define the `aws_region` value for your installation. This should be the same as the value you used for the network module and the backend configuration. You'll also need to set the source parameter to point to your GitHub-hosted module.

Update the *main.tf* file of your sandbox environment so that it uses the Kubernetes module you've just created. You can add the module reference immediately after the

#EKS Configuration placeholder we put in the file earlier. You'll also need to replace the token **{YOUR_EKS_MODULE_PATH}** with the path to your module's GitHub repository (see Example 7-18).

Example 7-18. env-sandbox/main.tf (Kubernetes)

```
...

# Network Configuration
...

# EKS Configuration
module "aws-eks" {
  source = "*github.com/{YOUR_EKS_MODULE_PATH}*"

  ms_namespace      = "microservices"
  env_name          = local.env_name
  aws_region        = local.aws_region
  cluster_name      = local.k8s_cluster_name
  vpc_id            = module.aws-network.vpc_id
  cluster_subnet_ids = module.aws-network.subnet_ids

  nodegroup_subnet_ids    = module.aws-network.private_subnet_ids
  nodegroup_disk_size     = "20"
  nodegroup_instance_types = ["t3.medium"]
  nodegroup_desired_size  = 1
  nodegroup_min_size      = 1
  nodegroup_max_size      = 3
}

# GitOps Configuration
```

Now you can commit and push this file into your CI/CD infrastructure pipeline and create a working EKS cluster. Don't forget that you'll need to use a tag to get the build to kick off. For example, you can run the following commands to create a 1.1 version of the infrastructure:

```
$ git add .
$ git commit -m "initial k8s release"
$ git push
$ git tag -a v1.1 -m "k8s build"
$ git push origin v1.1
```

Be prepared to wait for a few minutes for a result as provisioning a new EKS cluster can take up to 10 to 15 minutes. When it's done, you'll have a powerful container-based infrastructure up and running, ready to run your microservices resiliently.

The AWS EKS cluster we've defined here will accrue charges even when it's idle. We recommend that you destroy the environment when you are not using it. You'll find instructions for doing that in "Cleaning Up the Infrastructure" on page 177.

You can test that the cluster has been provisioned by running the following AWS CLI command:

```
$ aws eks list-clusters
```

If all has gone well, you'll get the following response:

```
{
    "clusters": [
        "ms-cluster-sandbox"
    ]
}
```

Our final step is to install a GitOps deployment tool that will come in handy when it's time to release our services into our environment's Kubernetes cluster.

Setting Up Argo CD

As we mentioned earlier, we're going to complete our infrastructure setup with a GitOps server that we'll use later in the book. We'll continue to follow the module pattern by creating a Terraform module for Argo CD that we can call to bootstrap the server in our sandbox environment. Unlike the other modules, we'll be installing Argo CD on the Kubernetes system that we've just instantiated.

To do that, we'll need to let Terraform know that we're using a different host. Up until now, we've been using the AWS provider, which lets Terraform communicate with AWS through its API. For our Argo CD installation we'll use a Kubernetes provider; this enables Terraform to issue Kubernetes commands and install the application to our new cluster. We'll also use a package-management system called Helm to do the installation. We'll introduce Helm a little bit later, but for now, we'll need to set up Terraform to use it as a provider.

We'll install this resource into the Kubernetes cluster rather than on the AWS platform.

That means we won't be using the AWS provider. Instead, we'll use Terraform's Kubernetes and Helm providers.

 A completed version of this module is available in this book's GitHub repository (*https://oreil.ly/Microservices_UpandRunning_argo_mod*).

Create a file called *main.tf* file in the root directory of the `module-argo-cd` Git repository that you created earlier. Add the code in Example 7-19 to set up the providers we need for the installation.

Example 7-19. module-argo-cd/main.tf

```
provider "kubernetes" {
  load_config_file      = false
  cluster_ca_certificate = base64decode(var.kubernetes_cluster_cert_data)
  host                  = var.kubernetes_cluster_endpoint
  exec {
    api_version = "client.authentication.k8s.io/v1alpha1"
    command     = "aws-iam-authenticator"
    args        = ["token", "-i", "${var.kubernetes_cluster_name}"]
  }
}

provider "helm" {
  kubernetes {
    load_config_file      = false
    cluster_ca_certificate = base64decode(var.kubernetes_cluster_cert_data)
    host                  = var.kubernetes_cluster_endpoint
    exec {
      api_version = "client.authentication.k8s.io/v1alpha1"
      command     = "aws-iam-authenticator"
      args        = ["token", "-i", "${var.kubernetes_cluster_name}"]
    }
  }
}
```

To configure the Kubernetes provider, we're using the properties of the EKS cluster that we provisioned earlier. These properties let Terraform know it needs to use the AWS authenticator to connect to the cluster along with the certificate that we've provided.

As we mentioned earlier, we're also using a provider for Helm. Helm is a popular way of describing a Kubernetes deployment and for distributing Kubernetes applications as packages. It's similar to other package-management tools, such as `apt-get` in the Linux world, and is designed to make installation of Kubernetes-based applications simple and easy. To configure our Helm provider, we simply need to provide a few Kubernetes connection parameters.

A Helm deployment is called a *chart*. We'll be using a Helm chart provided by the Argo CD community to install the Argo CD server. Add the code in Example 7-20 to the *main.tf* file to complete the installation declaration.

Example 7-20. module-argo-cd/main.tf (Helm)

```
resource "kubernetes_namespace" "example" {
  metadata {
    name = "argo"
  }
}

resource "helm_release" "argocd" {
  name       = "msur"
  chart      = "argo-cd"
  repository = "https://argoproj.github.io/argo-helm"
  namespace  = "argo"
}
```

This code creates a namespace for the Argo CD installation and uses the Helm provider to perform the installation. All that's left to complete the Argo CD module is to define some variables.

Variables for Argo CD

Create a file called *variables.tf* in your Argo CD module repository and add the code in Example 7-21.

Example 7-21. module-argo-cd/variables.tf

```
variable "kubernetes_cluster_id" {
  type = string
}

variable "kubernetes_cluster_cert_data" {
  type = string
}

variable "kubernetes_cluster_endpoint" {
  type = string
}

variable "kubernetes_cluster_name" {
  type = string
}

variable "eks_nodegroup_id" {
  type = string
}
```

We need to define these variables so that we can configure the Kubernetes and Helm providers in our code. So we'll need to grab them from the Kubernetes module's output when we call it in our sandbox's Terraform file. Before we get to that step, let's format and validate the code we've written in the same way as we did for our other modules:

```
module-argocd$ terraform fmt
[...]
module-argocd$ terraform init
[...]
module-argocd$ terraform validate
Success! The configuration is valid.
```

When you are satisfied that the code is valid, commit your code changes and push them to the GitHub repository so that we can use the module in our sandbox environment:

```
$ git add .
$ git commit -m "ArgoCD module init"
$ git push origin
```

Now, as we've done before, we just need to call this module from our sandbox definition.

Installing Argo CD in the sandbox

We want the Argo CD installation to happen as part of our sandbox environment bootstrapping, so we need to call the module from the Terraform definition in our sandbox environment. Add the code in Example 7-22 to the end of your sandbox module's *main.tf* file to install Argo CD. Don't forget to use your module's GitHub repository path in the source property of the module definition.

Example 7-22. env-sandbox/main.tf (Argo CD)

```
...

# Network Configuration
...

# EKS Configuration
...

# GitOps Configuration
module "argo-cd-server" {
  source = "*github.com/{YOUR_ARGOCD_MODULE_PATH}*"

  kubernetes_cluster_id        = module.aws-eks.eks_cluster_id
  kubernetes_cluster_name      = module.aws-eks.eks_cluster_name
  kubernetes_cluster_cert_data = module.aws-eks.eks_cluster_certificate_data
  kubernetes_cluster_endpoint  = module.aws-eks.eks_cluster_endpoint
  eks_nodegroup_id = module.aws-eks.eks_cluster_nodegroup_id
}
```

Now, you can tag, commit, and push the Terraform file into your CI/CD pipeline just like you've done before. For example, the following command will push a v1.2 tag into the repository and kick off the pipeline process:

> You'll need to wait for the EKS build to complete before tagging and committing these Argo CD sandbox changes. Otherwise, there won't be a Kubernetes cluster for Argo CD to be deployed to.

```
$ git add .
$ git commit -m "initial ArgoCD release"
$ git push origin
$ git tag -a v1.2 -m "ArgoCD build"
$ git push origin v1.2
```

When our pipeline is finished applying changes, you'll have a GitOps server that will help deploy microservices easier and more reliably. With that step completed, we've finished defining and provisioning the sandbox environment. All that's left is to test it and see if it works.

Testing the Environment

Before we finish with our infrastructure implementation, it's a good idea to run a test and make sure that the environment has been provisioned as expected. We'll do this by verifying that we can log in to the Argo CD web console. That will prove that the entire stack is running and operational. But in order to do that, we'll need to set up our kubectl CLI application.

Earlier in this chapter, when we were creating the Terraform code for our Kubernetes module, we added a local file resource to create a *kubeconfig* file. Now, we need to download that file so that we can connect to the EKS cluster using the kubectl application.

To retrieve this file, navigate to your sandbox GitHub repository in your browser and click on the Actions tab. You should see a list of builds with your latest run at the top of the screen. When you select the build that you just performed, you should see an artifact called "kubeconfig" that you can click and download.

> If you're having trouble finding the page to download the artifact, try following the instructions in the GitHub documentation (*https://oreil.ly/czDRi*).

GitHub will package the artifact as a ZIP file, so after downloading it you'll need to decompress the package. Inside the ZIP file you should find a file called *kubeconfig*. To use it, you just need to set an environment variable called KUBECONFIG that points to it. This will let the Kubernetes command-line application know where to find it. For example, if the *kubeconfig* file is in your *~/Downloads* directory, use the following value:

```
$ export KUBECONFIG=~/Downloads/kubeconfig
```

 If you like, you can copy the *kubeconfig* file to *~/.kube/config* and avoid having to set an environment variable. Just make sure you aren't overwriting a Kubernetes configuration you're already using.

You can test that everything runs as expected by issuing the following command:

```
$ kubectl get svc
```

You should see something like the following in response:

```
NAME         TYPE        CLUSTER-IP    EXTERNAL-IP   PORT(S)   AGE
kubernetes   ClusterIP   172.20.0.1    <none>        443/TCP   2h
```

This shows us that our network and EKS services were provisioned and we were able to successfully connect to the cluster. To get this information, kubectl makes an API call to the Kubernetes cluster we've just created. Getting this response back is proof that our cluster is up and running. As a final test, we'll check to make sure that Argo CD has been installed in the cluster. Run the following command to verify that the Argo CD pods are running:

```
$ kubectl get pods -n "argo"
NAME                                                  READY  STATUS    RESTARTS
msur-argocd-application-controller-5bddfb78fc-9jpzj   1/1    Running          0
msur-argocd-dex-server-84cd5fc9b9-bjzrm               1/1    Running          0
msur-argocd-redis-dc867dd9c-rpgww                     1/1    Running          0
msur-argocd-repo-server-75474975cc-j7lws              1/1    Running          0
msur-argocd-server-5cc998b478-wvkrr                   1/1    Running          0
```

 A Kubernetes Pod represents a deployable unit, consisting of one or more container images.

Later in the process, we'll get a chance to use Argo CD, the Kubernetes cluster, and the rest of the infrastructure we've designed. But now that we know our pipeline and configurations work, it's time to tear it all down. Don't worry, though: with our code written, it will be easy to create our environment again when we need it.

Cleaning Up the Infrastructure

We now have our infrastructure up and running. But, if you aren't planning on using it right away, it's a good idea to clean things up so you don't incur any costs to have it running. In particular, the elastic IP addresses that we used for our network can be costly if we leave them up. Since our environment is now completely defined in Terraform declarative files, we can re-create it in the same way whenever we need it, so destroying the existing environment is a low-risk activity.

Terraform will automatically destroy resources in the correct order for us because it has internally created a dependency graph. To destroy the sandbox environment, use the following steps:

1. Navigate to the working directory of your sandbox environment code on your machine. This is the same directory you used in "Installing Argo CD in the sandbox" on page 174.

2. Pull the latest version of the code from the repository:

   ```
   env-sandbox$ git pull
   ```

   Install the Terraform providers that our environment code uses (we'll need these so we can destroy the resources):

   ```
   env-sandbox$ terraform init
   ```

3. After Terraform has finished downloading plug-ins, enter the following command to destroy the sandbox environment:

   ```
   env-sandbox$ terraform destroy
   ```

4. Terraform will display the resources that it will destroy. You'll need to say yes to continue to the removal process. It will probably take about five minutes to complete. When it's done all of the AWS resources that we created will be gone.

    We're able to destroy these AWS resources from our local machine because we have AWS access and secret keys stored in a local credentials file. This shouldn't be the case for a production or secured environment.

5. When it's done, you'll see a message that looks like this:

   ```
   Destroy complete! Resources: 29 destroyed.
   ```

6. To verify that the EKS resources have been removed, you can run the following AWS CLI command to list EKS clusters:

   ```
   $ aws eks list-clusters
   ```

You should get back a response indicating that there are no EKS clusters left in your instance:

```
{
    "clusters": []
}
```

You can also run the following commands to double-check that the other billable resources have been removed:

```
$ aws ec2 describe-vpcs --filters Name=cidr,Values=10.10.0.0/16
$ aws elbv2 describe-load-balancers
```

 It's not absolutely necessary to run these CLI commands if terraform destroy returns successfully. We have included them so you can double-check that they are really gone, so you will not be billed unexpectedly.

If something has gone wrong, you'll need to use the AWS console and remove the resources manually. Consult the AWS documentation (*https://docs.aws.amazon.com*) if you have trouble deleting resources through the console.

Summary

We did a lot in this chapter. We created a Terraform module for our software-defined network that spanned two availability zones in a single region. Next, we created a module that instantiates an AWS EKS cluster for Kubernetes. We also implemented an Argo CD GitOps server into the cluster using a Helm package. Finally, we implemented a sandbox environment as code that uses all of these modules in a declarative, immutable way.

We went into a lot of detail with the Terraform code in this chapter. We did that so you could get a feel for what it takes to define an environment using infrastructure as code, immutability, and a CI/CD pipeline. We also wanted you to get hands on with the Terraform module pattern and some of the design decisions you'll need to make for your infrastructure. As we learn more about the microservices we are deploying, we may need additional infrastructure modules, but later in the book we'll use prewritten, hosted code instead of walking through it all line by line.

In Chapter 8, we'll get back to our example microservices and start the work of developing them. When we're done, we'll be able to release them into the infrastructure we've just designed.

Developer Workspace

In Chapter 1 we discussed how a microservices architecture is typically most beneficial when it is applied to complex systems, and explained some of the underlying reasons supporting this observation.

In any reasonably complex system, the only sustainable way to ensure that well-intentioned participants behave in a way that leads to positive and predictable collaboration is to make the right behaviors the absolute easiest and most intuitive ones. If doing the "right thing" is hard, over time most people will choose the path of least resistance—which will steer them the wrong way. It is therefore essential to invest early in setting up repeatable, predictable, standardized development processes that avoid unnecessary complexity and create an intuitively comfortable structure for your developers.

Investing in an exceptional developer experience that aims at a consistent and intuitive approach for all developers to easily "do the right thing" is one of the most underappreciated prerequisites of facilitating a successful microservices culture.

This is why developing robust continuous integration and continuous deployment (CI/CD) pipelines, for both your code as well as infrastructure, is a key enabler for your microservices efforts. Because of the modular nature of the architecture and the emphasis on independent deployability of each microservice, you will end up with many pipelines. One thing you should certainly avoid is every team creating a pipeline for their microservice in their own way, without any consistency with the code-bases of other microservices. Creating a new microservice should be a quick and predictable process. Ideally, it should be a templated process in which the majority of things are fully automated.

Robust CI/CD pipelines are crucial, but just as important is how the local development workspace is set up and what practices teams use for creating code. Most software engineers spend the majority of their time writing code on their laptops. Tapping into this process early and ensuring that the right guidance and tooling are provided at this stage can also have tremendous benefits later in the process. To be clear, we do not mean you should dictate every aspect of a developer's workflow. For instance, if you ever try to standardize the code editor that members of any sizable team must use, you will quickly make a lot of passionate enemies and achieve nothing. However, without becoming an overbearing tyrant we can and should declare some fundamental principles the team must stick with.

In this chapter, we will start by introducing a set of 10 highly opinionated rules and guidelines for a developer workspace setup that we have used with great success on some of our past microservices projects. Next, we'll walk you through setting up local containerized environments on multiple platforms. We will show you how to kickstart both vanilla Docker as well as a lightweight Kubernetes locally. Finally, we will show you an advanced example of containerization: how to install a local Cassandra database in the newly minted Docker setup.

By the end of this chapter, you should have a fully functioning, containerized infrastructure that's ready for writing some microservices code. More importantly, you will gain a solid understanding of the principles we use to set up projects for easy and intuitive development. We will use these principles in Chapter 9 to properly lay out our code, when we get into the development phase of our implementation.

Coding Standards and the Developer's Setup

When trying to introduce any organizational standards, it's useful to clarify and agree on goals, so people can relate to the "why" of the process before they are presented with the actual mechanics, the "how" and "what" of it.

We recommend following three high-level goals as a starting point:

Code can be set up in a short time frame
> There are few things more frustrating than joining a new team and spending a week or more on being able to set up an environment that allows you to start coding in the new codebase. Whether you are joining a new company, or just jumping in to give a helping hand to a team next to you in your current job, there are few more certain ways of killing any excitement and momentum than getting stuck on "How do I even run it?" Alas, this happens way too often. Our goal is that a new developer unfamiliar to the code should be able to set up a microservice, or a collection of microservices forming a logical subsystem, in under an hour!

New microservices can be created quickly, easily, and predictably

There is a lot of boilerplate related to jump-starting a new service. You need proper code templates for each supported tech stack, such as Java, Go, Node, Python, etc.; an automated testing and data management setup; dependencies such as data storage configured; and a skeleton of a pipeline bootstrapped; to name just a few. The worst-case scenario would be for a developer starting a new microservice to have to figure out all of these aspects from scratch, every single time.

Actually, an even worse scenario would be different developers varying these aspects unnecessarily for similar microservices. When you have a large codebase, one of the most impactful things you can do to avoid chaos is to establish consistency and familiarity. Providing well-thought-out templates for each of the standard tech stacks is a powerful way of achieving such consistency and high quality, while also increasing development speed.

Quality control must be automated

Enforcement of a company's software development quality standards must be automated and not left to human error.

Based on these goals, we can derive a set of fundamental guidelines for a developer workspace setup.

10 Workspace Guidelines for a Superior Developer Experience

The following guidelines are fairly opinionated and are based on the experience of the authors of this book. We recommend that you use these guidelines as a starting point.

After you have had experience building services with our guidelines, we expect that you may consider modifying some of them to better fit your individual needs and experiences:

1. *Make Docker the only dependency.*

   The "works for me" syndrome plagues many developer teams. It's essential that anybody be able to easily create the same environment. As such, elaborate, manual setups should be banned.

   We live in the era of containerization and teams should leverage it. To set up code, we should only expect to see the Docker runtime and Docker Compose on the host machine—nothing else! It should not matter if the machine is running Windows, macOS, or Linux and what libraries are present. Such assumptions are exactly what lead to broken setups. For instance, there should be no set expectations about a specific version of Python, Go, Java, etc., being present on the developer's machine. Setup instructions must be automated, not codified in *READ.ME* files.

2. *Remote or local should not matter.*

Setup should work regardless of whether a developer runs code on their own laptop or on a cloud server via an IDE's remote development/SFTP plug-ins. This should hold true by default and if there is a case in which this cannot be done, a cause for an exception must be justified and documented.

3. *Ensure a heterogeneous-ready workspace.*

A good setup should accommodate multiple microservices written in multiple programming languages, using multiple data storage systems. A microservices architecture assumes the ability to combine heterogeneous microservices; it doesn't mean just putting one codebase in one container or standardizing on one technology stack. Too often we see "[some-language] microservices framework" in marketing materials. Well, guess what—if 100% of your microservices are written in Java, there is something wrong with the setup, and no, you don't get to chuckle if all your services are written in a "cool" language like Go.

Now, for the record: this does not in any way mean that in a well-managed microservices environment you should see every team picking whatever language and databases they feel like and going for it. Quite the opposite: when uncertain, definitely try to exercise caution and go with two, at most three, stacks. The point here is that you *should* be able to introduce a new stack if you genuinely needed it, so in your example setup, you have to show that you actually can, that is, by implementing more than one stack.

 The Rule of Twos

We have found proactively practicing heterogeneity in a microservices setup to be a great approach. For any critical component in your system, make sure that you are using at least two alternatives in production at the same time—even when you only need one. You should also make sure that you have an infrastructure to support the two alternatives as easily as you would use a single one. We call this approach the "Rule of Twos" (*https://oreil.ly/_vYfU*).

Say that most of your APIs are written in Node.js—a truly wonderful, I/O-optimized stack for writing APIs. See if some of them could be implemented in Go, or Java, or Rust, etc., maybe because they do something more CPU-bound, which Node is not great at. While you practice heterogeneity, however, do make sure that you limit the selection of your programming languages and database systems across the entire application to two or three. Otherwise, you can run a high risk of confusing your teams with too much choice and creating serious maintenance overheads.

4. *Running a single microservice and/or a subsystem of several ones should be equally easy.*

   Let's say an airlines reservation system is implemented as three microservices. A developer should be able to check out any particular microservice individually and work on it, or check out an entire subsystem of interacting microservices (the reservation system implementation) and work on that. Both of these tasks should be very easy.

5. *Run databases locally, if possible.*

   For the sake of isolation, for any database system's local, Docker-ized alternatives should be provided, and it should be trivial to switch over to cloud (e.g., AWS) services via a configuration change. As an example, MinIO (*https://min.io*) can act locally as a drop-in replacement for S3. Many AWS service alternatives can be installed via this GitHub site (*https://oreil.ly/Lyasd*).

6. *Implement containerization guidelines.*

   Not all containerization approaches are equal. Anybody can haphazardly stick code into a Docker container, but making a containerized coding environment developer-friendly takes more effort. Following are some principles that we have found essential:

   a. Even though the code runtime is containerized, developers must be able to edit code on a host machine (e.g., their laptop, an EC2 dev server), with any code editor. However, during execution a full run/test/debug should be executed in a container.

   b. Since Docker Compose can generally do anything a Dockerfile can, they can easily be confused by developers. As such, it is important to establish the difference between the two. We recommend the following formula:

      Use a Dockerfile for building a container image, and Docker Compose for running things locally, including complex integrations. An image built with a Dockerfile should be directly runnable on Kubernetes, AWS ECR, Swarm, or any other production-grade runtime. Please note that just because it can be doesn't mean the local/dev image will always necessarily be the same as the one running in production. Teams do often optimize the former for usability and the latter for security and performance. A good example of this approach is the usage of multistage builds.

   c. Multistage builds (*https://oreil.ly/qI1Dp*) must be utilized in Dockerfiles to accommodate usage of slim images in production and usage of more full-featured images for local development.

   d. Developer user experience is critical. Implementing hot-reloading of the code and/or the ability to connect a debugger out of the box is an important feature.

7. *Establish rules for painless database migrations.*

It is extremely important to manage databases and the data in them in a way that supports and enhances team collaboration. Changes to data schemas must be codified and applied without any manual steps. The following list of principles facilitate painless data management in a microservices environment:

a. Any and all changes to a database schema must be codified in a series of "database migration" scripts. Migration files should be named and ordered by date.

b. Database migrations should support both schema changes as well as sample data insertion.

c. Running database migrations should be part of the project launch (via `Make start`, see the next section) and must be enforced.

d. Running database migrations must be automated and should be part of any build (integration, feature branch builds for PR, etc.).

e. It should be possible to indicate which migrations run on which environments (or which ones can be skipped), so that migrations that deal with sample data creation can be skipped in production, for example.

f. These rules apply to all data storage systems: relational, columnar, NoSQL, and so forth.

g. Some examples:

    a. Flyway hosts this introduction to database migrations (*https://flywaydb.org*)

    b. See this blog post (*https://oreil.ly/Vg41z*) by Daniel Miranda et al. about database migrations for Cassandra

    c. Check out this example (*https://oreil.ly/EqTxj*) of using Node's db-migrate-sql for a MySQL database

8. *Determine a pragmatic automated testing practice.*

Automated testing is a complex subject. We have certainly seen both extremes of the spectrum: some teams giving up entirely on automated testing, and others being overzealous on test-driven development to the extent of it becoming a problem. We advocate for a measured, pragmatic approach to automated testing, one that balances developer experience with quality metrics and accommodates the differing personal preferences of various developers on the team.

a. Test-first, test-as-you-code, or test-after-code should all be acceptable practices as long as all code is covered with a reasonable amount of meaningful tests before it is merged with the main branch.

b. Teams should use a testing approach and frameworks that is idiomatic for the platform/stack in which code is being developed (e.g., JUnit for Java). Codebases of the same stack (e.g., Go, Java, etc.) should use a uniform approach and various microservices in the same language should not be doing different things based on who wrote them and when.

c. Using external tools, especially for acceptance or performance testing, is fine with proper justification, given an important caveat: these tools (e.g., Cucumber) must be fully integrated in the code/repository of the service itself and using and running them must be as easy as a native solution. An average developer of the service should not need to set anything up to get things going and should be able to easily run tests with a command like `make test-all`.

d. Special attention and care should be given to automated tests that span the boundaries of individual microservices. They will have to be applied either at a higher level (e.g., an API that invokes microservices, or a UI), or in some cases, a dedicated repository may need to be set up to house testing orchestration and automation for such tests.

e. Code linting/static analysis tooling should be set up and a consistent configuration for the linter must be adapted for the organization's style.

9. *Branching and merging.*

Virtually everyone these days uses some form of code version control system. While the basics of version control–driven development are well-understood, it's worth reminding ourselves of some core principles of good branching hygiene that all team members should observe for a happy collaboration:

a. All development should happen on feature and bug branches.

b. Merging of a branch to the main branch should not be allowed without all tests (including integration tests in a temporary integration cluster spun up for the branch) passing on that branch.

c. The status of the test runs (after each commit/push) must be readily visible for code reviewers during pull requests.

d. Linting/static analysis errors should prevent code from being pushed to a branch, and/or merged into the main branch.

10. *Common targets should be codified in a makefile.*

Every code repository (and generally there should be one repository per microservice) should have a makefile that makes it easy for anybody to work with the code, regardless of the programming language stack used. This makefile should have standard targets, so that no matter what codebase, in whatever language the developer clones, they should know that by running `make run` they can bring that codebase up, and by running `make test` they can run automated tests.

We recommend defining and implementing the following standard targets for your microservice makefiles:

- `start`: Run the code.
- `stop`: Stop the code.
- `build`: Build the code (typically a container image).
- `clean`: Clean all caches and run from scratch.
- `add-module`
- `remove-module`
- `dependencies`: Ensure all modules declared in dependency management are installed.
- `test`: Run all tests and produce a coverage report.
- `tests-unit`: Run only unit tests.
- `tests-at`: Run only acceptance tests.
- `lint`: Run a linter to ensure conformance of coding style with defined standards.
- `migrate`: Run database migrations.
- `add-migration`: Create a new database migration.
- `logs`: Show logs (from within the container).
- `exec`: Execute a custom command inside the code's container.

Check out example microservices in Go (*https://oreil.ly/SY_ph*) and Node (*https://oreil.ly/IMfBj*) that follow the aforementioned pattern, and a sample setup of a multi-microservice workspace that follows the recommendations defined on this GitHub site (*https://oreil.ly/rJyPX*). For your convenience, we have also published this template on Github (*https://oreil.ly/kd2VT*) in Markdown format, so you can easily link and refer to it from your projects if you need to.

Let's review what we have learned so far. First, we recognized that the developer experience is paramount for building happy, highly productive, and autonomous teams. Next, we identified three core goals for achieving a superior developer experience. Last, but not least, we delved into 10 principles that, in our experience, fulfill the promises of these goals. The result is a repeatable blueprint for developing highly user-friendly developer workspaces for teams, regardless of which technology stack or specific tools end up being chosen. This is a solid foundation that will help you delight your teams and create an early team bond when you start building microservices organization or when you reorganize your existing teams into a microservices structure.

One of the principles that allows us to create repeatable, reliable, and comfortable development setups is code containerization with Docker. In the following section, we will dive into how to set up a solid containerized environment on major platforms, such as Linux, macOS, and Windows.

Setting Up a Containerized Environment Locally

Earlier in this chapter, we mentioned that the presence of Docker (and possibly of make for running makefiles) should be the only expectation for a developer environment. Everything else should be easily installable off of that. Let's see how we can get a complete Docker toolset, or even single-node Kubernetes, if needed, on various platforms.

Installing Docker on a Linux machine is fairly straightforward (*https://oreil.ly/2jdq6*), but what are some ways of getting it on your macOS or Windows machine?

When Docker4Mac (*https://oreil.ly/gXDWu*) and Docker4Windows (*https://oreil.ly/oLSzW*) came out they were truly revolutionary: bringing the cutting-edge power of Docker to the everyday desktop environments most people use. Eventually they started supporting Kubernetes as well, and it looked like the world could not be more perfect for a backend web developer, especially those moving into microservices.

The easiest way to get Docker and Kubernetes on your macOS or Windows is still Docker4Mac and Docker4Windows. There are, however, other choices that may be appealing to you.

An unfortunate reality is that the day-to-day experience of using Docker4Mac and Docker4Windows can be quite hit-and-miss. Even on fairly modern, powerful hardware we have experienced high CPU usage and battery drain. For some it may also be a problem that Docker4Mac only allows you to install one Docker instance and one Kubernetes. If you experiment a lot, you may want to have more freedom to break things.

Thankfully, there are alternatives. The obvious one is to install your own VMs with VirtualBox or its commercial alternatives. My experience, however, has been that these are even heavier than Docker4Mac/Win packages.

One of the more interesting alternatives that I have recently started experimenting with, however, is Multipass (*https://multipass.run*), a slick tool from Canonical, the creators of Ubuntu, that allows you to very quickly launch Ubuntu-based Docker hosts on your macOS or Windows machine (or even Linux). Multipass supports a number of underlying VMs, but most importantly it defaults to HyperKit on macOS, and Hyper-V on Windows (Windows Pro required!), which in our experience are more lightweight.

Installing Multipass

Multipass installers for various platforms can be downloaded from the website (*https://multipass.run*). Once you have it installed, check out the following interesting things you can do on macOS or Windows Subshell for Linux.

To launch a new Ubuntu environment:

```
→ multipass launch -n docker
Launched: docker
→ multipass list
Name                    State           IPv4            Image
docker                  Running         192.168.64.3    Ubuntu 20.04 LTS
```

By default, Multipass allocates 1 GB RAM, 5 GB disk, and 1 CPU core to the new machine. These may not be sufficient. In our experience, if you are using something like Node.js or Python with MySQL, 1 GB may be OK, but if you start using heavy Java applications with Java-based database systems such as Cassandra, you'll need more memory. We can override the defaults at launch:

```
→ multipass launch -m 4G -n dubuntu
Launched: dubuntu
→ multipass list
Name                    State           IPv4            Image
docker                  Running         192.168.64.3    Ubuntu 20.04 LTS
dubuntu                 Running         192.168.64.4    Ubuntu 20.04 LTS

→ multipass exec dubuntu -- bash

ubuntu@dubuntu:~$ free -m
              total       used       free     shared  buff/cache   available
Mem:           3945         79       3640          0         225        3653
```

 While Multipass does allow you to indicate more than one CPU with, say, -c 2, for us this resulted in broken containers on macOS. We assume it may have something to do with limitations on the Hypervisor implementation, but proceed with caution. Increasing memory has been no problem.

You could also increase the memory of an existing container without reinstalling everything you already have set up. You have to be careful, since this process can be fragile, but generally speaking, you need to stop a Multipass process via `launchctl` (otherwise it will overwrite your changes) and edit the configuration JSON, then relaunch the Multipass process:

```
→ sudo launchctl unload /Library/LaunchDaemons/com.canonical.multipassd.plist
→ sudo vi "/var/root/Library/Application
  Support/multipassd/multipassd-vm-instances.json"
→ sudo launchctl load /Library/LaunchDaemons/com.canonical.multipassd.plist
```

The JSON file you will be editing (*multipassd-vm-instances.json*) should look something like this:

```
{
    "dubuntu": {
        "deleted": false,
        "disk_space": "5368709120",
        "mac_addr": "52:54:00:27:53:b4",
        "mem_size": "4294967296",
        "metadata": {
        },
        "mounts": [
        ],
        "num_cores": 1,
        "ssh_username": "ubuntu",
        "state": 4
    }
}
```

As you might guess, `mem_size` is what you want to override (in bytes). To be on the safer side, we recommend indicating a number that is properly divisible by 1 GB. Since 1 GB is 1024 * 1024 * 1024 = 1,073,741,824 bytes, you should indicate a number that is a multiple of 1,073,741,824; e.g., for 8 GB enter 1073741824 * 8 = 8589934592.

Entering the Container and Mapping Folders

You can launch any command within your container with a command like `multipass exec <containername> -- <command launched inside>`. For instance, to see free memory in the container or to launch a bash shell, use the following:

```
→ multipass exec dubuntu -- free -m
              total        used        free      shared  buff/cache   available
Mem:           3945          77        3640           0         226        3654
Swap:             0           0           0

→ multipass exec dubuntu -- bash

ubuntu@dubuntu:~$ ls -al
total 36
drwxr-xr-x 5 ubuntu ubuntu 4096 .
drwxr-xr-x 3 root   root   4096 ..
-rw------- 1 ubuntu ubuntu  107 .bash_history
-rw-r--r-- 1 ubuntu ubuntu  220 .bash_logout
-rw-r--r-- 1 ubuntu ubuntu 3771 .bashrc
drwx------ 2 ubuntu ubuntu 4096 .cache
drwx------ 3 ubuntu ubuntu 4096 .gnupg
-rw-r--r-- 1 ubuntu ubuntu  807 .profile
drwx------ 2 ubuntu ubuntu 4096 .ssh
ubuntu@dubuntu:~$ exit
```

```
exit
→
```

Launching a shell of the primary container can be made easier by indicating which of your containers you want to set as primary. Then you can just type `multipass shell`:

```
→ multipass set client.primary-name=dubuntu
→ multipass shell

ubuntu@dubuntu:~$
```

To map your home folder (on macOS) to a folder in the container, you can run:

```
→ multipass mount $HOME dubuntu:/home/ubuntu/mac
Enabling support for mounting -

→ multipass exec dubuntu -- ls -ald mac
drwxr-xr-x 1 ubuntu ubuntu 3936 mac
→ multipass info dubuntu
Name:           dubuntu
State:          Running
IPv4:           192.168.64.4
Release:        Ubuntu 18.04.4 LTS
Image hash:     2f6bc5e7d9ac (Ubuntu 18.04 LTS)
Load:           0.00 0.08 0.07
Disk usage:     1.1G out of 4.7G
Memory usage:   81.9M out of 3.9G
Mounts:         /Users/irakli => /home/ubuntu/mac
→ multipass exec dubuntu -- ls -al mac
total 240120
drwxr-xr-x 1 ubuntu ubuntu     3936 .
drwxr-xr-x 6 ubuntu ubuntu     4096 ..
-rw-r--r-- 1 ubuntu ubuntu    10244 .DS_Store
drwx------ 1 ubuntu ubuntu       64 .Trash
drwxr-xr-x 1 ubuntu ubuntu      512 .atom
drwxr-xr-x 1 ubuntu ubuntu      128 .aws
```

Now that we have a functioning virtualized Linux via Multipass, installing Docker (or even local Kubernetes) becomes quite easy. Let's see in the next section how we would go about it.

Installing Docker

You can install Docker inside a container by following the usual Docker installation process:

```
→ multipass shell

ubuntu@dubuntu:~$ sudo apt-get update && sudo apt-get upgrade -y
ubuntu@dubuntu:~$ sudo apt-get install build-essential -y

# Sanity Check
```

```
ubuntu@dubuntu:~$ sudo apt-get remove docker \
                  docker-ce-cli docker-engine docker.io containerd runc

# Install Docker and Docker Compose
ubuntu@dubuntu:~$ sudo snap install docker
ubuntu@dubuntu:~$ echo 'export PATH=/snap/bin:$PATH' >> ~/.bashrc
ubuntu@dubuntu:~$ source ~/.bashrc
```

After completing these steps, you should have a working Docker installation, but it can only be run as root (via sudo), which is both insecure as well as inconvenient. To fix it you should grant the default, nonprivileged user (ubuntu for this installation) group access to Docker, as shown in the following code. Note that you must log out of Ubuntu and log back in for this change to take effect:

```
ubuntu@dubuntu:~$ sudo groupadd docker
ubuntu@dubuntu:~$ sudo usermod -aG docker $USER
ubuntu@dubuntu:~$ exit
logout
→ multipass restart
→ multipass shell

ubuntu@dubuntu:~$ docker ps
CONTAINER ID   STATUS    IMAGE    PORTS    NAMES

ubuntu@dubuntu:~$ docker version
Client:
 Version:          19.03.11
 API version:      1.40

ubuntu@dubuntu:~$ $ docker-compose --version
docker-compose version 1.25.5, build unknown
```

To test our new Docker setup, let's now use it for bringing up a MySQL database with Docker Compose.

Testing Docker

First, let's create a *mysql-stack.yml* file with instructions for Docker Compose:

```
version: '3.1'

services:
  db:
    image: mysql
    restart: always
    environment:
      MYSQL_ROOT_PASSWORD: rootPass
    ports:
      - 33060:3306
```

We should mention here that, by default, this file would be called *docker-compose.yml*, but we *can* use a custom name as long as we indicate the name we used with a special

-f flag when we try to execute Docker Compose. Let's now launch MySQL in a Docker container with the following:

```
ubuntu@dubuntu:~$ docker-compose -f mysql-stack.yml up -d

ubuntu@dubuntu:~$ docker ps
CONTAINER ID    STATUS         IMAGE     PORTS
e08f6f072c89    Up 3 seconds   mysql     33060/tcp, 0.0.0.0:33060->3306/tcp
```

At this point you should have a working Docker and Docker Compose setup. In the next section, we will show you how to use these tools to easily install advanced components, such as a local Cassandra database, should you need to do so.

Advanced Local Docker Usage: Installing Cassandra

We have already discussed how to use Docker Compose for running a containerized MySQL database, but let's look now at a somewhat more complex example of running a Cassandra database in a container. Considering the popularity and versatility of Cassandra, it is probably something you will have to deal with at some point in your cloud native microservices development journey.

 Cassandra requires more than the default 1 GB RAM, so make sure your Multipass container has more memory (e.g., 6–8 GB).

First, create a *docker-compose.yml* file with the following content anywhere in the container:

```
version: '3'

services:
  cassandra-seed:
    container_name: cassandra-seed
    image: cassandra:3.11
    ports:
      - "9042:9042"   # Native protocol clients
    # - "7199:7199"   # JMX
    # - "9160:9160"   # Thrift clients
    volumes:
      - local_cassandra_data_seed:/var/lib/cassandra

volumes:
  local_cassandra_data_seed:
```

Then run it and check that it worked:

```
ubuntu@dubuntu:~/cassandra$ docker-compose up -d
Creating network "cassandra_default" with the default driver
```

```
Creating cassandra-seed ... done
ubuntu@dubuntu:~/cassandra$ docker-compose ps
Name                    Command              State           Ports
-----------------------------------------------------------------------------
cassandra-seed    docker-entrypoint.sh cassa ...    Up      7000/tcp, 7001/tcp

ubuntu@dubuntu:~/cassandra$ docker exec -it cassandra-seed cqlsh
Connected to Test Cluster at 127.0.0.1:9042.
[cqlsh 5.0.1 | Cassandra 3.11.6 | CQL spec 3.4.4 | Native protocol v4]
Use HELP for help.
cqlsh> DESCRIBE keyspaces;
```

The last command, DESCRIBE keyspaces, will show all of the existing keyspaces in the newly minted Cassandra installation. At this point, you should have a fully working, local Cassandra setup. Next we will show you how to get a local Kubernetes environment installed when you need one.

Installing Kubernetes

For most cases, Docker Compose provides ample capabilities in orchestrating various components and microservices that make up your overall application. For more advanced cases, Kubernetes is a popular solution, with a much wider spectrum of functionality. It does, however, come with a proportionally higher level of complexity.

Avoid Using Kubernetes Locally Unless You Must

Generally, we do not recommend using local Kubernetes for everyday coding. Docker and Docker Compose can complete most containerization-related tasks more easily and they have more straightforward tooling for building container images. Kubernetes excels in orchestrating a runtime fleet of containers, which is rarely needed in a Dev environment, but which is crucial for environments such as production, preproduction, staging, performance testing, etc. However, in some circumstances you may want to use Kubernetes locally, especially for targeted testing.

You cannot simply install the official Kubernetes distribution on a single machine. Kubernetes is designed to be deployed on a cluster of servers. However, there are multiple nice side projects that bypass the requirement and get a functioning Kubernetes setup on a single machine. The default one, created by the same community that maintains Kubernetes, is Minikube (*https://oreil.ly/O9SON*). It is not the only solution, however. Two of our other favorites, based on simplicity and reliability, are Rancher's k3s (*https://k3s.io*) and Canonical's MicroK8s (*https://microk8s.io*).

To install Kubernetes locally with k3s, use the following:

```
ubuntu@dubuntu:~$ curl -sfL https://get.k3s.io | sh -
[INFO]  Finding release for channel stable
[INFO]  Using v1.17.4+k3s1 as release
[INFO]  Downloading hash \
https://github.com/rancher/k3s/releases/download/v1.17.4+k3s1/...
[INFO]  Downloading binary \
https://github.com/rancher/k3s/releases/download/v1.17.4+k3s1/k3s
[INFO]  Verifying binary download
[INFO]  Installing k3s to /usr/local/bin/k3s
...

ubuntu@dubuntu:~$ sudo k3s kubectl get nodes
NAME      STATUS   ROLES    AGE    VERSION
dubuntu   Ready    master   104s   v1.17.4+k3s1
```

With MicroK8s, the steps are similar but we are also adding a current user to a spe-cific group, and will need to log in again just like we did with Docker:

```
ubuntu@dubuntu:~$ sudo snap install microk8s --classic
microk8s v1.18.1 from Canonical✓ installed
ubuntu@dubuntu:~$ sudo usermod -a -G microk8s $USER
ubuntu@dubuntu:~$ sudo chown -f -R $USER ~/.kube
ubuntu@dubuntu:~$ exit
logout
→ multipass shell

ubuntu@dubuntu:~$ microk8s.kubectl get services --all-namespaces
NAMESPACE  NAME        TYPE        CLUSTER-IP     PORT(S)  AGE
default    kubernetes  ClusterIP   10.152.183.1   443/TCP  3m22s
```

And that's pretty much all you need to have a functioning Kubernetes setup on a development machine.

As we mentioned in the beginning of this section, an out-of-the box Kubernetes envi-ronment does not have tooling to build container images. It requires supplying a URI of a pre-built image from a registry. This shortcoming makes Kubernetes a cumber-some choice for active development, since there is no obvious solution for facilitating a streamlined build-run-test cycle. Kubernetes is really more of a tool for sophistica-ted orchestration in nondevelopment (QA, staging, preprod, prod, etc.) environ-ments. That said, several years after Kubernetes was released, an open source toolset called Skaffold (*https://skaffold.dev*) was developed to make building container images pluggable into Kubernetes life cycles.

We will not use local Kubernetes in most coding examples in this book, but if you would like to take a look at a sample open source project implementing such a setup, check out the Skaffold microservices (*https://oreil.ly/WHcqP*) repository that we cre-ated for demonstration purposes.

Summary

In this chapter, we outlined goals for designing a developer-friendly workspace to ensure that the space in which most developers spend the majority of their time (except maybe for meetings) is comfortable, reliable, and effective. Based on those goals, we introduced 10 principles for building efficient developer workspaces and demonstrated some of the steps for laying the containerized foundation for a variety of major operating systems: macOS, Windows, and Ubuntu Linux.

These concepts and skills will allow you to create delightful collaborative environments for your development teams, make on-boarding of new developers a pleasant experience, and facilitate good coding practices. In Chapter 9, we will come back to the goals and principles outlined here as we demonstrate the finer details of how we put together the code and the underlying project.

Developing Microservices

Let's put to work some of the techniques we've been discussing and implement a sample multimicroservices project. The implementation of the microservices in this sample project will be greatly simplified. We will show just enough code to suffice for demonstration purposes, but the steps and approaches we'll discuss can be directly applied on much larger, real projects.

We will start by identifying fitting candidates for microservices based on a bounded contexts analysis using Event Storming, similar to the process described in Chapter 4. Next we'll go through the seven steps of the SEED(S) design methodology that we discussed in Chapter 3, culminating in writing the code for both of the sample microservices. In the implementation of these services we will employ the data-modeling guidance from Chapter 5. And last, but not least, we will show how a user-friendly development environment for the microservices is properly set up and configured, applying many of the recommendations from Chapter 8, including the creation of an umbrella project—a way to execute multiple microservices together in a developer workspace.

Designing Microservice Endpoints

Let's assume that an Event Storming session that you conducted for a flight management software product identified two major bounded contexts:

- Flights management
- Reservations management

As we discussed in Chapter 4, in the initial stages it pays off to design microservices in a coarse-grained way. Specifically, we often align them with bounded contexts; i.e., our first two microservices can be ms-flights and ms-reservations!

Now that we have the target microservices identified, we need to use the SEED(S) design process (introduced in Chapter 3) for them. According to the first step of the SEED(S) methodology, we need to identify various actors. For our purposes, we'll assume the following actors:

- The customer trying to book the flight
- The airline's consumer app (web, mobile, etc.)
- The web APIs that the app interacts with (In Chapter 3, we mentioned that some call these "backends for frontends" or BFF APIs.)
- The flights management microservice: ms-flights
- The reservations management microservice: ms-reservations

Let's look at some sample JTBDs that our product team may have collected from customer interviews and business analysis research.

1. *When* a customer interacts with the UI, the *app needs* to render a seating chart showing occupied and available seats, *so the customer can* choose a seat.
2. *When* a customer is finalizing a booking, the *web app needs* to reserve a seat for the customer, *so the app can* avoid accidental seat reservation conflicts.

Recall from Chapter 3 that we recommended BFF APIs be a thin layer with no business logic implementation. They mostly just orchestrate microservices. So there are usually jobs for which a BFF API needs microservices. The following list of jobs, the more technical JTBDs, describes the needs between the BFF APIs and microservices:

1. *When* the API is asked to provide a seating chart, the *API needs* ms-flights to provide a seating setup of the flight, *so the API can* retrieve availabilities and render the final result.
2. *When* the API needs to render a seating chart, the *API needs* ms-reservations to provide a list of already reserved seats *so the API can* add that data to the seating setup and return the seating chart.
3. *When* the API is asked to reserve a seat, the *API needs* ms-reservations to fulfill the reservation, *so the API can* reserve the seat.

Key Decision: Avoid Microservices Calling Each Other Directly

Note that we don't let ms-flights call ms-reservations to assemble the seating chart, and instead have the BFF API handle the interaction. This refers back to the recommendation in Chapter 3 that direct microservice-to-microservice calls be avoided.

Following the SEED(S) methodology, next we describe the interactions represented by various jobs, using UML sequence diagrams in PlantUML format:

```
@startuml

actor Customer as cust
participant "Web App" as app
participant "BFF API" as api
participant "ms-flights" as msf
participant "ms-reservations" as msr

cust -[#blue]-> app ++: "Flight Seats Page"
app -[#blue]-> api ++ : flight.getSeatingSituation()
api -[#blue]-> api: auth
api -> msf ++ : getFlightId()
msf --> api: flight_id
api -> msf: getFlightSeating()
return []flightSeating
api -> msr ++ : getReservedSeats()
return []reservedSeats
return []SeatingSituation
return "Seats Selection Page"
|||
cust -[#blue]->app ++: "Choose a seat & checkout"
app-[#blue]->app: "checkout workflow"
app-[#blue]->api ++: "book the seat"
api -[#blue]->api: auth
api->msr ++: "reserveSeat()"
return "success"
return "success"
return "Success Page"
@enduml
```

This can be rendered (e.g., using LiveUML (*http://liveuml.com*)) into the UML diagram shown in Figure 9-1.

As you can clearly see from this diagram, the first JTBD is to present a customer with a "seats on the flight" page. To fulfill this job, an app (or a website) will need to call a frontend (BFF) API that returns the seating "situation": a list of seats with indicators for which ones are occupied or vacant. The API will first authenticate the call to ensure the app is authorized to ask such questions. If the auth passes, it will first try to get a flight_id from the ms-flights microservice. This is necessary because customers usually just enter the nonunique flight number (identifying a route more than a specific flight on a specific date) and flight date. With the unique flight_id returned, the API will then get the list of seats from ms-flights. To make sure we can show occupied seats, it will separately query ms-reservations for existing reservations on the flight.

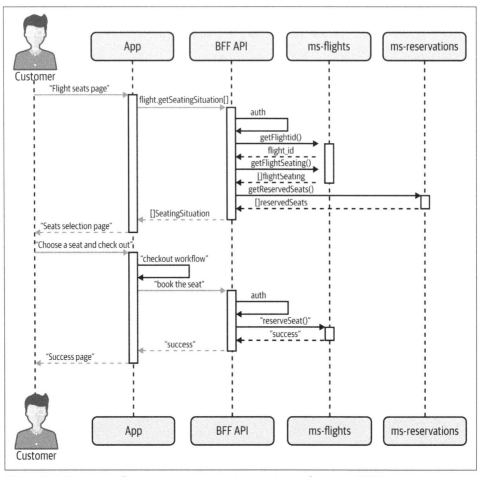

Figure 9-1. Sequence diagram representing interactions of various JTBDs

Of particular importance here is how we're practicing the principle described in Chapter 3 regarding microservices not calling each other directly and instead being orchestrated by a thin API layer. This is entirely why ms-flights is not querying the list of reserved seats from ms-reservations directly. Once the API collects all of the required information it can return the rich data to the app/website so the latter can render the desired screen for the customer.

In the second part of Figure 9-1, we describe the second JTBD for the customer: once they see the current seating situation, they want to pick a specific (available) seat and reserve it. To fulfill this task, API will again need to auth and then call a microservice, ms-reservations, returning the status, success, or failure to the app, based on the result of the booking attempt. This allows the app to let the customer know whether their request could be completed or not.

Once we have the JTBDs, and understand the interactions, we can translate them into queries and actions. We will do this for both ms-flights and ms-reservations. In Chapter 3, we explained that you should also design actions and queries for the BFF API, not just microservices, but we will leave that task as an exercise to the reader.

Flights Microservice

To compile actions and queries for ms-flights:

Get flight details
- *Input*: `flight_no`, `departure_local_date_time` (ISO8601 format and in the local time zone)
- *Response*: A unique `flight_id` identifying a specific flight on a specific date. In practice, this endpoint will very likely return other flight-related fields, but those are irrelevant for our context, so we are skipping over them.

Get flight seating (the diagram of seats on a flight)
- *Input*: `flight_id`
- *Response*: Seat Map object in JSON format[1]

Reservations Microservice

To compile actions and queries for ms-reservations:

Query already reserved seats on a flight
- *Input*: `flight_id`
- *Response*: A list of already-taken seat numbers, each seat number in a format like "2A"

Reserve a seat on a flight
- *Input*: `flight_id`, `customer_id`, `seat_num`
- *Expected outcome*: A seat is reserved and unavailable to others, or an error fired if the seat was unavailable
- *Response*: Success (`200 Success`) or failure (`403 Forbidden`)

As discussed in Chapter 3, the beauty of writing down actions and queries is that they bring us much closer to being able to create the technical specifications of the services than when jobs are presented in their business-oriented, jobs (JTBD) format.

---

1 For demonstration purposes we are using the Seat Map object structure from Sabre's Seat Map RESTful API (*https://oreil.ly/oQA29*), a gold standard of the industry.

Now that we have the actions and queries for our microservices, we can proceed with describing the microservices we intend to build in a standard format. In our case, we will build RESTful microservices and describe them with an OAS. In the next section, we'll see what this specification for our two microservices could look like.

Designing an OpenAPI Specification

Based on the query and commands specification we just designed, translation into an OpenAPI Specification (OAS) becomes fairly straightforward. The top part of the specification is usually some meta information:

```
openapi: 3.0.0
info:
  title: Flights Management Microservice API
  description: |
    API Spec for Flight Management System
  version: 1.0.1
servers:
  - url: http://api.example.com/v1
    description: Production Server
```

For the `/flights` endpoint you will want to provide `flight_no` and `depar ture_date_time` input parameters in the query string of the request. The schema should also describe the response JSON's structure, containing `flight_id`, the origin airport's identifier code, the destination airport's code, and the HTTP code (200) for a successful response. This part in OpenAPI format may look like:

```
paths:
  /flights:
    get:
      summary: Look Up Flight Details with Flight No and Departure Date
      description: |
        Look up flight details, such as: the unique flight_id used by the
        rest of the Flights management endpoints, flight departure and
        arrival airports.

        Example request:
        ```
          GET http://api.example.com/v1/flights?
              flight_no=AA2532&departure_date_time=2020-05-17T13:20
        ```
      parameters:
        - name: flight_no
          in: query
          required: true
          description: Flight Number.
          schema:
            type : string
          example: AA2532
        - name: departure_date_time
```

```
      in: query
      required: true
      description: Date and time (in IS08601)
      schema:
        type : string
      example: 2020-05-17T13:20


  responses:
    '200':    # success response
      description: Successful Response
      content:
        application/json:
          schema:
            type: array
            items:
              type: object
              properties:
                flight_id:
                  type: string
                  example: "edcc03a4-7f4e-40d1-898d-bf84a266f1b9"
                origin_code:
                  type: string
                  example: "LAX"
                destination_code:
                  type: string
                  example: "DCA"

          example:
            flight_id: "edcc03a4-7f4e-40d1-898d-bf84a266f1b9"
            origin_code: "LAX"
```

When you design the specification for the `/flights/{flight_no}/seat_map` endpoint, it can take the `flight_no` input parameter in the URL path itself, instead of in the query part of the URL. In the response object, for demonstration purposes, we are using a SeatMap object structure that mimics that of the industry gold standard, Sabre's Seat Map API (*https://oreil.ly/ySRA0*). If you were really building a commercial API, you would need to design your own implementation or acquire permission for reuse from the design's original author:

```
/flights/{flight_no}/seat_map:
  get:
    summary: Get a seat map for a flight
    description: |
      Example request:
      ```
        GET http://api.example.com/
            v1/flights/AA2532/datetime/2020-05-17T13:20/seats/12C
      ```
    parameters:
      - name: flight_no
```

```
        in: path
        required: true
        description: Unique Flight Identifier
        schema:
          type : string
        example: "edcc03a4-7f4e-40d1-898d-bf84a266f1b9"

    responses:
      '200':    # success response
        description: Successful Response
        content:
          application/json:
            schema:
              type: object
              properties:
                Cabin:
                  type: array
                  items:
                    type: object
                    properties:
                      firstRow:
                        type: number
                        example: 8
                      lastRow:
                        type: number
                        example: 23
                      Wing:
                        type: object
                        properties:
                          firstRow:
                            type: number
                            example: 14
                          lastRow:
                            type: number
                            example: 22
                  CabinClass:
                    type: object
                    properties:
                      CabinType:
                        type: string
                        example: Economy
                  Column:
                    type: array
                    items:
                      type: object
                      properties:
                        Column:
                          type: string
                          example: A
                        Characteristics:
                          type: array
                          example:
```

```
                              - Window
                        items:
                           type: string
              Row:
                type: array
                items:
                  type: object
                  properties:
                    RowNumber:
                      type: number
                      example: 8
                  Seat:
                    type: array
                    items:
                       type: object
                       properties:
                         premiumInd:
                           type: boolean
                           example: false
                         exitRowInd:
                           type: boolean
                           example: false
                         restrictedReclineInd:
                           type: boolean
                           example: false
                         noInfantInd:
                           type: boolean
                           example: false
                         Number:
                           type: string
                           example: A
                         Facilities:
                           type: array
                           items:
                              type: object
                              properties:
                                Detail:
                                  type: object
                                  properties:
                                    content:
                                       type: string
                                       example: LegSpaceSeat
```

You can view the full source of the specification at this book's GitHub site (*https://oreil.ly/Microservices_UpandRunning_api_yml*).

The OAS can be rendered with a number of editors; for instance, Swagger Editor (*https://editor.swagger.io*). Rendering the preceding specification produces a result that looks like Figure 9-2.

Figure 9-2. OAS for ms-flights rendered with Swagger Editor

Similarly to the OAS of the flights microservice, the designs for the endpoints of the reservation system would be something along the lines of:

```
openapi: 3.0.0
info:
  title: Seat Reservation System API
  description: |
    API Spec for Fight Management System
  version: 1.0.1
servers:
  - url: http://api.example.com/v1
    description: Production Server
paths:
  /reservations:
    get:
```

```yaml
    summary: Get Reservations for a flight
    description: |
      Get all reservations for a specific flight
    parameters:
      - name: flight_id
        in: query
        required: true
        schema:
          type: string
    responses:
      '200':    # success response
        description: Successful Response
        content:
          application/json:
            schema:
              type: array
              items:
                type: object
                properties:
                  seat_no:
                    type: string
                    example: "18F"
              example:
                - { seat_no: "18F" }
                - { seat_no: "18D" }
                - { seat_no: "15A" }
                - { seat_no: "15B" }
                - { seat_no: "7A" }
put:
  summary: Reserve or cancel a seat
  description: |
    Reserves a seat or removes a seat reservation
  requestBody:
    required: true
    content:
      application/json:
        schema:
          type: object
          properties:
            flight_id:
              description: Flight's Unique Identifier.
              type : string
              example: "edcc03a4-7f4e-40d1-898d-bf84a266f1b9"
            customer_id:
              description: Registered Customer's Unique Identifier
              type : string
              example: "2e850e2f-f81d-44fd-bef8-3bb5e90791ff"
            seat_num:
              description: seat number
              type: string
          example:
            flight_id: "edcc03a4-7f4e-40d1-898d-bf84a266f1b9"
```

```
              customer_id: "2e850e2f-f81d-44fd-bef8-3bb5e90791ff"
              seat_num: "8D"
      responses:
        '200':
          description: |
            Success.
          content:
            application/json:
              schema:
                type: object
                properties:
                  status:
                    type: string
                    enum: ["success", "error"]
                    example:
                      "success"
        '403':
          description: seat(s) unavailable. Booking failed.
          content:
            application/json:
              schema:
                type: object
                properties:
                  error:
                    type: string
                  description:
                    type: string
                example:
                  error: "Could not complete reservation"
                  description: "Seat already reserved. Cannot double-book"
```

Now that we have our service designs and the corresponding OASs, it's time to proceed to the last step in the SEED(S) process: writing the code for the microservices.

As we implement the flights and reservations microservices, we will practice the principles discussed earlier in this book. Specifically, we will use different tech stacks for these services, so we can demonstrate their ability to support heterogeneous implementation. The reservations microservice will be implemented in Python and Flask, while the flights microservice will be implemented in Node/Express.js.

Implementing the Data for a Microservice

To emphasize the need for data independence that we discussed at length in Chapter 5, not only will we ensure the two microservices do not share any data space, but we will intentionally implement them using entirely different backend data systems: Redis for the reservations and MySQL for flights. We will also explain how each of these microservices benefits from the choice of data storage mechanisms. Let's start with the data for the reservations system microservice.

Redis for the Reservations Data Model

In the reservations system, we need to be able to capture a set of seat reservations for a flight, and reserve a seat if it is not already booked. Redis has a perfect, simple data structure that fits our use case very well: *hashes*.

Redis hashes are optimized for storing mappings of lists of key/value pairs, where both keys and values are of the string type. They are often used to store flat objects such as a user with first name, last name, email, etc. For us, it can serve as robust storage for seat reservations information. We can have a hash object saved for each `flight_id` (specific flight) where keys of the hash are the seat numbers on the flight and the value is the `customer_id` for the customer that the seat is already reserved for. Redis has commands to set a new value in a hash and to get all set values (for when we need to know all reserved seats), and, very conveniently, a command that allows us to set a value only if the value for the same key (seat) is not already set. That's perfect for us, since we typically do not want to allow double-booking a seat on a flight.

Key Decision: Use Redis to Implement the Reservations Database

Use Redis as the data store for reservations to leverage its unique simplicity and flexibility, characteristics fitting for the implementation of this microservice.

Let's see an example of reserving several seats on a flight uniquely identified with the `flight_id` of `40d1-898d-bf84a266f1b9`. If you have a working Redis installation, or use the Redis CLI (*https://oreil.ly/ZmFAQ*) from the reservations microservice's workspace by invoking `make redis` after you check out that GitHub repository, you should be able to run the following commands:

```
> HSETNX flight:40d1-898d-bf84a266f1b9 12B b4cdf96e-a24a-a09a-87fb1c47567c
(integer) 1
> HSETNX flight:40d1-898d-bf84a266f1b9 12C e0392920-a24a-b6e3-8b4ebcbe7d5c
(integer) 1
> HSETNX flight:40d1-898d-bf84a266f1b9 11A f4892d9e-a24a-8ed1-2397df0ddba7
(integer) 1
> HSETNX flight:40d1-898d-bf84a266f1b9 3A 017d40c6-a24b-b6d7-4bb15d04a10b
(integer) 1
> HSETNX flight:40d1-898d-bf84a266f1b9 3B 0c27f7c8-a24b-9556-fb37c840de89
(integer) 1
> HSETNX flight:40d1-898d-bf84a266f1b9 22A 0c27f7c8-a24b-9556-fb37c840de89
(integer) 1
> HSETNX flight:40d1-898d-bf84a266f1b9 22B 24ae6f02-a24b-a149-53d7a72f10c0
(integer) 1
```

The `HSETNX` command we use here sets the value of the `HSET` key, we indicate, to the specified value only if the key doesn't already have a value. This way we avoid reserving seats that are already assigned.

Let's see how we would get all of the occupied seats on a specific flight:

```
> HKEYS flight:40d1-898d-bf84a266f1b9
1) "12B"
2) "12C"
3) "11A"
4) "3A"
5) "3B"
6) "22A"
7) "22B"
```

If we wanted to get both keys and values, we can also do this:

```
> HGETALL flight:40d1-898d-bf84a266f1b9
 1) "12B"
 2) "b4cdf96e-a24a-a09a-87fb1c47567c"
 3) "12C"
 4) "e0392920-a24a-b6e3-8b4ebcbe7d5c"
 5) "11A"
 6) "f4892d9e-a24a-8ed1-2397df0ddba7"
 7) "3A"
 8) "017d40c6-a24b-b6d7-4bb15d04a10b"
 9) "3B"
10) "0c27f7c8-a24b-9556-fb37c840de89"
11) "22A"
12) "0c27f7c8-a24b-9556-fb37c840de89"
13) "22B"
14) "24ae6f02-a24b-a149-53d7a72f10c0"
```

Let's now see what happens if we try to double-book an already reserved seat, such as 12C:

```
> HSETNX flight:40d1-898d-bf84a266f1b9 12C 083a6fc2-a24d-889b-6fc480858a38
(integer) 0
```

Notice how the response to this command is `(integer) 0` instead of the `(integer) 1` we got for earlier HSETNX commands. This indicates that 0 fields were actually updated and that is because 12C had already been reserved.

As you can see, choosing Redis as the data store for ms-reservations has made the implementation easy and natural. We were able to use well-fitting data structures, such as `HSET`, that effortlessly and elegantly met our needs. The `HSETNX` command allowed us to avoid accidental double-bookings in a reliable and straightforward way.

Redis is a fantastic key/value store that can be used in a wide variety of use cases, which is why it has a huge fan base among programmers. However, it is not going to be the perfect database for every single use case. Sometimes we may have data needs that are better met by other popular databases.

To demonstrate this, in the next section, we will implement the data for the ms-flights microservice using a traditional SQL database.

MySQL Data Model for the Flights Microservice

The first data model we need here should contain seat maps. As we saw in the OAS for the flights microservice, the seat map is a complex JSON object. MySQL can be a better storage for such data than standard Redis. As of MySQL 5.7.8, MySQL has robust, native support for JSON data types. This support has expanded and improved in the latest 8.x version of MySQL. It now also supports in-place, atomic updates of JSON values and JSON Merge Patch syntax. In comparison, Redis only supports JSON with a RedisJSON module that doesn't come pre-built with the standard Redis distribution.

A well-implemented JSON data type provides tangible advantages over storing JSON data in a string column: validation of JSON documents during inserts, internally optimized binary storage, ability to look up subobjects and nested values directly by a key, and so on.

Additionally, in the lookup endpoint we need to query data by two fields: `flight_no` and `datetime`. A relational database is a more natural structure for such queries. In Redis, we would probably need to create a compound field to achieve the same. All in all, while we could technically implement this service with Redis as well, there are reasons to choose MySQL for doing this, among them that MySQL also helps us demonstrate usage of different databases for different services. Real-life situations will obviously be more complex, with more aspects to consider.

Let's look at the `seat_maps` table:

```
CREATE TABLE `seat_maps` (
  `flight_no` varchar(10) NULL,
  `seat_map` json NULL,
  `origin_code` varchar(10) NULL,
  `destination_code` varchar(10) NULL,

  PRIMARY KEY(`flight_no`)
);
```

Another table we need is the mapping of `flight_ids` with `flight_nos` and `date times`. The creation script for this table may look something like the following:

```
CREATE TABLE `flights` (
  `flight_id` varchar(36) NOT NULL,
  `flight_no` varchar(10) NULL,
  `flight_date` datetime(0) NULL,

  PRIMARY KEY (`flight_id`),
  INDEX `idx_flight_date`(`flight_no`, `flight_date`)

  FOREIGN KEY(flight_no)
    REFERENCES seat_maps(flight_no)
);
```

Let's insert our first sample seat map:

```
INSERT INTO `seat_maps`(`flight_no`, `seat_map`, `origin_code`, /
`destination_code`) VALUES ('AA2532', '{\"Cabin\": [{\"Row\": [{\"Seat\": /
[{\"Number\": \"A\", \"Facilities\": [{\"Detail\": {\"content\": /
\"LegSpaceSeat\"}}], \"exitRowInd\": false, \"premiumInd\": false, /
\"noInfantInd\": false, \"restrictedReclineInd\": false}], \"RowNumber\": /
8}], \"Wing\": {\"lastRow\": 22, \"firstRow\": 14}, \"Column\": /
[{\"Column\": \"A\", \"Characteristics\": [\"Window\"]}], \"lastRow\": 23, /
\"firstRow\": 8, \"CabinClass\": {\"CabinType\": \"Economy\"}}]}', /
'LAX', 'DCA');
```

Once we have the proper JSON value in the database, we can easily select specific values in it or filter by specific values. For instance:

```
select seat_map->>"$.Cabin[0].firstRow" from seat_maps
```

Now that we have a working data model for both of our microservices, we can dive deeper into the implementation of code for them.

Implementing Code for a Microservice

Now we'll work toward the second goal that is the foundation of the "10 Workspace Guidelines for a Superior Developer Experience" on page 181 and start new microservices quickly, using well-tested templates for each relevant tech stack. For the Node.js-implemented flights microservice we'll use a popular bootstrapper, Node-Bootstrap (*https://nodebootstrap.io*). For the Python-based reservation microservice we're going to use a GitHub template repository (*https://oreil.ly/g1LIk*) that contains most of the boilerplate code that we'll need.

> ### Key Decision: Start Microservices with Reusable Templates
>
> Use code templates to jump-start a microservice development in each programming language supported in your ecosystem. Using templates helps with speed of development without sacrificing quality, and keeps various microservices uniform in their key traits.

Based on the 10 guidelines, using any templates assumes that you have a working Docker installation and the GNU Make, since we use both of them. There are no other expectations, however. In Chapter 8, we showed how to set up Docker on multiple platforms. GNU Make usually comes preinstalled on macOS and Linux/Unix systems. There are multiple ways to get GNU Make on Windows. The one we recommend is Windows Subsystem for Linux (*https://oreil.ly/1JERY*).

Edit Code on a Host Run Inside Containers

Note that in all further examples in this chapter, we assume that you perform work on your host machine, without needing to log in to Docker containers.

As you work on a containerized project, your favorite code editor would be installed on your macOS, Windows, or Linux machine and you will be executing various make commands on that machine. Docker should be installed/available and most results of the commands you issue will execute inside the containers, but there's rarely a need for you to explicitly shell into the containers, unless you are debugging something low level.

The Code Behind the Flights Microservice

To use NodeBootstrap for jump-starting a Node/Express microservice, either install its bootstrapper with `node install -g nodebootstrap` (if you already have Node available on your system), or clone this GitHub template repository (*https://oreil.ly/ Hi-wn*).

While the former may be somewhat easier, we will do the latter since we do not want to assume that you had to set up Node on your system. Go ahead and click "Use this template" on the nodebootstrap-microservice's main repository page, as shown in Figure 9-3.

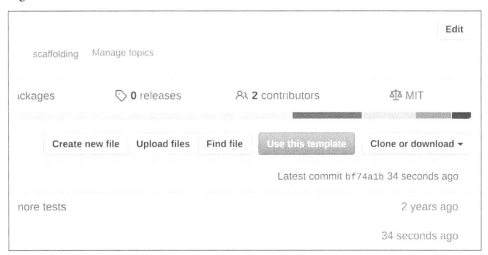

Figure 9-3. The nodebootstrap-microservice's main repository page

Once you have created a new repository for the ms-flights microservice, at the destination of your choosing, let's check it out on your developer machine and start modifying things by writing code.

A nice thing about the NodeBootstrap template is that it comes with full support for an OAS of the microservices. Let's take the specification we designed earlier and put it into the *docs/api.yml* file, replacing the sample specification we already find there. Make sure you are in the *docs* subfolder and then run `make start`:

```
→ make start
docker run -d --rm --name ms-nb-docs -p 3939:80 -v \
ms-flights/docs/api.yml:/usr/share/nginx/html/swagger.yaml \
-e SPEC_URL=swagger.yaml redocly/redoc:v2.0.0-rc.8-1
49e0986e318288c8bf6934e3d50ba93537ddf3711453ba6333ced1425576ecdf
server started at: http://0.0.0.0:3939
```

This will render the specification to a beautiful HTML template and make it available at *http://0.0.0.0:3939*. The rendering will probably look like Figure 9-4.

Figure 9-4. Rendered OAS of the ms-flights microservice

The Nodebootstrap microservice comes with a sample "users" module, located under the *lib/users* folder. Since we don't need a user management module and do need a flights management one, let's rename that folder *flights* and delete another default module, *lib/homedoc*, as we won't need that one, either. When you remove the *lib/homedoc* folder you need to also remove its plug from *appConfig.js* in the root folder. This appears around line 24, and reads something like:

```
app.use('/',     require('homedoc')); // Attach to root route
```

Likewise, change the hookup for the flights module in the same file, so that the line reads as follows:

```
app.use('/flights', require('flights')); // Attach to sub-route
```

Once you are done making these modifications, edit *lib/flights/controllers/mappings.js* to introduce some input validation and indicate functions from the actions module of the microservice that will be invoked for each of your two API endpoint routes:

```
const {spieler, check, matchedData, sanitize} = require('spieler')();

const router      = require('express').Router({ mergeParams: true });
const actions     = require('./actions');

const log = require("metalogger")();

const flightNoValidation = check('flight_no',
  'flight_no must be at least 3 chars long and contain letters and numbers')
  .exists()
  .isLength({ min: 3 })
  .matches(/[a-zA-Z]{1,4}\d+/)

const dateTimeValidation = check('departure_date_time',
  'departure_date_time must be in YYYY-MM-ddThh:mm format')
  .exists()
  .matches(/\d{4}-\d{2}-\d{2}T\d{2}:\d{2}/)

const flightsValidator = spieler([
  flightNoValidation,
  dateTimeValidation
]);
const seatmapsValidator = spieler([
  flightNoValidation
]);

router.get('/', flightsValidator, actions.getFlightInfo);
router.get('/:flight_no/seat_map', seatmapsValidator, actions.getSeatMap);

module.exports = router;
```

As you can see, in this file we are setting up routes for our two main endpoints and validators that ensure that our input parameters are present, as well as properly formatted. When they are not, NodeBootstrap also has standard error messaging to let the client know.

Let's now implement some logic. First we need to create MySQL tables and some sample data. As you may guess, Nodebootstrap provides an easy solution for this as well, in the form of database migrations: scripts that codify database modifications and allow you to apply them in any environment later.

We can create several database migrations with some make commands, as follows:

```
→ make migration-create name=seat-maps
docker-compose -p msupandrunning up -d
ms-flights-db is up-to-date
Starting ms-flights ... done
docker-compose -p msupandrunning exec ms-flights
```

```
    ./node_modules/db-migrate/bin/db-migrate create seat-maps --sql-file
[INFO] Created migration at /opt/app/migrations/20200602055112-seat-maps.js
[INFO] Created migration up sql file at
    /opt/app/migrations/sqls/20200602055112-seat-maps-up.sql
[INFO] Created migration down sql file at
    /opt/app/migrations/sqls/20200602055112-seat-maps-down.sql
sudo chown -R $USER ./migrations/sqls/
[sudo] password for irakli:

➜ make migration-create name=flights
docker-compose -p msupandrunning up -d
ms-flights-db is up-to-date
ms-flights is up-to-date
docker-compose -p msupandrunning exec ms-flights
    ./node_modules/db-migrate/bin/db-migrate create flights --sql-file
[INFO] Created migration at /opt/app/migrations/20200602055121-flights.js
[INFO] Created migration up sql file
    at /opt/app/migrations/sqls/20200602055121-flights-up.sql
[INFO] Created migration down sql file
    at /opt/app/migrations/sqls/20200602055121-flights-down.sql
sudo chown -R $USER ./migrations/sqls/

➜ make migration-create name=sample-data
docker-compose -p msupandrunning up -d
ms-flights-db is up-to-date
ms-flights is up-to-date
docker-compose -p msupandrunning exec ms-flights
    ./node_modules/db-migrate/bin/db-migrate create sample-data --sql-file
[INFO] Created migration at
    /opt/app/migrations/20200602055127-sample-data.js
[INFO] Created migration up sql file at
    /opt/app/migrations/sqls/20200602055127-sample-data-up.sql
[INFO] Created migration down sql file at
    /opt/app/migrations/sqls/20200602055127-sample-data-down.sql
sudo chown -R $USER ./migrations/sqls/
```

After *this*, we should open the corresponding SQL files and insert the content in Examples 9-1, 9-2, and 9-3 into each one of them.

Example 9-1. /migrations/sqls/[date]-seat-maps-up.sql

```
CREATE TABLE `seat_maps` (
  `flight_no` varchar(10) NOT NULL,
  `seat_map` json NOT NULL,
  `origin_code` varchar(10) NOT NULL,
  `destination_code` varchar(10) NOT NULL,
  PRIMARY KEY (`flight_no`)
) ENGINE=InnoDB DEFAULT CHARSET=utf8;
```

Example 9-2. /migrations/sqls/[date]-flights-up.sql

```sql
CREATE TABLE `flights` (
  `flight_id` varchar(36) NOT NULL,
  `flight_no` varchar(10) NOT NULL,
  `flight_date` datetime(0) NULL,

  PRIMARY KEY (`flight_id`),

  FOREIGN KEY(`flight_no`)
      REFERENCES seat_maps(`flight_no`)
) ENGINE=InnoDB DEFAULT CHARSET=utf8;
```

Example 9-3. /migrations/sqls/[date]-sample-data-up.sql

```sql
INSERT INTO `seat_maps`
VALUES ('AA2532', '{\"Cabin\": [{\"Row\": [{\"Seat\": [{\"Number\": \"A\",
        \"Facilities\": [{\"Detail\": {\"content\": \"LegSpaceSeat\"}}],
        \"exitRowInd\": false, \"premiumInd\": false, \"noInfantInd\": false,
        \"restrictedReclineInd\": false}], \"RowNumber\": 8}],
        \"Wing\": {\"lastRow\": 22, \"firstRow\": 14},
        \"Column\": [{\"Column\": \"A\", \"Characteristics\": [\"Window\"]}],
        \"lastRow\": 23, \"firstRow\": 8,
        \"CabinClass\": {\"CabinType\": \"Economy\"}}]}', 'LAX', 'DCA');
```

Once you have these files, you can either just restart the project with make restart so that the migrations will be automatically applied (the new ones get applied at every project start to keep various installations consistent), or you can explicitly run a task to apply migrations with make migrate.

For the rest of the modifications, you will want to:

1. Change ms-nodebootstrap-example to ms-flights in a variety of files, if you didn't install the project with the nodebootstrap utility, and just clone the repository (the former approach does renaming for you).

2. Modify the rest of the source code to implement the flights and seat_maps endpoints and hook them up with the database.

ms-flights Full Source Code

You can see a working version of the sample ms-flights code on this book's GitHub repository (*https://oreil.ly/Microservices_UpandRunning_msflights*).

When everything is working, you should be able to access your /flights endpoint locally at a URL like the following:

```
http://0.0.0.0:5501/flights?flight_no=AA34&departure_date_time=2020-05-17T13:20
```

The `seat_maps` endpoint should appear in a URL:

```
http://0.0.0.0:5501/flights/AA2532/seat_map
```

Be sure to check out all of the makefile targets. Try testing one to get a sense of the user experience provided by the template project and what kind of facilities you should strive to provide to your developers with your templates. For the `make test` to work, additional modifications are required, related to us deleting functionality from the sample project. We aren't covering those changes in detail here, so it's best to just check out this book's /ms-flights repository (*https://oreil.ly/Microservices_UpandRun ning_msflights*), which has every modification required. Feel free to submit bug requests if you run into any problems.

Health Checks

To manage the life cycle of the containers that the app will be deployed into, most container-management solutions (e.g., Kubernetes, which we will use later in this book) need a service to expose a health endpoint. In the case of Kubernetes, you should generally provide liveness and readiness endpoints.

Key Decision: Starting Microservices from Reusable Templates

To implement a health-check endpoint, we are going to use the draft RFC (*https://oreil.ly/nF9T-*) and a Node.js implementation of it (*https://oreil.ly/ZyfBZ*).

The NodeBootstrap template already has a sample implementation (*https://oreil.ly/EzEIi*) for it, we just need to modify it for the ms-flights codebase.

Let's start by replacing lines 13–17 in *appConfig.js* with code like the following:

```
// For Liveness Probe, defaults may be all you need.
const livenessCheck = healthcheck({"path" : "/ping"});
app.use(livenessCheck.express());

// For readiness check, let's also test the DB
const check = healthcheck();
const AdvancedHealthcheckers = require('healthchecks-advanced');
const advCheckers = new AdvancedHealthcheckers();

// Database health check is cached for 10000ms = 10 seconds!
check.addCheck('db', 'dbQuery', advCheckers.dbCheck,
  {minCacheMs: 10000});
app.use(check.express());
```

This will create a simple "Am I live?" check at /ping (known as a *liveness probe* in Kubernetes) and a more advanced "Is the database also ready? Can I actually do useful things?" check (known as the *readiness probe* in Kubernetes) at /health. Using two probes for overall health is very convenient since a microservice being up doesn't always mean that it is fully functional. If its dependency, such as a database, is not up yet or is down, it won't be actually ready for useful work.

The fourth argument {minCacheMs: 10000} in the .addCheck() call sets minimal cache duration on the server side, indicated in milliseconds. This means you can tell the health-check middleware (the module we use) to only run an expensive, database-querying health-check probe against MySQL every 10 seconds (10,000 milliseconds), at most!

Even if your health-probing infrastructure (e.g., Kubernetes) calls your health-check endpoint very frequently, the middleware will only trigger the calls you deemed light enough. For more heavy calls (e.g., database calls like the one to MySQL), the middleware (Maikai module) will serve cached values, avoiding stress on downstream systems like the database. To complete the setup, also edit the *libs/healthchecks-advanced/index.js* file and rename the function to dbCheck. Then update the SQL query so that lines 7–10 read:

```
async dbCheck() {
  const start = new Date();
  const conn = await db.conn();
  const query = 'select count(1) from seat_maps';
```

If everything was done correctly and the microservice is up and running in a healthy way, if you now run curl http://0.0.0.0:5501/health, you should get a health endpoint output that looks like the following:

```
{
  "details": {
    "db:dbQuery": {
      "status": "pass",
      "metricValue": 15,
      "metricUnit": "ms",
      "time": "2020-06-28T22:32:46.167Z"
    }
  },
  "status": "pass"
}
```

If you run curl http://0.0.0.0:5501/ping instead, you should get a simpler output:

```
{ "status": "pass" }
```

If you run into any issues while modifying the code yourself, you can see the full microservice implementation on this book's GitHub repository (*https://oreil.ly/Micro services_UpandRunning_msflights*).

Now that we have a fully functioning ms-flights microservice implemented with Node.js and MySQL, let's switch to the code behind the ms-reservations microservice.

Introducing a Second Microservice to the Project

We are going to implement a second microservice (ms-reservations) in Python and Flask using the Redis data store. Again following the second goal from "10 Workspace Guidelines for a Superior Developer Experience" on page 181, we will use a template GitHub repository (*https://oreil.ly/rjRhK*) for a Python/Flask stack.

As you can see, this template has a lot of the same characteristics as the NodeBootstrap one we just used for ms-flights: it only requires working with Docker and make, has all of the make targets to support a smooth development experience, just like NodeBootstrap, and has a working setup for common tasks such as testing, linting, etc. One thing it lacks, however, is support for database migrations.

Unlike MySQL, Redis doesn't really use database schemas, so there's no burning need to codify various data definitions for "table" creations. You could still use migrations to create test data in various environments, but we will leave that task to the reader to figure out and have fun with. It is one way this template is different from the ones you would see that do use SQL databases.

Just like with ms-flights, we'll start our code modifications by placing the proper OAS we developed earlier in this chapter into the *docs/api.yml* of the new ms-reservations repository. After running `make start` in the *docs* folder (note: this is a separate makefile from the main one!), you should see the API specification for reservations rendered at *http://0.0.0.0:3939*, appearing as shown in Figure 9-5.

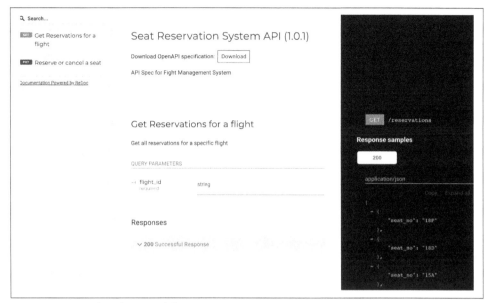

Figure 9-5. Rendered OAS of the ms-reservations microservice

We will start modifying our template microservice by implementing the reservation creation endpoint.

Open *service.py* and replace the mapping for the update_user POST /users endpoint with the one for PUT /reservations, like this:

```
@app.route('/reservations', methods=['PUT'])
def reserve():
    """Endpoint that reserves a seat for a customer"""
    json_body = request.get_json(force=True)
    resp = handlers.reserve(json_body)
    if (resp.get("status") == "success"):
        return jsonify(resp)
    else:
        return Response(
            json.dumps(resp),
            status=403,
            mimetype='application/json'
        )
```

As you can see, based on the result of the reservation, we'll output a success or an error and provide a corresponding HTTP error code.

To fully implement this endpoint, we also need to create a handler for the mapping (usually tasked with error validation, but for brevity we'll skip it) in *src/handlers.py*. We'll do this by replacing the save_user user creation handler with the following:

```
def reserve(json_body):
    """Save reservation callback"""
    return model.save_reservation(json_body)
```

Most importantly, we need to implement the actual save to the database in *src/models.py* by replacing the save_user function with something like the following:

```
def save_reservation(reservation):
    """Saves reservation into Redis database"""

    seat_num = reservation['seat_num']
    try:
        result = this.redis_conn.hsetnx(
            this.tblprefix + reservation['flight_id'],
            seat_num,
            reservation['customer_id'])
    except redis.RedisError:
        response = {
            "error" : f"Unexpected error reserving {seat_num}"
        }
        log.error(f"Unexpected error reserving {seat_num}", exc_info=True)
    else:
        if result == 1:
            response = {
                "status": "success",
            }
        else:
            response = {
                "error" : f"Could not complete reservation for {seat_num}",
                "description" : "Seat already reserved. Cannot double-book"
            }

    return response
```

This code implements the same hsetnx command in Python that we manually executed earlier in the Redis CLI, when we were demonstrating the benefits of using Redis for the data model of the reservations microservice. Redis's hsetnx method only sets the value if one is not already set. This is how we reliably avoid accidental double-booking. When hsetnx is rejected due to an already set key, it returns 0 (as in: "0 records modified"); otherwise it returns 1, letting us know whether a conflict occurred.

You should also declare the table-level prefix for reservations in the module scope by adding the following code around line 19 of *src/models.py*, right after the this = sys.modules[__name__] declaration:

```
this = sys.modules[__name__] # Existing line
this.tblprefix = "flights:" # New line
```

The microservice template we used readily contains all of the code required to grab the relevant credentials and configuration from the environment and connect to a

---

Redis database. This is implemented in accordance with the popular guidance outlined in the manifesto for building better cloud native applications, known as the Twelve-Factor App (*https://12factor.net/config*). Specifically, the template aligns with the third factor of the document, which addresses preferred ways of configuration management. The fact that the template we used already had this best practice fully implemented demonstrates once again the significant benefits of leveraging code templates for microservices development.

Once you make all the required changes, the endpoint should work. You should be able to run make from the top level of the source code, which will build and run the project at 0.0.0.0:7701.

If you encounter issues at any point or would like to check out the application logs for some reason, you can do this using the logs-app make target:

```
↪ make logs-app
docker-compose -p ms-workspace-demo logs -f ms-template-microservice
Attaching to ms-template-microservice
ms-template-microservice    | [INFO] Starting gunicorn 20.0.4
ms-template-microservice    | [INFO] Listening at: http://0.0.0.0:5000 (1)
ms-template-microservice    | [INFO] Using worker: sync
ms-template-microservice    | [INFO] Booting worker with pid: 15
```

You may notice that the logs say the service is running on port 5000, but that is true inside the Docker container; it's not port 5000 on the host machine! We map the standard Flask port 5000 to 7701 on the host machine (your machine). You can view the combined app and database logs by running make logs, or just the database logs by running make logs-db.

Now let's run several curl commands to insert a couple of reservations:

```
curl --header "Content-Type: application/json" \
  --request PUT \
  --data '{"seat_num":"12B","flight_id":"werty", "customer_id": "dfgh"}' \
  http://0.0.0.0:7701/reservations

curl --header "Content-Type: application/json" \
  --request PUT \
  --data '{"seat_num":"12C","flight_id":"werty", "customer_id": "jkfl"}' \
  http://0.0.0.0:7701/reservations
```

We can also test that our protection against accidental double-bookings works. Let's verify this by attempting to reserve an already reserved seat (e.g., 12C):

```
curl -v --header "Content-Type: application/json" \
  --request PUT \
  --data '{"seat_num":"12C","flight_id":"werty", "customer_id": "another"}' \
  http://0.0.0.0:7701/reservations
```

It will respond with HTTP 403 and an error message:

```
→ curl -v --header "Content-Type: application/json" \
>    --request PUT \
>    --data '{"seat_num":"12C","flight_id":"werty", "customer_id": "another"}' \
>    http://0.0.0.0:7701/reservations
*    Trying 0.0.0.0:7701...
* TCP_NODELAY set
* Connected to 0.0.0.0 (127.0.0.1) port 7701 (#0)
> PUT /reservations HTTP/1.1
> Host: 0.0.0.0:7701
> User-Agent: curl/7.68.0
> Accept: */*
> Content-Type: application/json
> Content-Length: 64
>
< HTTP/1.1 403 FORBIDDEN
< Server: gunicorn/20.0.4
< Connection: close
< Content-Type: application/json
< Content-Length: 111
<
* Closing connection 0
{"error": "Could not complete reservation for 12C",
"description": "Seat already reserved. Cannot double-book"}
```

Perfect!

Since we now have some data in the Redis store, we can proceed to implementing the reservation retrieval endpoint as well. Again, we will start with the mapping definition in *service.py*, replacing the default /hello/<name> greeter endpoint with the following:

```python
@app.route('/reservations', methods=['GET'])
def reservations():
    """ Get Reservations Endpoint"""
    flight_id = request.args.get('flight_id')
    resp = handlers.get_reservations(flight_id)
    return jsonify(resp)
```

The implementation of the handler in *src/handlers.py* will again be simple since we are skipping input validation, for the sake of brevity:

```python
def get_reservations(flight_id):
    """Get reservations callback"""
    return model.get_reservations(flight_id)
```

The model code will look like the following:

```python
def get_reservations (flight_id):
    """List of reservations for a flight, from Redis database"""
    try:
        key = this.tblprefix + flight_id
        reservations = this.redis_conn.hgetall(key)
    except redis.RedisError:
```

```
        response = {
            "error" : "Cannot retrieve reservations"
        }
        log.error("Error retrieving reservations from Redis",
            exc_info=True)
    else:
        response = reservations

    return response
```

To test this endpoint, we can issue a curl command and verify that we receive the expected JSON response:

```
→ curl -v  http://0.0.0.0:7701/reservations?flight_id=werty
*   Trying 0.0.0.0:7701...
* TCP_NODELAY set
> GET /reservations?flight_id=werty HTTP/1.1
> Host: 0.0.0.0:7701
> Accept: */*
>
< HTTP/1.1 200 OK
< Server: gunicorn/20.0.4
< Connection: close
< Content-Type: application/json
< Content-Length: 90
<
{
  "12B": "dfgh",
  "12C": "jkfl",
}
* Closing connection 0
```

ms-reservations Full Source Code

You can see a working version of the sample ms-reservations code on this book's GitHub site (*https://oreil.ly/Microservices_UpandRunning_msreservations*).

Please take a look and try to use various make targets available in the repository to get a better feel for what you get from the template this code was bootstrapped from.

You should also use this opportunity to take a break and pat yourself on the back— you just created and executed two perfectly sized, impeccably implemented, and beautifully separate-stack microservices! Hooray!

Now what we need to do is figure out a way to execute these two microservices (and any additional future components you may create) as a single unit. For this, we will introduce the notion of an "umbrella project" and explain how to develop one.

Hooking Services Up with an Umbrella Project

Developing individual microservices is how teams should be spending most of their time. It's essential for providing team autonomy, which leads to the ever-important coordination minimizations, and most of our system design work in the microservices style should indeed target the minimization of coordination needs. That said, at some point we do need to try the entire project—all microservices working together. Even if this need is relatively rare, it is very important to make doing so easy, which is why principle four of the "10 Workspace Guidelines for a Superior Developer Experience" on page 181 states: "Running a single microservice and/or a subsystem of several ones should be equally easy."

We need an easy-to-use *umbrella project*, one that can launch all of our microservice-specific subprojects in one simple command and make them all work together nicely, until such time as we decided to shut down the umbrella project with all of its components. This obviously should also be very easy to do. Everything we want our developers to do without mistakes should be easy!

To deploy an easy-to-use umbrella project, we'll use the microservices workspace template available at this GitHub site (*https://oreil.ly/VpyDJ*) and start a workspace for us at this book's GitHub repository (*https://oreil.ly/Microservices_UpandRunning_workspace*) instead.

Key Decision: Use Faux Git Submodules

To check out repositories of individual microservices under the umbrella repository, we use the open source project Faux Git Submodules (*https://oreil.ly/ic_c0*). The idea is to make it easy to descend into a subfolder of your workspace repository containing a microservice and treat it as a fully functioning repository, which you can update, commit code in, and push to. The basic intent is identical to that of regular Git submodules, except anyone who has used them knows that the actual submodules can behave unpredictably and tend to be major pains in the neck. Faux submodules, in our opinion, are much simpler and work more predictably.

We'll start by indicating the two repos we've just created as the components of the new workspace, by editing the *fgs.json* file to look something like the following:

```
{
  "ms-flights" : {
    "url"  : "https://github.com/implementing-microservices/ms-flights"
  },

  "ms-reservations" : {
    "url" : "https://github.com/implementing-microservices/ms-reservations"
```

```
    }
}
```

In the last configuration we indicated ms-flights and ms-reservations using the read-only "http://" protocol. This was done so that you can follow the example. In real projects, you would want to pull your repositories with the read/write "git://" protocol so you can modify them.

Now that we have configured *repos.json*, let's pull the ms-flights and ms-reservations microservices into the workspace:

```
→ make update
git clone -b master \
  https://github.com/implementing-microservices/ms-flights ms-flights
Cloning into 'ms-flights'...

git clone -b master \
  https://github.com/implementing-microservices/ms-reservations ms-reservations
Cloning into 'ms-reservations'...
```

 This operation also helpfully adds the checked-out repositories to the *.gitignore* of the parent folder, to prevent the parent repository trying to double-commit them into the wrong place.

We also need to edit the *bin/start.sh* and *bin/stop.sh* scripts to make changes from the default. We'll edit *bin/start.sh* as shown in Example 9-4.

Example 9-4. bin/start.sh

```
#!/usr/bin/env bash
set -eu

export COMPOSE_PROJECT_NAME=msupandrunning

pushd ms-flights && make start
popd
pushd ms-reservations && make start
popd

make proxystarts
```

Edit *.bin/stop.sh* as in Example 9-5.

Example 9-5. bin/stop.sh

```
#!/usr/bin/env bash
set -eu
```

```
export COMPOSE_PROJECT_NAME=msupandrunning

pushd ms-flights && make stop
popd

pushd ms-reservations && make stop
popd

make proxystop
```

To keep things simple yet powerfully automated, our workspace setup is using the Traefik edge router (*https://oreil.ly/I-ddh*) for seamless routing to the microservices. It gets installed by our *docker-compose.yml* file (*https://oreil.ly/vBvwS*). Also, we will need to add Traefik-related labels to the *docker-compose.yml* files of both microservices to ensure proper routing of those services, as shown in Examples 9-6 and 9-7.

Example 9-6. ms-flights/docker-compose.yaml

```
services:
  ms-flights:
    container_name: ms-flights
    labels:
      - "traefik.enable=true"
      - "traefik.http.routers.ms-flights.rule=PathPrefix(`/reservations`)"
```

Example 9-7. ms-reservations/docker-compose.yaml

```
services:
  ms-reservations:
    container_name: ms-reservations
    labels:
      - "traefik.enable=true"
      - "traefik.http.routers.ms-reservations.rule=PathPrefix(`/reservations`)"
```

We also need to update the umbrella project's name (which serves as the namespace and network name for all services) in the workspace's makefile, so that instead of `project:=ms-workspace-demo`, it says:

```
project:=msupandrunning
```

Once you bring up the workspace by running `make start` at the workspace level, you will be able to access both microservices in their attached-to-workspace form. We mounted Traefik to local port 9080, making *http://0.0.0.0:9080/* our base URI. Therefore, the following two commands are querying the reservations and flights systems:

```
> curl http://0.0.0.0:9080/reservations?flight_id=qwerty
> curl \
```

```
http://0.0.0.0:9080/flights?\
flight_no=AA34&departure_date_time=2020-05-17T13:20
```

You can see the full source of the umbrella project at this book's GitHub site (*https://oreil.ly/Microservices_UpandRunning_workspace*).

Summary

In this chapter we brought together a lot of system design and code implementation guidance that we had been teasing out to provide an end-to-end implementation of a couple of powerful microservices, together with an umbrella workspace that allows us to work on these services either individually or as a unified project. We did this through a step-by-step implementation of the powerful SEED(S) methodology and the design of individual data models, and learned how to quickly jump-start code implementations from robust template projects.

The ability to put together well-modularized components quickly and efficiently can make a material difference in your ability to execute microservice projects successfully. There's a big difference between what you were able to achieve in this chapter, and somebody spending weeks figuring out the basic boilerplate or going down the rabbit hole of wrong decisions. This difference can be that of the success or failure of the entire initiative.

## CHAPTER 10

Releasing Microservices

We're getting to an exciting part of our microservices build—the point where we actually bring everything together. So far, we've built an operating model, a microservice design, an infrastructure foundation, and two working microservices. Now, we'll take all those pieces and put them together in a single implementation.

We'll be covering a lot of ground in this chapter. We'll build a new infrastructure environment called *staging*. Next, we'll augment our code repository with a container delivery process. With a container ready to go, we'll implement a deployment process using the Argo CD GitOps tool. When we're done, we'll have an architecture that looks like Figure 10-1.

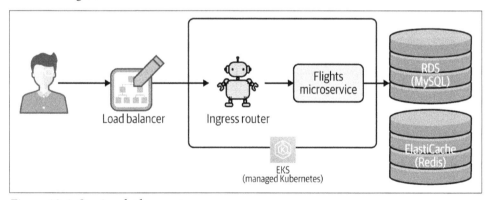

Figure 10-1. Staging deployment

 Because of the scope of what we need to cover, we'll only deploy the flight information microservice. However, you can use all the mechanisms we describe here to deploy the reservations service as well.

To make all this work, we'll be using three different GitHub repositories with their own pipelines and assets (as shown in Figure 10-2). One of the reasons we've done it this way is that it matches up well with the operating model we defined in Chapter 2 and gives each of our teams their own responsibilities and domains to work in.

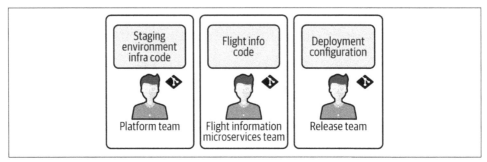

Figure 10-2. Three code repositories for deployment

There's a lot to cover, so let's dive in with our first step: provisioning the AWS-based staging environment.

Setting Up the Staging Environment

Up until now, we've been deploying microservices into a local developer environment. Now we'll take the same services we've built and tested locally and deploy them into an AWS-based cloud infrastructure. In this section, we'll build the staging infrastructure using the process shown in Figure 10-3.

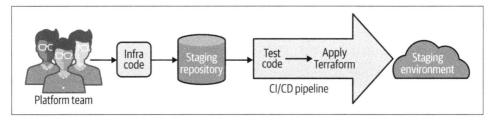

Figure 10-3. Building a staging environment

We started this work when we built the sandbox environment in Chapter 7. Now, we'll need to update that infrastructure code to reflect the needs of the flight information and flight reservation microservices. We'll be adding three new components to our Terraform code to support our microservices:

- An ingress controller and edge router that sends requests to microservices in Kubernetes
- An AWS-based MySQL database instance for the flights microservice's data

- An AWS-based Redis database instance for the reservations microservice's data

This kind of nontrivial change could be risky. But this is where our immutable infrastructure and infrastructure as code (IaC) approach really starts to pay off! We know exactly what our current environment build looks like, because all of it is in our Terraform code. All we need to do now is create modules for each of these new components, update an environment definition, and run the build through our CI/CD pipeline.

In Chapter 7, we walked through the process of writing each Terraform module together. But since we've already covered that in detail, this time we'll use code and configuration assets that we've already written for you. You'll just need to customize them a bit to fit your needs.

Let's start by taking a quick tour of the new modules we'll be using to provision our new components, starting with the ingress gateway module.

The Ingress Module

In Chapter 9, we used an edge router called Traefik to route messages to our container-based microservices. We're going to implement a similar architecture in our AWS-based infrastructure. There are plenty of tools available to perform ingress routing. For example, many practitioners use the Nginx ingress controller (*https://oreil.ly/QyHmJ*). Traefik is also a fine choice: since we've already started using it in the development stage, we'll make the decision to implement it as our controller in the AWS environment as well.

Key Decision: Implement a Traefik Ingress Controller

We'll use Traefik to route messages from the load balancer to microservices deployed in Kubernetes.

To save time, we've already written a Terraform module that will install the Traefik ingress controller into the environment. We'll be able to use this module in our Terraform environment code, in the same manner as the network, EKS, and Argo CD modules we used in Chapter 6. The code for the Traefik module is available at this GitHub site (*https://oreil.ly/8YXIW*).

We won't have time to implement a "backend for frontend" (BFF) API as part of our example build. But the ingress we're setting up lends itself well to being extended for that purpose in the future. For example, you can provision an AWS API Gateway (*https://oreil.ly/KATjx*) in front of the ingress controller to compose services into a single API. In fact, we've implemented Traefik using an AWS Network Load Balancer, which makes that kind of connectivity easier to implement.

We'll get a chance to use this ingress module in "Forking the Staging Infrastructure Project" on page 234 when we build the staging environment. For now, let's see how we'll support our database needs.

The Database Module

Each of our microservices use different databases, so we'll need to provision two different databases in the infrastructure environment. We'll need both a MySQL and a Redis database to support the needs of our microservices teams. For our build, we've decided to use AWS managed versions of these database products. That way, our platform team can offer two databases in an *x*-as-a-service manner to the microservices teams that need them.

Key Decision: Use Shared and Managed Database Services

The platform team will create Terraform-based modules to provision AWS hosted and managed database services for each environment.

In our database module, we'll use the AWS ElastiCache service to provision a Redis data store and the AWS Relational Database (RDS) to provision a MySQL instance. We've already written a module that does this, which you can find in this book's Git-Hub repository (*https://oreil.ly/Microservices_UpandRunning_mod_awsdb*). The module provisions both types of databases as well as the network configuration and access policies that the database service needs for operation.

When the module is applied to the staging environment, we'll have both a Redis and a MySQL database instance running and ready for use. All that's left now is to use our modules in a Terraform code file and provision an environment. That's what we'll cover in the next section.

Forking the Staging Infrastructure Project

The staging environment we need for releasing our microservices will be very similar to the sandbox environment we created in Chapter 7. We'll continue to use the same methods and principles we applied earlier. We'll use Terraform to define the environment in code and we'll use the modules we wrote for the network, Kubernetes cluster, and Argo CD. We'll complement those modules with the new database and ingress controller modules we've just described. Finally, we'll use a GitHub Actions pipeline to provision the environment, just like we did for our sandbox environment.

We explained how to create a GitHub Actions pipeline in Chapter 6, and walked through the process of writing and using Terraform code in Chapter 7. So there's no need to do all of that again. Instead, we'll use a staging environment skeleton project that we've already created for you (see Figure 10-4). We'll need to make a few small changes to the code so that it will work in your AWS environment. To do that, we'll fork the repository so you can have your own copy that you can change as you like.

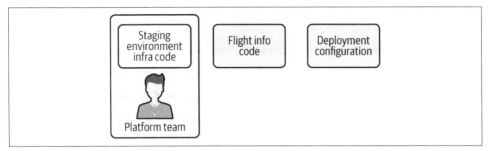

Figure 10-4. Starting with the staging environment repository

In GitHub, a *fork* lets you make a copy of someone else's code project in your own account. To fork the staging environment repository, follow these steps:

1. Open your browser and sign in to your GitHub account.

2. Navigate to this book's GitHub repository (*https://oreil.ly/Microservices_Upan dRunning_infrastaging_env*).

3. Click the Fork button in the top-right corner of the screen.

 You may want to duplicate this repository instead of forking it. This will allow you to change the access mode of the repository to private instead of public. Instructions on duplicating a GitHub repository are available in the GitHub documentation on the topic (*https://oreil.ly/HbZMN*).

Once the operation is complete you'll have your own forked copy of `infra-staging-env`. But it's not yet configured to use your AWS account or resources. The first thing we'll need to update is the GitHub Actions workflow.

Configuring the Staging Workflow

The forked CI/CD workflow we've just created won't be able to access your AWS account without credentials. So we'll need to add AWS access management credentials and a MySQL password to the repository's secrets. You should have your AWS operator account credentials from the pipeline setup work we did in Chapter 6. If you don't have those keys anymore, you can open the AWS management console in a browser and create a new set of credentials for your operations user.

When you have your credentials in hand, navigate to the Settings pane of your forked GitHub repository and choose Secrets from the lefthand navigation menu. Add the secrets in Table 10-1 by clicking the New secret button.

Table 10-1. Infrastructure secrets

Key	Value
AWS_ACCESS_KEY_ID	The access key ID for your AWS operator user
AWS_SECRET_ACCESS_KEY	The secret key for your operator user
MYSQL_PASSWORD	microservices

Make sure you type these key names exactly as described in Table 10-1. If you don't, the pipeline won't be able to access your AWS instance and create resources. Use the value microservices for the MYSQL_PASSWORD secret. This password will be used when we provision the AWS RDS database.

When we forked the infra-staging-env repository, GitHub made a copy of the Actions workflow that defines the CI/CD pipeline. But, for security reasons, GitHub doesn't automatically enable the GitHub Actions feature when you fork a repository (see Figure 10-5). So, you'll need to get it running by doing the following:

- Click the Actions tab in the management console for your forked repository.
- If challenged, instruct GitHub to enable the workflow that we've forked.

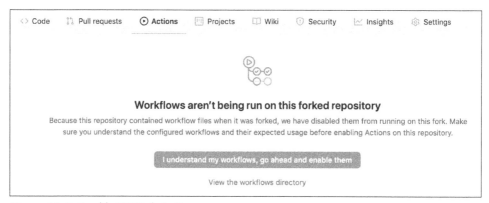

Figure 10-5. Enable GitHub Actions

 GitHub changes its user experience quite often, so the specific steps and screens you encounter might be different.

Our forked infrastructure pipeline is now activated and ready to be triggered. Now we just need to make a few adjustments to the Terraform code that creates the staging environment.

> The staging workflow we've built for you will automatically generate a *kubeconfig* file as part of the provisioning process. This file contains connection information so you can connect to the Kubernetes cluster that we'll create on EKS. Since this code repository is public, that file will be available to anyone who visits your repository. In theory, this shouldn't be a problem. Our EKS cluster requires AWS credentials to authenticate and connect. That means even with the *kubeconfig* file an attacker shouldn't be able to connect to your cluster, unless they also have your AWS credentials.

Editing the Staging Infrastructure Code

The Terraform code that we've written for you will provision a staging environment. But, it won't work properly until we set some local variable values that will be specific to your AWS account and environment. To do that, we'll work on the files in your local environment. Also, you'll need to create a clone of your forked infra-staging-env repository. We'll leave it to you to do that.

> If you aren't sure how to clone your repository, follow the instructions for your OS in the GitHub documentation (*https://oreil.ly/ hvEWn*).

We'll be editing the *main.tf* file that defines the staging environment. You'll need to change the values of a few local variables that we've defined in Table 10-2.

Table 10-2. Staging environment values in main.tf

Resource	Property name	Description
terraform	bucket	The name of the S3 bucket for your Terraform backend
terraform	key	The identifier to use for your backend data in S3
terraform	region	Your AWS region
locals	aws_region	Your AWS region

> These values will be identical to the configuration we created in Chapter 7, so if you have that code handy, you can copy and paste from there.

To make these changes, edit *main.tf* in your favorite text editor and update it with the appropriate values. All the values you need to replace are in the terraform and locals sections, at the top of the file. You can also use this step to review the Terraform file and learn more about what it does. When you're done, the top of your file should look similar to Example 10-1.

Example 10-1. An updated main.tf for the staging environment

```
terraform {
backend "s3" {
  bucket = "rm-terraform-backend"
  key = "terraform-env"
  region = "eu-west-2"
  }
}

locals {
  env_name = "staging"
  aws_region = "eu-west-2"
  k8s_cluster_name = "ms-cluster"
}
```

Our staging Terraform code is now ready to be applied. But it won't work if we try to use it. That's because our AWS operator account doesn't have the right privileges. We've added some new database modules, but the operator account we're using isn't allowed to create or work with those AWS resources. If we tried to run our Terraform right now, we'd get access errors from AWS.

To solve that problem, we'll need to give our AWS operator a few more permissions. We'll do this by creating a new IAM group for database work. When the group is set up, we'll add our operator account to the group so it inherits those permissions.

Run the following AWS CLI command to create a new group called DB-Ops:

```
$ aws iam create-group --group-name DB-Ops
```

Next, we can run the following command to attach access policies for RDS and ElastiCache to the group:

```
$ aws iam attach-group-policy --group-name DB-Ops\
  --policy-arn arn:aws:iam::aws:policy/AmazonRDSFullAccess &&\
aws iam attach-group-policy --group-name DB-Ops\
  --policy-arn arn:aws:iam::aws:policy/AmazonElastiCacheFullAccess
```

Finally, use a CLI command to add our Ops account to the group we've just created:

```
$ aws iam add-user-to-group --user-name ops-account --group-name DB-Ops
```

With those permissions set, we're just about ready to go. But before we commit, let's do a quick test to make sure our updated infrastructure code works. Run the following Terraform commands to format and validate our updated code:

```
infra-staging-env$ terraform fmt
[...]
infra-staging-env$ terraform init
[...]
infra-staging-env$ terraform validate
[...]
infra-staging-env$ terraform plan
[...]
```

Now we're ready to commit the infrastructure code and kick off the CI/CD pipeline. Let's start by committing our updated Terraform code to your forked repository:

```
$ git add .
$ git commit -m "Staging environment with databases"
$ git push origin
```

If you recall in Chapter 6, our workflow gets triggered when we push a release tag that starts with a v. Use the following Git commands to create a new v1.0 tag and push it to your forked repository:

```
$ git tag -a v1.0 -m "Initial staging environment build"
$ git push origin v1.0
```

With that, your staging provisioning process should be kicked off. You can validate the status of your pipeline run in the browser-based GitHub console. If the pipeline job has succeeded, you now have a staging environment with a Kubernetes cluster and MySQL and Redis databases running and ready to use. We'll need that Kubernetes cluster for our microservices deployment. So our next step will be to validate that it is up and running.

Testing access to the Kubernetes cluster

In order to communicate with the staging Kubernetes cluster we'll need the configuration details for the kubectl application. To get those details we'll use the same process we used in "Testing the Environment" on page 175—we'll download a configuration file and update our local environment settings.

Make sure the CI/CD pipeline has completed successfully before trying to connect to the Kubernetes cluster.

Set up your Kubernetes client environment by downloading the *kubeconfig* file that our GitHub Actions staging pipeline generated. Then set the KUBECONFIG environment variable to point to the configuration that you've just downloaded:

```
$ export KUBECONFIG=~/Downloads/kubeconfig
```

When the environment is set up, run kubectl get svc --all-namespaces to confirm that our staging cluster is running and the Kubernetes objects have been deployed. You should see a result that looks similar to Example 10-2.

Example 10-2. get svc result

```
$ kubectl get svc --all-namespaces
NAMESPACE    NAME                                        TYPE          CLUSTER-IP
argocd       msur-argocd-application-controller ClusterIP    172.20.133.240
argocd       msur-argocd-dex-server                      ClusterIP     172.20.74.68
default      ms-ingress-nginx-ingress                    LoadBalancer 172.20.239.114
[... lots more services ...]
```

In the result you should see a list of all the Kubernetes services that we've deployed. That should include services for the Argo CD application and the Nginx ingress service. That means that our cluster is up and running and the services we need have been successfully provisioned.

Create a Kubernetes secret

The last step we need to take care of is setting up a Kubernetes *secret*. When our flight information microservices connects to MySQL, it will need a password. To avoid storing that password in plain text, we're going to store it in a special Kubernetes object that keeps it hidden from unauthorized viewers.

Run the following command to create and populate the Kubernetes secret for the MySQL password:

```
$ kubectl create secret generic \
mysql --from-literal=password=microservices -n microservices
```

 The built-in secrets functions of Kubernetes are useful, but we recommend that you use something more feature rich for a proper implementation. There are lots of options available in this area, including HashiCorp Vault (*https://oreil.ly/YeiHQ*).

We now have a staging environment with an infrastructure that fits the needs of the microservices we've developed. The next step will be to publish those microservices as containers so that we can deploy them into the environment.

Shipping the Flight Information Container

In Chapter 9, we used make to test, build, and run microservices locally in a development environment. But in order to build and deploy our services into testing, staging, and beyond, we'll want a more repeatable and automated process.

 We've already built a containerized version of the flights microservice (*https://oreil.ly/7LHnY*) for you to use. So, if you aren't interested in building a Docker Hub deployment workflow yourself, you can skip ahead to "Deploying the Flights Service Container" on page 246.

Using automation and DevOps techniques to build our services improves the predictability, quality, and speed of our microservice deployments. This is the same principle we applied to our infrastructure build. In this section, we'll build a continuous integration and continuous delivery (CI/CD) pipeline to build and publish the flights microservice to a container registry, as in Figure 10-6.

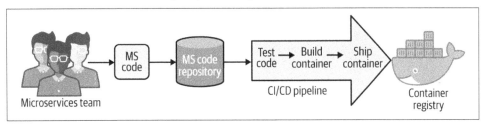

Figure 10-6. Microservices CI/CD

Let's start by taking a look at Docker Hub, the container registry we'll be using to host microservice containers.

Introducing Docker Hub

In Chapter 9, our make-based build process used both docker-compose and docker to produce containers for testing and release. In order to get those containers into our staging environment, we'll need a way to move them, or *ship* them over. Containers are a lot like binary applications, so we could just upload them into the filesystem of the target environment. But this would get messy when the number of containers we need to manage grows.

Instead, we'll ship our containers into a *container registry*. A registry is a software system that stores containers. A good registry keeps containers safe, and makes them easy to discover and to update and change. Docker even defines an API (*https://oreil.ly/sLI3B*) for registry operations and the Docker engine has built-in support for using it.

There are plenty of registry hosting options available that support the Docker registry API. All the major cloud providers can host a secure, private registry for you. You can also host your own registry server using Docker's open source implementation. For this book, we'll use Docker's publicly hosted registry called Docker Hub. We've chosen Docker Hub because it's free to use, it's popular, and it has good integration options with GitHub Actions.

Key Decision: Use Docker Hub as a Container Registry

We'll be shipping our microservice container into a Docker Hub container registry.

Configuring Docker Hub

Setting up a new Docker Hub registry is pretty easy. All you'll need to do is log in to Docker Hub and create one. You can create a repository for our flight application example by following these steps:

1. Go to the Docker Hub home page (*https://hub.docker.com*) in your browser.

2. Log in to Docker Hub.

3. Click the Create Repository button.

4. Give the repository the name "flights."

5. Click the Create button.

In order to use Docker Hub, you'll need to have a Docker account. If you installed Docker when you set up your developer environment, you'll have a Docker ID already. If you don't have an ID yet, visit *https://hub.docker.com* and create one.

If you run into problems during this process, visit the Docker documentation site (*https://oreil.ly/owCnP*). With a Docker account and a container repository, we're ready to build and push containers into it with a CI/CD pipeline.

Configuring the Pipeline

So far, we've been using GitHub Actions as our pipeline tool for all of our IaC-based provisioning work. It does the job well enough for our needs, so for the sake of consistency we'll use Actions again as the pipeline for our microservices container builds. As an added bonus, we'll be able to take advantage of actions that Docker has published that will make our workflow easier to integrate with Docker Hub.

In Chapter 9, we walked through the process of creating a flight information microservice. If you followed along with those steps, you should have a GitHub repository that contains the code and makefiles (see Figure 10-7). We'll create our GitHub Actions workflow inside the repository so that our CI pipeline can live right alongside the code. If you don't have your own flights service repository yet, you can create a fork of this book's example repository (*https://oreil.ly/Microservices_UpandRunning_msflights*).

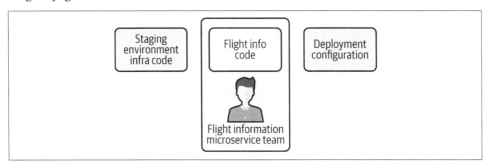

Figure 10-7. Build a container in the flight service repository

Just as we've done before, we'll start our pipeline configuration by adding credentials to the GitHub repository.

Configuring Docker Hub secrets

Our workflow will need to communicate with Docker Hub in order to publish a container. So we'll need to add our Docker Hub access information as secrets in the flights GitHub repository. Specifically, we'll need to create and populate two secret keys as defined in Table 10-3. These credentials are the same ones you would have used to log in to Docker Hub.

Table 10-3. GitHub secrets for Docker Hub

Key	Description
DOCKER_USERNAME	Your Docker account identity
DOCKER_PASSWORD	Your Docker account password

We've gone through the details of setting up secrets a few times already, but just as a reminder, you'll need to do the following:

1. Using your browser, navigate to the settings page of your forked ms-flights repository in GitHub.

2. Select Secrets from the side navigation.

3. Add the secret you want to define by clicking New Secret.

You may have noticed that we aren't adding any AWS account secrets to this repository. That's because we won't be deploying into an AWS instance in this pipeline. This workflow will only focus on pushing containers into the Docker Hub registry—not the deployment of the containers into our staging environment.

This is a useful separation to create because we want our microservice containers to be portable and environment agnostic (this means we won't add any environment-specific logic or values into the build). Using the same built container in all our test and release environments should improve the reliability of our system overall.

All we need to do now is create the workflow that does the work of building, testing, and shipping the container.

Shipping the flight service container

If you've forked the ms-flights repository, you'll find that we've already written a Git-Hub Actions workflow for you that builds and ships the container. All you need to do to is enable the workflow by navigating to the Actions tab in your forked repository, where you'll be prompted to enable the workflow. If you've built your own ms-flights repository, you can copy the workflow code (*https://oreil.ly/Microservices_UpandRunning_mainyaml*) into your own workflows directory.

The GitHub Actions workflow we've defined is triggered by a release tag, and has the following steps:

1. Runs unit tests on the code

2. Builds a containerized version of the microservices

3. Pushes the container to the Docker Hub registry

We've already added Docker Hub credentials to the repository, so the workflow is ready to run. All we'll need to do is push a tag called `v1.0` into the release to trigger the CI/CD workflow. We've done this a few times before using the command line and a local copy of the repository. But to save time we'll trigger this build using the Git-Hub browser-based UI.

In your browser, navigate to the Code tab of your forked ms-flights GitHub repository. On the righthand side of the screen, click the "Create a new release" link in the Releases section, as shown in Figure 10-8.

Figure 10-8. Create a new release

Next, enter the value v1.0 in the tag version field, as shown in Figure 10-9. Then click the Publish Release button at the bottom of the screen.

Figure 10-9. Setting the tag version

Publishing a GitHub release with a tag of v1.0 is the same as pushing the tag with the Git CLI. The end result should be that our GitHub Actions workflow will have kicked off. You can navigate to the Actions tab in your repository and verify that a workflow named CICD has started. It will take a few minutes to run the makefile and package up the container. When it's done, the flights service container will be pushed and ready to use in the Docker Hub registry.

To validate that the container has been shipped, access your Docker Hub account in the browser and take a look at your repositories. You should see an entry for the flights container that was just pushed. It will look something like Figure 10-10.

Figure 10-10. ms-flights container pushed

We now have a containerized ms-flights microservice ready to be deployed into our staging environment. With our microservices pushed into the container registry, we can move on to the work of deploying the container into our staging environment.

Deploying the Flights Service Container

We now have all the pieces in place to deploy the flights microservice. We've provisioned a test environment using our infrastructure pipeline and we've created a deployable containerized image for the service. To complete our deployment work, we'll use the Argo CD GitOps deployment tool we installed in our infrastructure stack in Chapter 7. When we're finished with this section we'll have a running version of the flight information microservice deployed and ready for use.

To make repeatable deployment easier, we'll be creating a new deployment repository that will contain Helm packages. We first introduced Helm in "Setting Up Argo CD" on page 171, when we were building our first environment. The Helm packages we build will describe how a microservice should be deployed. When they're ready and pushed into the deployment repository, Argo CD will use them to deploy containers into the staging environment (Figure 10-11).

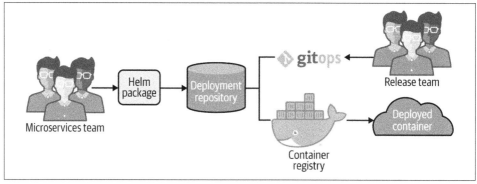

Figure 10-11. The Helm package will define the service deployment

All of this deployment work will happen within the world of Kubernetes, so let's get a basic understanding of what that means.

Understanding Kubernetes Deployments

In Chapter 7, we introduced and installed Kubernetes to help with operating and running container-based microservices. Kubernetes is popular because it handles a lot of the work that needs to be done to start containers, check on their health, find services, replicate them, and start them again when they fail. This gives our system the resilience and self-healing qualities that will help us meet our guiding principles.

But a Kubernetes cluster still needs to be told what to do. It can't deploy your microservices without knowing where to find the container image. It can't check on the health of a microservice without knowing which API to call. We also need to provide Kubernetes with some limits for the number of container instances we want it to create and how those services should be accessed over the network.

Kubernetes sees the world as a set of declarative configuration objects. To configure a microservices deployment, you will need to describe the optimal state for a running version of your container. Provided that you have described your running configuration correctly, Kubernetes will do the work behind the scenes to bring your service to life—and keep it that way.

This declarative approach is similar to the way we used Terraform to describe our infrastructure resources. In Kubernetes, we'll define a set of special deployment objects using the YAML format. The truth is that Kubernetes is incredibly complicated, so we won't be able to go into a lot of detail in this book. But it's helpful to cover a few of the core objects so that we can understand how our microservices will be deployed.

Understanding Kubernetes objects and controllers

There are many objects to learn about if you want to properly understand how to run a Kubernetes platform. But for our purposes, we'll just need a surface-level understanding of five key objects in order to create a simple deployment package for our flights microservice: Pods, ReplicaSets, Deployments, Services, and Ingress.

Pod
> A Pod is an object that describes a basic workload unit. It defines one or more Docker containers that need to be started and managed together.

ReplicaSet
> ReplicaSets let Kubernetes know how many instances of a specific Pod it should start up and run at the same time. You usually won't need to work with Replica Sets directly.

Deployment

> The Deployment controller declares a desired state for a Pod and associated Repli caSets. This is the main object you need to work with to create a Kubernetes Deployment.

Service

> A Service defines how applications in the Kubernetes cluster can access this Pod over the network—even when there are multiple replicas running at the same time. The Service object lets you define a single IP and port for accessing a group of replicated Pods. You'll almost always want to define a service for a microservice deployment.

Ingress

> The Ingress object allows you to identify an ingress route to your Service for applications outside the cluster. The Ingress declaration can include routing rules so that an ingress controller can route messages to the right Services.

In order to deploy our microservice, we'll need to write declarative configurations for the Ingress, Service, and Deployment objects. Although we won't be writing configurations for Pods and ReplicaSets as files in their own right, we'll be including their details in the Deployment object configuration. As we mentioned earlier, we'll be using Helm to package all of these files up.

Creating a Helm Chart

A Kubernetes Deployment can require a lot of communication with the cluster. You need to make multiple calls to the Kubernetes API, letting it know how, when, and where you want to deploy your containers. To help manage some of that complexity, we'll use the Helm packaging tool.

Helm is a package manager for Kubernetes. It gives us an easier way to manage the installation and deployment of application into a Kubernetes cluster. We used Helm earlier in the book to install off-the-shelf packages like Argo CD. Now we'll write our own Helm package so we can install our microservices just as easily.

To use Helm, we'll first need to understand the three important concepts of charts, templates, and values:

Charts

> A chart is a bundle of files that describe a Kubernetes resource or deployment. The chart is the core unit of deployment in Helm. We used pre-made charts earlier in the book when we deployed Kubernetes-based applications like Argo CD.

Templates

Templates are files in a chart that describe a specific Kubernetes resource. They're called templates because they contain special instructions that Helm uses to replace values in the file. For example, you can create a `Service` template for a microservice and make the port number of the `Service` a templated value.

Values

Every chart has a values file that defines the values that should be used to populate a template. Value files are a useful way of managing the differences between environments. Values can also be overridden when the Helm chart is installed.

To create a flights Helm package, we'll need to create a Helm chart. Within that chart, we'll define a set of template files that declare how the flights service should be deployed. Our template will have some parameterized values that will make it usable for different types of environments. Finally we'll create a values file for the staging environment that populates our templates.

As we described in "Deploying the Flights Service Container" on page 246, we want our Helm charts to be available for Argo CD to retrieve and use. So the first thing we'll need to do is create a microservices deployment repository to store and manage them.

Creating the Microservices Deployment Repository

We'll be keeping our Helm charts in a single "monorepo" of microservice deployments. This fits well with our operating model and allows the release team to manage the actual release of services in a holistic fashion. The microservices teams can still own their own Helm deployment charts and deploy into the deployment repository independently (see Figure 10-12).

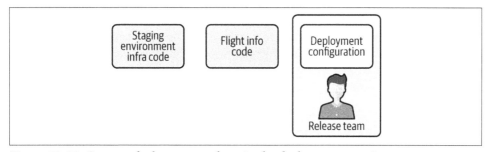

Figure 10-12. Create a deployment package in the deployment repository

To get started, create a new GitHub repository called ms-deploy. Once it's ready, create a local clone of the repository in your development environment. We've done this a few times already, so we won't go through all the details again. If you need help remembering the process for repository creation, the GitHub Quickstart documentation (*https://oreil.ly/TdrGG*) is a good place to start.

 The deployment repository you're creating now will become the "source of truth" for the Argo CD GitOps deployment tool that we'll set up later in the chapter.

You should now have an empty Git repository ready to be populated with Helm packages.

The easiest way to start working with Helm files is to use the Helm CLI application. Helm's CLI allows you to create, install, and inspect Helm charts by using the Kubernetes API. In our examples, we'll be using Helm version 3.2.4, which you can find at this GitHub site (*https://oreil.ly/ohMF7*).

If you don't have the Helm CLI already, download and install it on your local machine now. When you've done that, you'll be ready to create the ms-flights Helm chart.

Create a Helm chart

One of the nice things about the Helm CLI is that it provides a handy function for quickly bootstrapping a new chart. To create our skeleton chart, make sure you are in the root directory of your ms-deploy repository and run the following command:

```
ms-deploy $ helm create ms-flights
```

When it's done, Helm will have created a basic package that contains a *chart.yaml* file which describes our chart, a *values.yaml* file we can use to customize chart values, and a *templates* directory that contains a whole set of Kubernetes YAML templates for a basic deployment.

The great thing about using Helm is that most of the boilerplate code that we'd need to write for a basic microservices Kubernetes deployment has been handled for us already. We'll only need to make a few small changes to the templates that Helm has generated for us to have a working, deployable package.

In particular, we'll need to update the *templates/deployment.yaml* file just a little bit to make it more specific to the container that we want to deploy.

Update the flights deployment template

The */ms-flights/templates/deployment.yaml* file is a Kubernetes object description file that declares the target deployment state for a Pod. We've already mentioned that Kubernetes objects can get pretty complicated. The good news is that the file that Helm generated for us includes a lot of placeholder values that we can leave as is. But we'll need to make a few small changes for this deployment to work for our flights microservice.

Let's start by getting a basic understanding of some key YAML properties in the deployment object:

apiVersion
> Every Kubernetes YAML file specifies the version of a named Kubernetes API that this file uses.

kind
> This identifies the type of Kubernetes object. In this case, the Kubernetes object is Deployment.

spec
> The specification for the Kubernetes object—this is the heart of the description.

spec.replicas
> Specifies the number of replicas we want for this deployment. Kubernetes will create ReplicaSets for us based on this value.

spec.template
> The template property of the Deployment specification is the template for the Pod that we are planning to deploy. Kubernetes uses this template to provision the pods we are deploying.

spec.template.containers
> The containers property of a Pod template identifies the container image and environment values that Kubernetes should use when it creates a replica of a Pod.

For our simple deployment, we're going to use the default values that Helm has generated for most of the Deployment object's properties. But we'll need to update spec.template.containers so that it works for the ms-flights container that we've built.

Update the YAML for the containers property so that it contains the env, ports, livenessProbe, and readinessProbe values shown in Example 10-3.

Example 10-3. ms-flights template specification

```
spec:
[...]
  template:
  [...]
    spec:
    [...]
      containers:
```

```
- name: {{ .Chart.Name }}
  [...]
  imagePullPolicy: {{ .Values.image.pullPolicy }}
  env:
    - name: MYSQL_HOST
      value: {{ .Values.MYSQL_HOST | quote }}
    - name: MYSQL_USER
      value: {{ .Values.MYSQL_USER | quote }}
    - name : MYSQL_PASSWORD
      valueFrom:
        secretKeyRef:
          name: {{ .Values.MYSQLSecretName }}
          key: {{ .Values.MYSQLSecretKey }}
    - name: MYSQL_DATABASE
      value: {{ .Values.MYSQL_DATABASE | quote }}
  ports:
    - name: http
      containerPort: 5501
      protocol: TCP
  livenessProbe:
    httpGet:
      path: /ping
      port: http
  readinessProbe:
    httpGet:
      path: /health
      port: http
  [...]
```

A completed example of the ms-flights Helm chart is available at this book's GitHub site (*https://oreil.ly/Microservices_UpandRun ning_msflights*).

The update we've made to the `containers` section includes the following:

- A templated set of environment variables for connecting to a MySQL database (we'll set the actual values later)

- The TCP port that the flights microservice will bind to and our container exposes

- Liveness and readiness endpoints that Kubernetes will use to check if the Pod is still alive (as defined in Chapter 9)

That's all we need to customize to make the generated Helm templates work for us. With the deployment template we've created, we have a parameterized Kubernetes Deployment object defined. We'll only need to define some values to use in the template.

Set package values

One of the nice things about using a Helm package for deployment is that we can reuse the same template for lots of different environments by changing a few values. One way to set those values is through the Helm client at the time of installation. We did this earlier in the book when we installed the Helm package for Argo CD.

Another option is to create a file that serializes all of the values you want to use in a single place. This is the approach we'll take for our deployment package. This gives us the advantage of being able to manage our deployment value files as code. We'll use the *values.yaml* file that Helm has generated for us already. You'll find that file in the root directory of the ms-flights chart.

First, we'll need to update the details for the Docker image. Open the *values.yaml* file in your favorite text editor and find the image key at the beginning of the YAML file. Update image with the details in Example 10-4.

Example 10-4. Image example

```
replicaCount: 1

image:
  repository: "msupandrunning/flights"
  pullPolicy: IfNotPresent
  tag: "v1.0"
```

> This example uses the container we've already built for you. If you want to use your own, you'll need to change the values of reposi tory and tag.

Next, we'll add MySQL connection values so the microservice can connect to the staging environment's database services. Add the following YAML to your values file (you can add it immediately after the tag property):

```
image:
[..]

MYSQL_HOST: rds.staging.msur-vpc.com
MYSQL_USER: microservices
MYSQL_DATABASE: microservices_db
MYSQLSecretName: mysql
MYSQLSecretKey: password
```

Finally, find the ingress property near the end of the YAML file and update it with the following text:

```
ingress:
  enabled: true
  annotations:
    kubernetes.io/ingress.class: traefik
  hosts:
    - host: flightsvc.com
      paths: ["/flights"]
```

This definition lets our Ingress service know that it should route any messages sent to the host *flightsvc.com* with a URI of */flights* to the flight information microservice. We won't need to actually host the service at the *flightsvc.com* domain, we'll just need to make sure that HTTP requests have those values if we want them to reach our service.

For a production environment, we'd probably have more values and template changes we'd want to make. But to get up and running, this is more than enough.

Test and commit the package

The last thing we'll need to do is a quick dry-run test to ensure that we haven't made any syntax errors. You'll need to have connectivity to your Kubernetes cluster, so make sure you still have that environment accessible. Run the following command to make sure that Helm will be able to build a package:

```
ms-flights$ helm install --debug --dry-run flight-info .
```

If it works, Helm will return a lot of YAML that shows the objects that it would generate. It should end with something that looks like this:

```
[... lots of YAML...]
  backend:
            serviceName: flight-info-ms-flights
            servicePort: 80
NOTES:
1. Get the application URL by running these commands:
   http://flightsvc.com/flights
```

 If you're having trouble getting your Helm package to work, check out a reference example for the flights service package at this book's example repository (*https://oreil.ly/Microservices_UpandRunning_msflights_ex*).

If everything looks good, commit the finished Helm files to the GitHub repository:

```
ms-flights$ git add .
ms-flights$ git commit -m "initial commit"
ms-flights$ git push origin
```

Now that the package files are available in the deployment monorepo, we're ready to use them with the Argo CD GitOps deployment tool.

Argo CD for GitOps Deployment

So far, we've created a Helm chart that gives us a more consumable way of deploying microservices into the Kubernetes cluster. Helm comes with the capability of performing deployments into Kubernetes clusters, so we've already done enough to be able to deploy the flight information service into the staging environment.

But with what we have now, this would be a very manual operation and we'd need to use the Helm CLI for every deployment. We'd also need to somehow keep track of the current state and version of deployed services so that we'd know if a new deployment is necessary when our deployment repository is updated.

Instead, we can do something better. Earlier in Chapter 7, we introduced Argo CD as our continuous deployment tool. Now is our opportunity to use it and improve the way we deploy services into our environments.

Argo CD is a GitOps deployment tool, designed to use a Git repository as the source for the desired deployment state for our workloads and services. When it checks a repository that we've specified, it determines whether the target state we defined matches the running state in the environment. If it doesn't, Argo CD can "synchronize" the deployment to match what we declared in our Helm charts.

This declarative approach fits well with our principles and the other tools that we've adopted, like Terraform. To make all this magic happen, we just need to log in to the Argo CD instance that we've installed in staging, point to our ms-deploy repository, and set up a synchronized deployment.

 Make sure you've added the MySQL password Kubernetes Secret as described in "Create a Kubernetes secret" on page 240. Otherwise, the flight information service won't be able to start up.

Log in to Argo CD

Before we can log in to Argo CD, we'll need to get the password for the Argo administrative user. Argo CD does something clever and makes the default password the same as the name of the Kubernetes object that it runs on. Run the following `kubectl` command to find the Argo CD Pod:

```
$ kubectl get pods -n "argocd" | grep argocd-server
NAME                               READY   STATUS    RESTARTS   AGE
msur-argocd-server-c6d4ffcf-9z4c2  1/1     Running   0          51s
```

Copy the name of the Pod somewhere as that will be the password we'll use to log in. For example, in the result shown, the password would be `msur-argocd-server-c6d4ffcf-9z4c2`. In order to access the login screen and use our credentials, we'll need to set up a port-forwarding rule. That's because we haven't properly defined a way to access our Kubernetes cluster from the internet. But thankfully `kubectl` provides a handy built-in tool for forwarding requests from your local machine into the cluster. Use the following to get it running:

```
$ kubectl port-forward svc/msur-argocd-server 8443:443 -n "argocd"
Forwarding from 127.0.0.1:8443 -> 8080
Forwarding from [::1]:8443 -> 8080
```

Now you should be able to navigate to *localhost:8443* in your browser. You'll almost definitely get a warning indicating that the site can't be trusted. That's OK and is expected at this point. Let your browser know that it is OK to proceed and you should then see a login screen that looks like the one shown in Figure 10-13.

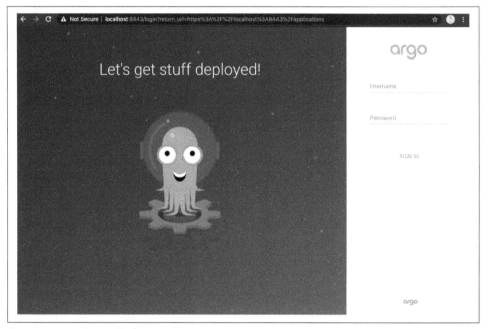

Figure 10-13. Argo CD login screen

Enter `admin` as your user ID and use the password you noted earlier and log in. If you can log in successfully, you'll see a dashboard screen. Now we can move on to creating a reference to our flight information service deployment.

Sync and deploy a microservice

In Argo CD, a microservice or workload that needs to be deployed is called an *application*. To deploy the flight-information microservice we'll need to create a new "application" and configure it with values that reference the Helm package in the Git repository that we created earlier.

Start by clicking the Create Application or New App button on the dashboard screen. When you click it, a web form will slide in from the righthand side of the screen that you'll need to populate. This is where you define the metadata for the application and the location of the Helm package. In our case, we'll want Argo CD to pull that from the deployments monorepo and the ms-flights directory within it.

Use the values in Table 10-4 to set up your flight-information microservice deployment. Make sure you replace the value YOUR_DEPLOYMENTS_REPOSITORY_URL with the URL of the deployment repository from "Creating the Microservices Deployment Repository" on page 249 so that Argo CD can access your Helm packages.

Table 10-4. Flight-information service values

Section	Key	Value
GENERAL	Application name	`flight-info`
GENERAL	Project	`default`
GENERAL	Sync policy	`manual`
SOURCE	Repository URL	`YOUR_DEPLOYMENTS_REPOSITORY_URL`
SOURCE	Path	`ms-flights`
DESTINATION	Cluster	`in-cluster` (*https://kubernetes.default.svc*)
DESTINATION	Namespace	`microservices`

When you are done filling in the form, click the Create button.

> If you run into any trouble, consult the Argo CD documentation (*https://oreil.ly/kZZJP*) for instructions on setting up an application.

If you've created the application successfully, Argo CD will list the flight-info application in the dashboard, as shown in Figure 10-14.

Figure 10-14. Flight-information application created

However, while the application has been created, it's not yet synchronized with the Deployment declaration, and the flight-info application in our cluster doesn't match the description in our package. That's because Argo CD hasn't actually done the Deployment yet. To make that happen, click the flight-info application that we've just created, click the Sync button, and then click the Synchronize button in the window that slides in, as shown in Figure 10-15.

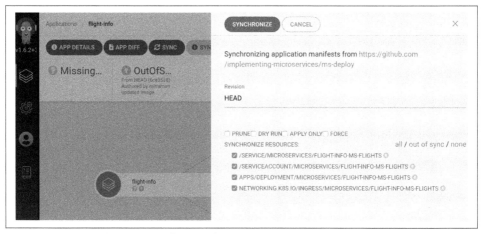

Figure 10-15. Synchronize the flight-information application

When you click Synchronize, Argo CD will do the work it needs to do to make your application match the state you've described in the Helm package. If everything goes smoothly, you'll have a healthy, synchronized, and deployed microservice, as shown in Figure 10-16.

Figure 10-16. Deployed flight service

If your deployment status isn't "healthy," try clicking the pod (the last node on the far right of the tree). You'll be able to view events and log messages that can help you troubleshoot the problem.

Our container has been deployed in the Kubernetes cluster, its health checks and liveness checks have passed, and it is ready to receive requests. This is a big milestone!

Now, let's try testing the flights service with a simple request.

Test the flights service

Our flights microservice is now up and running in our AWS-hosted staging environment. In order to test the service with a request message, we'll need to access Traefik's load balancer, which will route our request to the containerized service. The first thing we'll need is the load balancer's network address. Since we didn't set up a DNS entry, AWS will have given us a random address automatically. To get that address, run the following `kubectl` command:

```
$ kubectl get svc ms-traefik-ingress
```

You should get back something that looks like this:

```
NAME                  TYPE           CLUSTER-IP       EXTERNAL-IP
ms-traefik-ingress    LoadBalancer   172.20.149.191   ab.elb.amazonaws.com
```

The `EXTERNAL-IP` is the address of the Traefik load balancer. Make a note of it for our test request.

We'll be using curl to send a request message to the flights microservice. If you don't have a local copy of curl, you can get it from this site (*https://oreil.ly/xtfjJ*). If you've never used it before, curl is a powerful command-line tool for sending messages to URL-based addresses. We're using curl because it has a lot of useful options, including the ability to set a host header in the HTTP request. That's helpful for us because we need to set a host of *flightsvc.com* for our ingress routing rule to work.

Run the following curl command to send a test request message to the flights service (replacing *{TRAEFIK-EXTERNAL-IP}* with the address for your load balancer):

```
curl --header "Host: flightsvc.com" \
  {TRAEFIK-EXTERNAL-IP}/flights?flight_no=AA2532
```

If all has gone well, you'll get the details of that flight as a JSON-formatted response.

> You can use a dedicated API testing tool such as Postman or SoapUI to get a more user-friendly formatted version of the response message.

The HTTP request we've just made calls the ingress service, which in turn routes the message to the flights microservice based on the ingress rule we defined earlier in this chapter. The flights microservice retrieves data from the database service we provisioned and returns a result to us through the load balancer. With that request, we've been able to bring together all the parts of our architecture deployment and test an end-to-end microservices architecture!

All that's left is to clean up, so we don't end up paying for AWS resources that we aren't using.

> AWS bills you for EKS resources even when they aren't handling traffic, so make sure you tear down your infrastructure if you aren't using it.

Clean Up

As we've done before, we'll use a local Terraform client to bring down the infrastructure. Make sure you're in the directory where your staging Terraform files are and run the following command:

```
infra-staging-env $ terraform destroy
```

When it's successfully completed, our Kubernetes-based staging environment will be destroyed. You can check to make sure that the resources have been destroyed by using the AWS CLI or the AWS browser-based console. We gave you some examples of CLI commands you can run in Chapter 6.

Summary

At the beginning of this chapter we warned you that we'd be doing a lot of work. All that work paid off as we ended up with the end-to-end deployment of the microservices architecture that we've been building throughout this book. We also got to reuse some of the tools and practices we established earlier to get more done in less time.

In this chapter we updated our infrastructure template to support the dependencies from our microservices teams. We implemented a build and integration pipeline in our microservice code repositories, and we built a new deployment repository and tool-based process to get services deployed.

Hopefully, you've been able to see how the decisions we made at deployment time have been heavily influenced by the earlier decisions we made on principles, operating models, infrastructure, and design. They've all come together to form an end state that allowed us to build a running implementation.

But the real test of a microservices system is how it handles change. That's what we'll cover in our next chapter.

## CHAPTER 11

Managing Change

We have now built a microservices system that is optimized to reduce change costs. We've done it quite quickly and with a great variety of tools, technologies, and repositories. In this chapter, we'll take a step back and consider the system we've built from the perspective of change. We'll explore what change looks like for the system we've built. We'll take a look at the typical kinds of change you'll need to do and the patterns and methods that work well to support them.

Change is an important factor because of the impact it has. Poorly designed software can end up costing organizations a lot of pain. As we highlighted in Chapter 1, one of the benefits of a microservices system is that it makes change faster and safer.

Also, change will always have a cost. In a software system, that cost is a combination of time, money, and impact to people. To get the most out of our microservices system, we need to minimize change cost and make changes that have the greatest impact. Reducing the cost of change gives all of our teams more freedom to experiment, optimize, and improve. Focusing change activities gives us better results from a finite change budget.

Let's start by getting a better understanding of the kinds of changes we can expect in a microservices system and the best way to make decisions about change.

Changes in a Microservices System

In a microservices system, change should be a feature, not a problem or a bug. That means you should be able to change the system to make it better and get more value from the software you've built. When people think about software change, they often think about extrinsic drivers—the things that come from business or user input. For example, here are some common reasons to make changes in your system:

- Supporting a new product launch
- Resolving a logic bug that is degrading the user experience
- Integrating with a new partner

These are all important reasons to change and our architecture should facilitate these kinds of changes to make them as cost-effective as possible. But it's important to understand that the microservices style is an optimization technique. That means we should consider intrinsic drivers as well. The following changes come from our observation of the system itself:

- Splitting a microservice to reduce code complexity
- Redeploying infrastructure to avoid drifting from the infrastructure code
- Optimizing the CI/CD pipeline to deliver changes faster

There's no doubt that you'll need to support extrinsic change. But to get the best value from your system you'll need to plan for and execute intrinsic change as well. A good way to adopt this continual improvement mindset is to use data and measurements to guide your decisions.

Be Data-Oriented

A classic problem in software development is overengineering and premature optimization. This happens when we design software or architecture to resolve a problem that hardly ever occurs. Or when our solution to a predicted problem is more costly than the problem itself will ever be.

This can be a danger for a microservices system as well. That's why it's a good idea to use data and measurements to guide your decision making about when to make changes—especially the intrinsic improvement ones. Without data, you'll be guessing and you'll probably end up working hard to improve parts of the system that actually don't need any help. Meanwhile, other pressing problem areas may go undetected. With finite resources, you can't afford to work that way.

Product teams use data to make better informed decisions about the changes they want to make. Businesses use objective and key results (OKRs), key performance indicators (KPIs), net promoter scores, satisfaction surveys, and revenue numbers to help shape their strategic decision making and their backlog of changes.

You'll need something similar to inform your improvement and optimization plans. For example, consider collecting the following project, design, and runtime metrics to get a better understanding of your improvement opportunities:

- Change time per microservice
- Frequency of changes per microservice
- Number of microservices changed per change request
- Lines of code in a microservice (as a datapoint, not a constraint!)
- Runtime latency per microservice
- Dependencies between microservices

 We didn't implement observability or reporting in our microservices architecture. That's because we had limited space and wanted to focus on some of the more foundational elements. But the good news is that all the hooks are there for you to extend the system to give you some of the metrics we've been describing.

Collectively, these kinds of analytic metrics can give you a better, holistic picture of where improvements can be made. Then you can make a decision about where to best spend your efforts. Of course, you'll also need to balance the improvements you can make against the impact that a change will have.

The Impact of Changes

There are many potential impacts that come from software change, but four in particular seem to cause the most strife for modern organizations: implementation time, coordination time, downtime, and consumer impact. When we review change costs in a microservices system, it's a good idea to consider these focus areas. Let's take a quick look at each of them:

Implementation time
> A core part of any change cost is the time it takes to actually make the change. This includes the time required to understand the current state, make the desired changes, test changes, and update the production environment. A big factor for implementation time is the readability, learnability, and maintainability of the components to be changed.

Coordination time
> In order to implement a change, there will almost always be some form of communication between teams. Coordination time is a subset of implementation time, but it's worth calling out on its own. In fact, it's so important, we've mentioned it a few times in this book. Coordination time can include the amount of time spent getting access to resources and gaining permission and agreement on change activities and the general "organizational friction" that comes from

working in a large organization. Coordination time is often a factor of organizational design and structure.

Downtime

Downtime is a measurement of how long the system or a system component remains unavailable while a change is being implemented. Years ago, downtime was an accepted part of the software change process. But times and expectations have changed. Now there is increasing pressure on technology teams to minimize the downtime required for changes. In fact, in a microservices system it's common to strive for a "zero-downtime" change model in which the system remains constantly available.

Consumer impact

An often forgotten impact is the cost that a change has on the users of the system. Downtime captures one form of consumer impact, but even in a "zero-downtime" model there can be costly impacts that could have been avoided. For example, a change to an infrastructure module may have wide-reaching impact on microservice developer teams. Similarly, a change to an interface can break the code of every component that uses it.

Software architecture has a big role to play in the costs and impacts of change across all four of the lenses we've described. But another part of the story is the way that changes are applied. Microservices architectures, cloud infrastructures, and DevOps practices have enabled practices that are a huge leap forward. Let's take a look at two modern deployment patterns as well as an older one that has managed to stick around.

Three Deployment Patterns

There are lots of different ways to apply changes and deploy software components. Before we dive into the changeability of the architecture we've built, it's worth reviewing three deployment patterns that we'll use when we make changes in our system: blue-green, canary, and multiple versions. We'll start by looking at blue-green deployments.

Blue-green deployment

In a blue-green (*https://oreil.ly/zj7g-*) deployment, there are two parallel environments maintained. One is live and accepts traffic while the other is idle. Change is applied to the idle environment and when ready, traffic is routed to the changed environment. The two environments now switch roles with idle becoming live and live becoming idle, ready for the next change.

This is a useful deployment pattern because it allows you to make changes in a production environment safely. Switching the traffic over means that you don't have to worry about repeating the change in a live system. The actual colors of the environments are unimportant—the key to this pattern is that the two environments interchange roles between live and idle.

A benefit of this pattern is that it can vastly reduce downtime, all the way down to a zero-downtime model. However, maintaining two environments requires careful handling of persistent systems like databases. Persistent, changing data needs to be synchronized, replicated, or maintained entirely outside of the blue-green model.

Canary deployment

A canary deployment (*https://oreil.ly/QXtSZ*) is similar to a blue-green deployment, but instead of maintaining two complete environments, you release two components in parallel. The "canary" in this pattern is the version that acts as a "canary in a coal mine" (*https://oreil.ly/hr1Vk*), alerting you to danger early. For example, to perform a canary deployment of a web application, you'd release a new canary version of the web application alongside the original web application that continues to run.

Just like the blue-green pattern, canary deployments require traffic management and routing logic in order to work. After deploying the new version of an application, some traffic is routed to the new version. The traffic that hits the canary version could be a percent of the total load or could be based on a unique header or special identifier. However it's done, over time more traffic is routed to the canary version until it eventually gets promoted to full-fledged production state.

Although the canary pattern is similar to blue-green, it has the added advantage of being finer-grained. Instead of maintaining an entire duplicate environment, we can focus on a smaller, bounded change and make that change within a running system. This can cause problems if the canary we are deploying impacts other parts of our system. For example, if our canary deployment alters a shared system resource in a new way, even handling 1% of traffic in the canary could have catastrophic effects.

But in a system that's designed for independent deployment, the canary pattern can work quite well. When changes are made to components that are well bounded and own their own resources, the blast radius of damage is limited. So it's a good pattern to have in your tool belt if you are working with the right type of architecture. As we'll see, the canary pattern turns out to be a good fit for the microservices architecture we've built in this book.

Multiple versions

The last pattern to cover is one that considers users and clients as part of the change process—running multiple versions in parallel. The blue-green and canary deployment patterns we've covered already use a mechanism of temporarily running parallel instances (sometimes called the *expand and contract* pattern). But in both of those cases, you'd typically run your new and old instances privately, not sharing details of the new function until it's safe to use. The routing decision is *implicit* and hidden from users of the system.

The multiple versions pattern makes changes more transparent to the users and clients of the system. In this deployment pattern we *explicitly* version a component or interface and allow clients to choose which version of the component they want to use. In this way, we can support the use of multiple versions at the same time.

The main reason to employ this technique is if we're making a change that will require a dependent system to make a change as well. We use this pattern when we know people we don't coordinate with will need to do work for the change to be completed. A classic example of this situation is when you want to change an API in a way that will break client code. In this scenario, managing migration for all parties would require significant coordination effort. Instead, we can keep older versions running so that we don't need to wait for every client to change.

There are some significant challenges to using this approach. Every version of a component we introduce brings added maintenance and complexity costs for our system. Versions need to be able to run safely together and parallel versions need to be continually maintained, supported, documented, and kept secure. That overhead can become an operational headache and can slow down changeability of the system over time. Eventually, you'll need to migrate users of old versions and do some contraction of versions.

 There are some systems that almost never contract their versions. For example, at the time of this writing, the Salesforce SaaS API is on version 49 and supporting 19 previous versions in parallel!

We now have a decent framework for assessing the impact of change and a set of typical deployment patterns we can use to describe how change might be handled. Now we can dive into an evaluation of the architecture we've built from a change perspective across infrastructure, microservices, and data. We'll start by examining the changeability of our infrastructure platform.

Considerations for Our Architecture

If you followed along with the instructions in this book, you'll have built a pretty advanced microservices architecture in a fairly short amount of time. That speed of engineering is a testament to the incredible tools, services, and software that are available for us to use. But building something fast is no good if it doesn't do the job it's supposed to do. For us, this means the architecture we built should hold its own when it comes to changeability.

In this section, we'll take a tour of the system and get a closer look at how the decisions we've made have impacted the changeability of the architecture. We'll look at change through the factors of implementation costs, coordination time, downtime, and consumer impacts that we introduced earlier in this chapter. To make things easier, we'll split the architecture into three subsystems: infrastructure, microservices, and data, considering each in turn. Let's start by examining our infrastructure.

Infrastructure Changes

In Chapter 7, we developed a Terraform-based platform for our microservices that included networking, Kubernetes, and a GitOps deployment tool. Later, we added MySQL and Redis databases to the stack based on the emerging needs of the microservices teams. It's realistic to expect the infrastructure platform to continue to change as the needs of users and teams evolve, and demand patterns and business goals change.

For our infrastructure, we can divide change into two categories: changes that extend the platform with new resources and changes that alter existing platform resources. Creating new resources is a form of extension that has little impact on the running system, while changes to existing resources need to be managed more carefully.

Examples of adding new resources to our architecture would be:

- Implementing a new event-streaming infrastructure using AWS SNS for new microservices that are being developed
- Provisioning an Elastic Container Service (ECS) instance and VPC for the installation of a third-party application
- Adding a new operator account to the IAM system

Here are some examples of changes that would alter an existing resource:

- Changing the network design of the VPC our EKS service is deployed within
- Upgrading the MySQL version of our RDS instance
- Modifying the configuration of the Kubernetes cluster

We'll need to consider both types of changes when we assess the changeability of our infrastructure. Let's start by looking at implementation costs.

Infrastructure change: Implementation costs

The implementation cost of making infrastructure changes is a function of how difficult a change is to both understand and execute. This is where the investment we
made in our infrastructure design helps. Our decisions to embrace the principle of
immutable infrastructure, build a CI/CD pipeline, and write IaC combine to greatly
reduce the cost of making changes.

When it comes time for you to make an infrastructure change, you can employ a
change process that looks something like this, thanks to the tools we've implemented:

1. Decide on the infrastructure change you want to make.
2. Identify the infrastructure code you need to change (e.g., do you need to create a
   new Terraform module? Are you just updating an environment definition?).
3. Test the infrastructure change in an infrastructure development environment.
4. Try to deploy applications and microservices to the updated infrastructure.
5. Run tests and release (e.g., integration tests, performance tests, and end-to-end
   tests).

By adopting the principle of IaC, the changeability of our infrastructure design has
improved significantly. We only ever make changes through the infrastructure pipeline, so we know that if it's not in the code, it's not in the infrastructure.

We use the same code modules in every environment, so we know that if your infrastructure changes work in a development environment, they should work in the production environment as well. Finally, our automated pipeline ensures that our
infrastructure code and tests will be run in the same way consistently and repeatedly.

What we've done in our system is to drive variation out of the change process. With
less uncertainty for us to worry about, we can focus more on making the change
itself. Writing IaC requires a bit more up-front effort, but the payoff when it comes to
changes makes it a worthwhile investment.

Overall, the infrastructure implementation costs should be lower with our architecture than they would be if we had just made changes directly using the AWS console.

Infrastructure change: Coordination costs

When we developed our operating model in Chapter 2, we made an important decision about how infrastructure work would be done. We decided that a single team
called the platform team would be responsible for designing, maintaining, and running our cloud-based infrastructure. Centralizing the infrastructure design within
this team means that we'll pay a relatively low coordination cost for decision making.
That's because we won't need to gain consensus among all of the parties in your system whenever an infrastructure change is needed. Instead the platform team has

independent authority and autonomy (and responsibility!) over infrastructure changes.

In practice, it's difficult to offer an infrastructure platform in a pure *x*-as-a-service manner. Enablement, engagement, and agreement are bound to be needed for microservices teams to use the platform for delivery. The centralized nature of the platform team is also a potential problem. What happens when teams require conflicting changes? How are new changes tested across all the teams?

The platform model only works if there are tools and processes to properly enable a self-service, low-coordination mode of interaction. That requires a lot of up-front and continual work and shouldn't be underestimated. For example, a Terraform-based environment shouldn't be offered to the microservices teams without appropriate documentation, issue tracking, and a reasonable level of support.

 In a full-fledged microservices system for any reasonably sized organization, infrastructure changes almost always incur additional coordination costs from gating processes. The potential impact of a poor infrastructure decision is high, so it's common to require security, business, and risk checks before an infrastructure change can be deployed. One practical way to reduce coordination costs is to treat these groups as consumers of the platform and design the solution accordingly.

Infrastructure change: Downtime

It's difficult to make infrastructure changes without introducing a little bit of downtime. That's because infrastructure is such a foundational part of a software system. For example, how do you upgrade a Kubernetes server or make a major network change without bringing the system down temporarily?

The infrastructure system we've built can handle extensions and additions pretty easily. All that's needed is some Terraform code that will run through the pipeline. However, our system isn't great at handling changes to existing parts without at least a small outage.

A big challenge for us is the immutable nature of our infrastructure. If we want to make even a small change to a component, we need to first destroy it. That can be a problem if we're hoping to handle workload and traffic at the same time.

To make these kinds of in situ infrastructure changes, we could adopt the blue-green deployment pattern (see "Blue-green deployment" on page 266). In fact, we'd even take it a step further and use a phoenix deployment pattern (*https://oreil.ly/enM_P*). This pattern is similar to blue-green, but instead of having an environment idling, we'll create new environments as needed using our IaC pipeline.

This means we could spin up a new environment with our changes. After some testing we could deploy all our microservices into it and if everything looked good, we could switch our live traffic over to the new environment. For example, an API gateway or load balancer would give us the traffic-routing features we'd need to facilitate this kind of maneuver.

But our big problem is data. We don't have a clean separation between our data instance and our application instances. For the sake of brevity and simplicity, we've thrown all of our databases in the same network as the microservice instances. That means we don't have an easy way of spinning up a new environment without doing some heavy data replication work. That's going to add a lot of complexity to the change process.

If zero downtime is an important principle for you, you'll need to reconsider the infrastructure design from the data perspective.

Infrastructure change: Consumer impact

Consumers of our applications won't interact with the infrastructure directly. However, since we've made the decision to offer the infrastructure "as a service" within our operating model, we need to consider the impact of changes on our microservices teams.

When you change any part of the infrastructure, you'll need to consider how that change might impact all of the microservices teams consuming and using the platform as a service. This can turn out to be a big coordination activity as the number of microservices in your system grows.

In truth, the architecture we've built doesn't do a lot to address this problem. If you use the architecture as is, you'll need to do some work to make sure that infrastructure changes won't break existing microservices. There will need to be some testing involved whenever changes are made.

In order to keep coordination costs light, the platform and microservices teams need to establish a method of communicating changes, keeping automated tests up to date, and sharing the responsibility for overall reliability and quality in the system. As always, that requires a mix of Team Topologies, architecture, and good tools and technologies.

One thing we can expect for certain is that the number of microservices will grow beyond the two services we used in our flight system example. So there will be lots of changes for the microservices teams to handle. Let's dive into those changes next.

Microservices Changes

Most of the changes you'll need to make in the system will be to the microservices themselves. When you want to offer new products, change the way that a user experience works, or just fine-tune the system, chances are you'll be making changes to the microservices subsystem. That may mean creating a new microservice, updating the logic of an existing service or even retiring, splitting, or combining services.

In our up and running architecture, it's easy to imagine that we may want to add more features to our travel system. For example, we might want to add train bookings to our search and reservation system. In that case, it's easy to imagine that we'd be creating a new cluster of microservices and updating the API in the gateway to support those new, extended features.

As we've seen across all of our domains, adding something new is usually the easiest kind of change we can make. Things get more complicated when we need to change a service that is already running. Consider the complications that might arise from these kinds of changes:

- Splitting the flight-information microservice into services for domestic and international flights
- Updating the flight-reservation service with a new "tentative" booking state
- Merging the flight-information and flight-reservation microservices together

In all of these cases, change management gets more complicated because these services are in use. Thankfully, the architecture we've built together does a great job of minimizing these impacts. Let's take a look at microservices changes through the lens of our four key change impacts.

Microservices: Implementation costs

When it comes to changing a microservice, the main implementation costs come from being able to understand, maintain, and test the code. In our architecture, we've made some important decisions to bring down the cost of implementation:

Used Event Storming to rightsize microservices
   Event Storming helped us define boundaries for our microservices that were internally consistent and addressed specific parts of our domain. The net effect is that code comprehension should be improved and changes can be implemented in smaller batches with speed.

All microservices use microservice-bootstrap

The `microservice-bootstrap` framework gives our teams a consistent way of documenting and testing the microservices they develop. By making this framework mandatory we've reduced some of the burden of making and testing changes across the organizations. Developers can quickly become familiar with the tool, and the work of testing and building services can become a common competency across teams.

Used CI/CD for microservices

Using a CI/CD pipeline means that all of our code changes are tested, linted, and validated. The net effect of this is a greater chance that the code is in a usable, maintainable state by the time it comes to make a new change.

Overall, the rightsizing of the service and the DevOps tooling we've put in place should greatly reduce the costs of making code changes to microservices in our architecture.

Microservices: Coordination costs

Coordination costs can be a big problem for making software changes. Over time, a simple piece of application code can grow to contain a mess of interdependencies with other libraries, components, and systems. Those interdependencies make it difficult to make changes quickly because of the organizational friction that comes from having to work with many other people and teams to understand if a change can be made safely.

In our architecture, we've made a few decisions that should help reduce this cost. In "What Are Microservices?" on page 2, we described a definition of microservice that highlighted characteristics of independence for our microservice engineering and release work. This line of thinking led us to make decisions that could increase the independence of a microservices team:

- Every microservice is owned by only one team.
- Every microservice has its own repository and CI/CD pipeline.

Taken together, these decisions increase the autonomy of teams that are making microservices code changes.

In addition to reducing interteam coordination, our decision to "rightsize" our service boundaries and keep team sizes constrained ensures that the coordination costs within our team should stay relatively low as well. It's fair to say that reducing coordination costs for microservices code changes has been a primary driver for the architecture we've built.

But there are two areas where coordination costs are difficult to avoid in our up and running architecture: life-cycle events and interface changes.

In Chapter 2, we introduced the system team that owns responsibility for the health and value of the system as a whole. The kinds of changes that come from the system team can result in high levels of coordination. For example, what happens when the system team decides that two microservices should be merged into one? Worse, what happens if those microservices are owned by two different teams? In our architecture, these types of changes will require much more negotiation, planning, and communication than code changes to an individual microservice.

We've deemed this to be an acceptable cost trade-off. In our experience, life-cycle and system-grooming changes are relatively rare compared to changing code to reflect new business or technology requirements. It makes sense to optimize the change model for the types of change that we expect to happen more frequently.

It's one thing to change the code of a microservice, but you'll often find yourself needing to change the interface of a microservice as well. In these cases, there may be additional coordination effort required due to the contractual nature of an API between consumer and provider. We'll touch on this change factor in more detail in "Microservices: Consumer impact" on page 276.

Finally, in Chapter 2, we made a decision to have a single release team that would own responsibility for updating the production environment. This decision has the most potential to go wrong! We established a release team to give special attention to changes and the coordination costs that often come with them. We've also tried to arm the release team with deployment tools to minimize any impacts to velocity. But ultimately if the release team becomes a bottleneck to change, the system design must be revisited. We'll reevaluate the topology and the tools that enable the release cycle.

Overall, the coordination costs of microservices change within our architecture are low. This is thanks to the operating model, tools, and design decisions we've made throughout this book.

Microservices: Downtime

Another change area that we've optimized for is in minimizing the downtime required when an individual microservice is changed. That's because of the tooling and infrastructure we introduced at the platform level. The key to bringing this cost down is our ability to use the canary deployment pattern ("Canary deployment" on page 267) for microservices releases. When it comes time to release a new version of a microservice you can use the tooling we've installed to perform the following change process:

1. Deploy the new version of the microservice as a canary, alongside the existing version.

2. Implement a traffic routing rule to send a small percentage of traffic to the new version.

3. Observe the health of the new version and verify that the results are as expected.

4. Promote the canary microservice by routing all traffic to the new version.

5. Drain and delete the older version of the microservice.

This pattern will work for most of the changes you need to make and you'll be able to use Argo CD to orchestrate the canary activities. However, be careful using this pattern when a new version of the microservice will make a change that could impact the older version. For example, if a new version changes data in a shared database, make sure that change is compatible with previous running versions.

Microservices: Consumer impact

So far, we've mostly focused on changes to microservices code. The logic, validation, and behavior of the service is reflected in code, so that's where a high frequency of our changes will be found. But sometimes you'll need to make changes to the interface (or API) of a microservice and that can cause some big problems.

Changing the interface of a microservice is almost inevitable. You'll eventually want to change the parameters of an operation or change the data that comes back from a call. The problem is that as other services and components start to depend on the interface, even small changes can result in a lot of work for everyone involved.

We haven't really built anything into our architecture to reduce the consumer impact of making changes. The best way to reduce the consumer impact of an API change is to adhere to some good design practices: don't change what you've already released, write client code that tolerates new data, and don't make new input parameters mandatory.

 Our favorite source for API design advice is Mike Amundsen. If you're interested in building evolvable APIs, we recommend learning from the API change patterns in his book *Design and Build Great Web APIs* (Pragmatic Bookshelf, 2020).

In addition to these kinds of design principles, some microservices practitioners have adopted contract testing as a way to minimize coordination costs between teams when changing interfaces. In contract testing, consumers and providers share a contract that describes how the interface will be used. This allows providers to run contract tests independently and validate that their changes will not impact existing clients of an API.

 In order to get our system up and running as quickly as reasonably possible, we didn't include a contract testing component in our architecture. But many practitioners have had success using Pact (*https://pact.io*) for consumer-driven contract testing. Tools like Pact allow your consumers and providers to continually share and test changes that are made to their interfaces.

But even with contract testing, chances are that you'll eventually need to introduce a change that will break someone's code. In that case, you'll need to implement some form of the multiple versions pattern (see "Multiple versions" on page 267) and maintain an old microservice until the client team can make the changes they need to.

Ultimately, our architecture doesn't do a whole lot to reduce the cost of consumer impact changes. API change is hard, and it will take good design thinking and good planning to make those changes affordable. Another area of danger is data and that's what we'll cover next.

Data Changes

One of the most difficult aspects of maintaining a microservices architecture is dealing with the data. Data models are notoriously difficult to change. A persistence layer is a much needed part of any software system, but when it comes time to change the structure of data, things can get complicated. Software components grow to be dependent on the data systems that they use and changing them can have a big cost and impact to the system.

We've tried to make decisions that improve this situation and lessen the cost of data model changes. Let's take a look at the data architecture we've built through our four lenses of change.

Data: Implementation costs

At its most basic level, the cost of changing a data model is a function of how complex the structure, formats, and relationships are and the tooling or language that's needed to make the change. The complexity of a model can increase when there are complicated values and many different data types, unique keys, or complicated values. The cost really comes from having to understand the model itself, so that changes can be made safely.

We haven't done much in our architecture explicitly to prevent a data model from getting too complicated. But we did make a decision that microservices should own their own data. This decision alone should help constrain the scope and size of a model, in the same way it should help us reduce the cost of a code change.

So, just as with code changes, you should get a great deal of implementation cost benefit from the decision to prioritize independence. But, just like with code, you'll need to keep measuring the implementation costs to ensure that the service and its data model don't grow to a size that negates the benefits of a strong boundary.

Data: Coordination costs

An even bigger benefit of prioritizing independence is the reduction in coordination costs. By deciding that microservices own their own data, we're free to make changes to our data structures without having to consult with other teams or system owners. This is in stark contrast to more traditional models where multiple teams may be using a shared data service and changes need to be coordinated carefully across all data users.

However, you should beware: there's a hidden cost to the independent data approach. We've optimized our architecture for high-speed, autonomous local changes. This made system-wide changes more costly. For example, if you need to globally change the definition of an airline identifier code, you'll need to coordinate across all of the teams who have implemented a data model that uses it. In our architecture, that could be more costly than if we had just used a shared database.

A good resource for understanding distributed data patterns is Martin Kleppmann's *Designing Data-Intensive Applications* (O'Reilly, 2017).

We decided to optimize for local changes because in our experience there is a higher change frequency of local changes. But you'll need to change that decision if the system you're building is likely to have sweeping, global changes.

If you find that you're often making changes to multiple data models in the system at the same time, it could be a sign that the boundaries of your microservices need to be reevaluated.

Data: Downtime

Our independent data model gives us some big advantages when it comes to coordination. But it isn't built for zero-downtime data model changes. That's especially true for the MySQL database that our flight-information microservice uses.

The root of our limitation is that we're using a shared database instance to serve multiple replicas of a microservice. When it comes time to make a change to a data model, it's difficult to do that without impacting existing microservices that are currently running. This may be easier to do with the Redis store that our reservations service uses, but we'll still need to be wary of making changes that will break existing versions.

In cases where we need to make an intrusive data model change, the simplest option may be to destroy the existing microservice versions and replace them with new instances that can implement the data change. In a Kubernetes environment, that can be performed with minimal impact to service. But if any and all downtime is out of the question, a more elaborate blue-green deployment would be needed.

Data: Consumer impact

Because we've made the decision that microservices should own their own data, the impact of a data model change is restricted to the service itself. So we can freely make changes without impacting the consumer of a service directly. Since the data model is encapsulated within the microservice, your microservice teams will have more autonomy to make changes to their model, although as we highlighted above, these changes may require a small amount of downtime.

In practice, a data model change is likely to require code and even interface changes. But we're free to separate or stagger these modifications so that a data model change can be made first, before we implement changes that will impact consumers directly.

Summary

Overall, we've seen that the architecture we've built is designed to make changes easier and cost-efficient. Change can come from extrinsic or intrinsic sources, but the key is to reduce the costs and impacts so that your teams have more freedom to improve the system and the products and experience that the system powers.

We've looked at our architecture across infrastructure, code, APIs, and data from the perspective of change. As you've seen in this chapter, the decisions we made throughout this book have combined to create a profile of changeability for this system. Some of our decisions were trade-offs that were made to optimize for certain types of change. Other decisions were trade-offs based on the constraints of the medium of a design in a book!

Regardless of the reasons, we've now been able to both build a microservices architecture and evaluate its usefulness and suitability. The only thing left to do with our architecture is to make it even better. That's what we'll cover in our final chapter.

## CHAPTER 12

A Journey's End (and a New Beginning)

Congratulations, you've made it to the final chapter! While you may be reaching the end of your journey with us, we hope it is only the beginning of a long and fruitful journey in successfully implementing microservices on real projects. We make no excuses for the fact that we are admirers of the microservices architecture and of the benefits it can bring when deployed in the right context, with the right intentions and skill. It is by no means the only choice and should never be implemented without understanding all the implications, but it can certainly be a very powerful choice in your arsenal of architectural tools.

We have witnessed many successful microservices projects. There is also no shortage of failed attempts to adopting microservices. Our main motivation in writing this book was to increase a reader's chances of success, if they so choose to implement their system in the microservices style. We tried to do it by providing step-by-step, pragmatic guidelines on when, why, and how to deploy microservices, explaining core concepts and demonstrating the implementation of those concepts, using simple examples. We hope we were successful in achieving the goal of turning abstract concepts into a more approachable step-by-step explanation, but most importantly, we hope you enjoyed reading this book, even if it provided only a handful of key ideas you think you can use when implementing your own systems.

Before we part ways, we wanted to share some final thoughts that summarize our understanding of the architectural decisions in microservices and an approach we recommend for continually measuring the progress of a transformation, if you do decide to embark on one.

On Complexity and Simplification Using Microservices

Throughout this book we have asserted that microservices are most applicable when utilized to implement large, complex, continuously changing systems. Intuitively, this statement makes sense: a microservices architecture itself is not simple, so embarking on that journey has to be worth it—maybe when it helps solve something even more complex. But what is the nature of complexity and how exactly do microservices decrease complexity, if at all?

A seminal work on software complexity is Fred Brooks's 1986 article, "No Silver Bullet" (*https://oreil.ly/4qh3l*), where he aptly notes:

> There is no single development, in either technology or management technique, which by itself promises even one order of magnitude improvement in productivity, in reliability, in simplicity.

Brooks continues to elaborate, explaining that the reason for this phenomena is the presence of essential complexity in software systems. While in any codebase there is always some accidental complexity (the complexity related to our own implementation choices), the majority of the complexity that we deal with in software systems is not accidental, it's related to the very essence of the complexity of modeling the problem domain itself. It is "essential complexity," by which Brooks means the sophisticated datasets, relationships among data items, algorithms, and invocation flows that represent the model a system is attempting to represent. If we tried to simplify a system beyond its essential complexity, we would be taking away from its core model, and it would no longer be the same system.

When dealing with microservices, early adopters are often attracted by the promise of microservices making building complex systems…wait for it…simpler! Most people would rather microservices make it easier for them to get their jobs done than make their lives unnecessarily difficult, so a promise of "it will be easier" is unsurprisingly a powerful motivator. Quick, off-the-cuff explanations are readily provided: by implementing a "larger" system as a collection of many simple microservices, we are making the whole process simpler! Skeptics may immediately note that while each microservice may be small and simple, orchestrating a large number of them into a coherent, complex system cannot be expected to be an easy task. And they are correct; but more importantly, for those of us who have read Brooks's "No Silver Bullet," one additional, troublesome question is: have microservices broken Brooks's conjecture that there is no way to take away essential complexity? Or is a microservices architecture purely addressing the accidental part of system complexity, and does such an amazing job that we can still feel the improvement?

The truth is that neither is the case. The microservices concept is not just about accidental complexity and not a methodology for better coding hygiene, it is an essentially different approach. And no—it does not invalidate Brooks's observation. Rather, it achieves its goals in accord with it. You see, you cannot eliminate essential complexity, but you can shift it: you can move essential complexity from one part of the system into another. This would not seem like a big deal, unless different parts of the system required different levels of effort.

Simply speaking, when building any software system there's the implementation part of it (the code) and the operational part of it (the deployment and orchestration). We can make the code simpler by breaking it up into many small microservices. Such change will make your operations equally harder. It would seem that we haven't gained much, since by simplifying one part we have made another one more difficult, but in reality this type of complexity shift can be quite beneficial if you can automate the part that you are making "harder" but not the one that you have made simpler. The increased complexity of operations matters much less if they can be automated. And that is indeed the gain.

In the last decade or so we've gotten very good at automating software operations. A vast arsenal of operation automation tooling such as Ansible, Puppet, Chef, Terraform, Docker, and Kubernetes, together with serverless functions and a wide variety of cloud services provided to us without us having to even think about it have made building complex operations materially simpler, beyond anything Brooks could have imagined in 1986. Actually designing and writing code, however, is more or less as difficult as it was in the 1980s. Don't get us wrong: there have been some advancements, sure, but nothing material. Therefore, if we shift complexity from coding into operations we can make things easier, in nontrivial ways.

Microservices Can Provide Simplification

A microservices architecture can be materially simpler than its alternatives when implementing complex systems. This does not violate Brooks's "No Silver Bullet" principle because microservices do not eliminate essential complexity. Rather, this architectural style is about *shifting* complexity from the area we cannot, yet, automate, design and code, into the area we have gotten very good at automating; operations. The net gain can be substantial.

Microservices Quadrant

Let's dig deeper into the subject of complexity. Systems Theory distinguishes the definition of a complicated system and a complex system. This was further expanded upon and popularized for decision making in the Cynefin framework (*https://oreil.ly/3Wx_M*). A complicated system can be very sophisticated and hard to understand, but in its essence is predictable and based on a finite number of well-defined rules. In contrast, a complex system is by essence nondeterministic, composed of many components that interact at a high degree of freedom, and can consequently produce emergent behaviors. If we were to classify monoliths and microservices in these terms, monoliths would be considered complicated, whereas microservices would be much more aligned with the definition of complex systems.

Another interesting classification is the notion of "easy" versus "simple." As most designers would passionately attest, these seemingly synonymous adjectives could not be any more different, in the context of design. Simple things are notoriously hard to design (think Apple's original iPod and iMac, or a simple invention such as the computer mouse), whereas easy designs are not necessarily simple to use.

Combining these two perspectives across the axis of architecture and implementation, a couple of years ago we created the "microservices quadrant" that you can see in Figure 12-1.

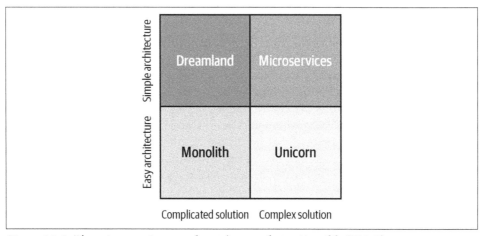

Figure 12-1. The microservices quadrant (source: https://oreil.ly/IO5t8)

This tongue-in-cheek quadrant visualization (beloved by business publications and MBA graduates) states that when we think of the overall complexity–simplicity continuum, we can align different solution types across four quadrants:

- Microservices would be a complex implementation, but a simple design (architecture).
- Monoliths would be a complicated implementation, with an easy (but not necessarily simple) architectural design.

As for the other two quadrants:

- Many software engineers would like to have a solution that has a simple architecture, and at the same time, a predictable, even if complicated, implementation. These would probably be the "dreamland"—nonmicroservices implementations that are elegant and successful, so you may not call them "monoliths" to avoid the now-established negative connotation. Candidly, these are quite rare; if your system is continuously and rapidly changing, achieving a solution in this quadrant is tantamount to achieving a dream.

- In the lower right quadrant, we have a situation where we got away with an easy design (think minimal effort), and ended up with a complex implementation that somehow still functions despite the easy architecture. Well, that would be a unicorn in more ways than one, including the need for the so-called "10x developers" to support and maintain it. But we are sure such things also exist.

The microservices quadrant gives a shorthand representation of where microservices and monolith solutions land vis-à-vis architectural simplicity compared to implementation complexity.

Having discussed the nature of microservices architectures through the lens of complexity, we would like to give the reader another important perspective: how to think about a microservice transformation over time.

In Chapter 11, we discussed both the role microservices architecture plays in helping teams tackle change in complex systems and techniques to manage change when implementing microservices. There is another important aspect of change in regards to microservices: the transformation that an organization as a whole needs to go through when transitioning from a nonmicroservices culture and adopting this novel organizational–technical structure. In the next section we will discuss how to be successful with a microservices transformation by taking a holistic look at one and avoiding the trap of technology-only blinders.

Measuring the Progress of a Microservices Transformation

When we discuss the migration to microservices, it's important to remember that we are talking about a style that encompasses complex technology and highly disruptive cultural transformations of an organization. If not carefully managed, the odds of getting it wrong are naturally much higher than those of accidentally getting lucky with it. If you have followed the various critical posts published about microservices in the past several years, you could observe a fairly discernible pattern. First, a company adopted a microservices architecture and wrote a cheerful blog post about its benefits and promise; this was followed by a blog post years later, complaining about microservices' complexity and praising a switch back to a monolith. While for some teams, projects, or companies, microservices may indeed be the wrong choice, the reality is that genuine poor fit is not always the cause of the failure. More often than not, flawed execution is the root cause of the disappointing results.

There is no turnkey software that teams can just buy from a vendor, or install with an open source license, that can magically make us "microservices" overnight. Moreover, there is not even some strict set of policies and guidelines that guarantee success. In reality, many traits of microservices architectures (*https://oreil.ly/_aFU8*) are aspirational and not directly quantifiable: independent deployability, decentralized governance, infrastructure automation, and evolutionary architecture, among others, are not things that any team can excel at right out of the gate or easily measure their progress toward! They take a long time and a fair amount of patience to mature, and are seldom perfect. It should not be a goal to perfect them in the early days of a transformation effort.

 One of the most damaging things an organization can do at the early stages of microservices adoption is to establish a "microservices police" that will strictly govern adherence to all of the microservices principles and traits. Migrating to microservices is a long process; it's a journey that requires patience and measurement.

The thinking that teams need to adopt when considering their level of maturity vis-à-vis microservices traits is largely similar to the philosophy we described in Chapter 4 when discussing rightsizing microservices: the size and granularity of a microservice evolves over time organically and forcing an attempt to start with a target granularity early on is detrimental. Similarly there are significant risks in prematurely insisting on a "perfect" microservices implementation as it relates to traits like independent deployability and automation too early in the transformation process. Instead, it is imperative for teams to remain pragmatic and ask themselves questions such as:

- While Kubernetes is undoubtedly the leading container orchestration solution, do we currently have the skills and developer capacity to support it? Even if it is provided by our cloud hosting solution? Or should we start with something much simpler (e.g., AWS ECS)?

- How automated does our infrastructure need to be in the early days? What level of self-healing is absolutely necessary in the early days?

- What systems can we delegate to a cloud provider to manage (e.g., databases, event streaming, etc.) even if eventually we may bring those back in-house? Do we absolutely need to start with a new, shiny database system, or can we instead initially use a less powerful, but cloud-provided database to cut down on maintenance overhead?

In most cases, the right thing to do in regard to these, and similar, questions is to cut yourself a fair amount of slack in the early days. It may be wise to stick to "boring" tech, and avoid upgrading MySQL to Cassandra or replacing Java with Golang at the same time you're also trying to adopt microservices, especially if your teams are unfamiliar with these new technologies. Instead, teams must concentrate on things that make business difference, and avoid getting bogged down by endless cycles of infrastructure setup, tech stack upgrades, and experimentation with cool new tools, critically delaying delivery of business value. Such delays can easily lead to stakeholders shutting down a transformation effort before it even gets properly started.

It is extremely important to remember that microservices architecture is a journey, not just a destination. In this journey, the trajectory of the progress means everything, and surprising as it may sound, current state is of much less significance. This is especially true in the early days of the transformation efforts.

We discussed in Chapter 1 that minimizing coordination costs is a core technique of a microservices architecture. It is so fundamental that teams that can demonstrate movement towards the diminishing levels of coordination needs are going to do well regardless of how many principles from Newman, Lewis, Fowler, or Mitra/Nadareishvili they adhere to initially. As long as they move in the right direction, the trajectory will win in the long run—every single time. The approach here is similar to the concept of Fitness Functions, as described in *Building Evolutionary Architectures* by Neal Ford, Rebecca Parsons, and Patrick Kua (O'Reilly).

How do we know if we are on the right trajectory? Sure, understanding that coordination costs are our main enemy is helpful, but we cannot directly measure "coordination cost" as a value. Some teams try measuring "speed" or "safety," but that is equally problematic, as these values are derivatives and measurements are indefensible. You will almost certainly notice a perceived increase in speed and safety, but to claim causality, what are you going to compare the new speed to? Nobody builds the same exact system once as a monolith and then as a microservices architecture. Any increase in speed will be intuitively rewarding but unscientific. The same idea applies to attempts of measuring increases in safety as well.

Instead, we propose measuring three values, two of which are directly related to the trajectory of increasing team autonomy, and the third that best indicates the overall efficiency of software teams (as described in *Accelerate* by N. Forsgren, J. Humble, and G. Kim (IT Revolution Press)):

- The average size of an autonomous team, across all teams
- The average length of time an autonomous team can work without getting halted on waiting for another team (waiting usually being caused by a critical dependency)

- The frequency of successful deployments

In a healthy microservices transformation that is on the right trajectory, you should see a gradual decrease in the size of autonomous teams and an increase in the amount of time that teams can work independently. For instance, you may observe that average autonomous team size in your organization used to be 15 to 20 members and after implementing microservices it starts to gradually decrease to 10, 8, 6…

Likewise, you should observe a decrease in frequency of coordination-related deadlocks. A *coordination deadlock* is a stoppage during which an autonomous team is waiting on another team for a shared capability to be made available for them; e.g., an infrastructure team provisioning a highly available Kafka or Cassandra cluster, or a security review team completing a code audit. Another common example of a team getting halted is when they need to wait for the outcome of a coordination meeting in which various stakeholders are making a critical decision.

Scheduling such meetings can take time due to varying priorities of the stakeholders. Tracking the number of dependencies that a team needs to clear before a code release to production is also a quantity worth measuring. Another important example of the type of event to track is whether teams need to often wait for other teams to make code changes, caused by the change in a shared data model. The triggers and duration of stoppages will vary depending on an organization and the business contexts. It's important to track both trigger types as well as stoppage duration, so that meaningful, actionable lessons learned can be derived and improvements can be made.

The third metric, deployment frequency, does not directly measure coordination costs, but is a general metric that has been scientifically proven by Forsgren et al. to be a powerful indicator of team agility. When applied to independently deployable microservices, in our experience it can also indicate the health of a microservices transformation trajectory.

By consistently measuring the three metrics and ensuring the transformation is on the right track, teams can free themselves from the anxiety of achieving perfection in every single microservices trait, freeing themselves for long-term success.

Summary

In this last, closing chapter of the book we shared with you how we think of microservices. Microservices can make your complex systems simpler, but it is no "silver bullet" and it is important to understand that the final effect is achieved by shifting complexity, not necessarily magically eliminating it. When we make such assertions, it also helps to be clear what we mean by "complexity," and it is different from the notion of "complicated" systems, and what role "easy" versus "simple" architectural approaches play in classifying various system delivery approaches.

We then shared our perspective on the importance of patience and a long-term outlook during a microservices transformation. It is a journey and a marathon, not a sprint, and teams intending to be successful need to be equipped with proper tools and concentrate on the trajectory of transformation much more than the current state. Make sure you get in the habit of measuring some reliable metrics to ensure you are still on the right track and that your trajectory is healthy.

We hope you have enjoyed reading this book. We hope it provided more hands-on and practical guidance than what has been previously available, and that you had fun going through the code and examples.

We wish you much success on your own microservices transformation journey and would love to hear from you—what you learn when you embark on implementing microservices in your own work.

All the best.

Index

branching, 185
merging, 185

X

X-as-a-service interaction mode, Team Topology, 23

Y

YAML, 126, 130
  deployment object, 247, 251
  kubeconfig file, 167
  spacing, 129
  templates, 250

About the Authors

Ronnie Mitra is an author, strategist, and consultant with over 25 years of experience working with web and connectivity technologies. He is the coauthor of *Microservice Architecture* and *Continuous API Management* (both O'Reilly).

Irakli Nadareishvili is the vice president of Core Innovation at Capital One Financial Corporation, leading the teams responsible for building Capital One's modern, cloud native, microservices-based core banking platform. Before Capital One, Irakli was cofounder and CTO of ReferWell, a successful New York City–based health technology startup, and held technology leadership roles at CA Technologies and NPR. Irakli is the coauthor of *Microservice Architecture* (O'Reilly). You can follow Irakli on Twitter at @inadarei.

Colophon

The animal on the cover of *Microservices: Up and Running* is the sparkling violetear hummingbird (*Colibri coruscans*). This hummingbird lives in a range that runs along the northwestern coast of South America, in higher-elevation habitats among the Andes mountains. Known in the Quechua language as *Siwar q'inti*, these hummingbirds have a place in local folklore as a sign of good luck.

Sparkling violetears are iridescent green with purple markings on the head and chest. The longer purple feathers at their ears extend outward from their heads during display. Large for hummingbirds, they average about five to six inches long, and weigh about a quarter ounce. Females lay two eggs in a nest of their own making, and incubate the eggs. The chicks fledge from the nest at three weeks.

Because they live at higher, colder altitudes, sparkling violetears are among the species of hummingbirds that enter a deep torpor each night to sleep. In this hibernation-like state of reduced body functions and a near-acclimation to surrounding cold temperatures, which it then reverses at dawn, the bird is able to survive long, cold nights without the food it would otherwise need to stay warm. The mechanisms by which they accomplish this complicated feat are the subject of ongoing scientific studies.

The sparkling violetear is common across its range, and is rated by the IUCN to be of Least Concern. Many of the animals on O'Reilly covers are endangered; all of them are important to the world.

The color illustration on the cover is by Karen Montgomery, based on a black-and-white engraving from *Wood's Natural History*. The cover fonts are Gilroy Semibold and Guardian Sans. The text font is Adobe Minion Pro; the heading font is Adobe Myriad Condensed; and the code font is Dalton Maag's Ubuntu Mono.